SECOND EDITION

PROFESSIONALISM IN EDUCATION

Hitting Your Mark

Editors

ANDREA P. BEAM, ED.D.
RUSSELL L. CLAXTON, ED.D.

Kendall Hunt
publishing company

MCEE main components on page 6 © Association of American Educators (AAE).

Ethical Considerations Principles appearing throughout text © 2016 National Association of State Directors of Teacher Education and Certification (NASDTEC). Reprinted by permission.

Cover image © Shutterstock.com

www.kendallhunt.com
Send all inquiries to:
4050 Westmark Drive
Dubuque, IA 52004-1840

Copyright © 2016 by Andrea P. Beam and Elyse C. Pinkie
Copyright © 2017 by Andrea P. Beam and Russell L. Claxton

ISBN 978-1-5249-1271-0

Kendall Hunt Publishing Company has the exclusive rights to reproduce this work, to prepare derivative works from this work, to publicly distribute this work, to publicly perform this work and to publicly display this work.

All rights reserved. No part of this publication may be reproduced, stored in a retrieval system, or transmitted, in any form or by any means, electronic, mechanical, photocopying, recording, or otherwise, without the prior written permission of the copyright owner.

Printed in the United States of America

CONTENTS

PREFACE V

ACKNOWLEDGEMENTS VII

ABOUT THE EDITORS IX

ABOUT THE AUTHORS XI

PART I: FOUNDATIONS OF PROFESSIONALISM 01

    CHAPTER 1: Professionalism 03

    CHAPTER 2: Integrity 11

    CHAPTER 3: Collaboration 25

    CHAPTER 4: Appropriate Relationships 39

    CHAPTER 5: Communication 53

    CHAPTER 6: Social Media 67

PART II: GETTING THE JOB 83

    CHAPTER 7: Resumes and Portfolios 85

    CHAPTER 8: Professional Dress 97

    CHAPTER 9: Interviewing Skills 107

    CHAPTER 10: What Administrators Look for When Hiring Teachers 121

PART III: KEEPING THE JOB 135

    CHAPTER 11: Commitment to Job, Students, and Profession 137

    CHAPTER 12: Social and Community Responsibility 155

    CHAPTER 13: Classroom Management 171

    CHAPTER 14: Time Management 185

    CHAPTER 15: Reflective Practice and Professional Development 199

CHAPTER 16: The Hats Teachers Wear 209

CHAPTER 17: Envisioning and Enacting a Servant Leadership Journey 223

APPENDIX. 233

GLOSSARY 241

PREFACE

Whether you are preparing for your first teaching position, already teaching, or seeking to advance your career in a new position, how you are perceived as professional can impact your effectiveness as an educator. Hitting your mark professionally can require preparation, self-reflection, and additional effort, but can significantly improve your interaction with students, their families, your colleagues, and your supervisors.

Professionalism is a term that all job requirements presume, but identifying what exactly is professionalism oftentimes may stir many variations. It is the hope that this book will enlighten all preservice teachers and newer teachers to not only prepare for their first years of teaching, but create an atmosphere that engages and exudes that of favorable practice and behavior. By discussing numerous aspects of professionalism for educators, including a complete definition of terminology, and leading into other areas of appropriate relationships and communication, teachers will be able to identify what is and what is not acceptable in our 21st century schools where we are working with a whole host of different constituents.

The following text will enable practitioners to consider suitable interaction with students, parents, supervisors, and colleagues, alike. While other professionalism textbooks are currently on the market, most are, unfortunately, geared to other professionals. This book will provide information to teachers on how to conduct themselves, what to say, what to avoid saying, how to manage students and parents, and just the "common sense" tactics that some teacher education programs fail to discuss. Furthermore, this book will approach professionalism from a "real world" perspective, helping even first-year teachers to feel comfortable walking into a classroom on day one!

This book can be used for preservice teachers—those seeking initial licensure, but could also be used for experienced educators or those starting in a new position who want to learn more about proper methods of conduct in K12 schools. Broken down into three distinct sections, this book will provide preservice teachers the "Foundations of Professionalism," but will then guide them into "Getting the Job" and ensure security with them "Keeping the Job." Information such as resume writing, interviewing skills, and common administrative expectations are all housed in this easy-to-read practitioner-based text. Although each chapter has a different topic, and the book was written by multiple authors, noticing common themes and areas of emphasis can help you identify some of the most important aspects of professionalism in education.

ACKNOWLEDGMENTS

This project could not be accomplished without the support of so many individuals. To a wonderful group of mentors, friends, colleagues, and teachers, we offer all of our thanks for your support throughout this process. A special thank you for the many authors who have contributed in making this project so invaluable.

Finally, an endeavor such as this would not be complete without the encouragement of our families. To each of you, we are forever grateful. Andrea would like to thank her husband, Allen, her children, Haley, Sydney, Lexi, and Sophie, and her dad, George, for never tiring of the unending stories and progress shared each and every day. Thank you for allowing her to "chew" on your ear and always appearing interested. Russ would like to thank his wife, Bunnie, and his kids, Emi and Lee, for their continuous support and encouragement, and his parents, Gerald and Rosemary, for guiding and supporting him down the path of becoming an educator.

ABOUT THE EDITORS

Andrea P. Beam, Ed. D. is an Associate Professor in the School of Education at Liberty University where she serves as the Chair of Secondary Education. With 22 years of experience in education, she has served as a special education teacher, served as an administrator at both the elementary and secondary level, and has served as a professor in many departments within the School of Education. Presently, she teaches courses in secondary curriculum, special education, and school law. Her numerous research efforts and publications keep her on the cutting edge in the field of education where she has published on the topics of inclusion, Multiple Intelligence, differentiation, Brain Gym, school law, and business programs for special education students. She holds degrees from George Washington University, Norfolk State University, and Old Dominion University.

Russell L. Claxton, Ed. D. is an Associate Professor and Department Chair in the School of Education at Liberty University in Lynchburg, VA. He currently teaches courses in school law, education policy, and leadership theory. Dr. Claxton has over 27 years of experience in education that includes serving as a high school business teacher, dean of students, assistant principal, and principal at the high school and middle school levels in the Atlanta, GA suburbs. He holds degrees from Liberty University, The University of West Georgia, and The University of Georgia.

ABOUT THE AUTHORS

Mr. Chris Amos is an Assistant Professor of Sport Management at Liberty University. Amos has worked over 12 seasons for the Washington Redskins as an Equipment and Staff Assistant. He has also worked as an Athletic Director and a Coach at various levels and was on staff with the Washington Nationals.

Dr. Andrea P. Beam is the Chair of Liberty University's Secondary Education Licensure Programs. She has taught in public school special education and has been an administrator in elementary and secondary schools in Virginia Beach. Presently, she teaches courses in curriculum, school law, and educational leadership and has published on multiple topics.

Dr. Bunnie Claxton is the Superintendent of Liberty University Online Academy. She is also an Adjunct Instructor for Liberty University. She currently teaches courses in Special Education including courses on Autism. Dr. Claxton has over 20-years of experience in the K–12 environment including public school, private school, and home school.

Russell L. Claxton is a Department Chair in the School of Education at Liberty University in Lynchburg, VA. He currently teaches courses in school law, education policy, and leadership theory. Prior to joining the faculty at Liberty University, Dr. Claxton served as a high school and middle school principal in the Atlanta, GA suburbs.

Dr. Susan Densmore-James is a 25-year educator. After 17 years of teaching in various K–12 settings, Dr. Densmore-James attended Florida State University and earned a dual Ph.D. in Reading and Language Arts. She specializes in secondary literacy and is known as The Book Dealer.

Dr. Kristina DeWitt earned her Ph.D. in Education from George Mason University, with a research focus in literacy, and earned a Masters of Education in Special Education from University of Mary Washington. She is currently an Associate Professor at Liberty University.

Mr. Allen Hackmann is currently a teacher in Lynchburg City Schools, an adjunct professor at Liberty University, and a wrestling coach at Liberty University. He has more than 20 years of experience in working with students with disabilities and general education, both at the elementary and secondary level.

Dr. Michael Kelly is currently a clinical associate professor for Virginia Tech in the School of Education. Prior to this appointment he was a principal of a middle school in Virginia. Under his helm, the school was identified as a "National Middle School to Watch" by the Virginia Department of Education and the National Middle School Association.

Dr. George Parker, III is currently serving as the superintendent of Caroline County Public School division which is located north of the city of Richmond, Virginia. Prior to his current position, he served as a teacher, principal and central office administrator in Virginia Beach City Public School System.

Dr. Tami Pratt has over 20 years of experience in PK–16 education. She has worked as an elementary teacher and reading specialist, middle school literacy coach, and most recently as an Associate Professor of Education at the University of Mary Washington where she taught graduate courses in literacy and literacy leadership.

Dr. Pamela Randall, with more than 30 years of experience, has had the pleasure of teaching all grade levels. She has had the honor of working as an administrator and now has the privilege of working at the collegiate level with pre-service teachers and those pursuing advanced degrees.

Dr. James Swezey is the Chair of Qualitative Doctoral Research at Liberty University. Along with research methods, he teaches courses on educational leadership. He has published widely in a variety of mediums and regularly presents at professional conferences. Before working in higher education, he worked as a K–12 teacher and administrator.

Dr. Russ Yocum has taught elementary students and graduate level courses for alternative certification teacher education in Florida. Currently, Dr. Yocum teaches doctoral level qualitative research and a variety of graduate level methods courses at Liberty University in Virginia.

PART 1

FOUNDATIONS OF PROFESSIONALISM

CHAPTER 1

PROFESSIONALISM

Andrea P. Beam and Russell L. Claxton

"There are three qualities that make someone a true professional. These are the ability to work unsupervised, the ability to certify the completion of a job or task and, finally, the ability to behave with integrity at all times."

~ Subroto Bagchi

INTRODUCTION

Professionalism may exemplify itself in many different manners for many different people. For educators, however, professionalism is paramount in the school environment. For those in the teaching realm, they must understand expectations before considering themselves to be true professionals. This chapter will discuss what it is to be a professional and display professionalism, why professionalism is important in the teaching field, as well as favorable practices and common mistakes surrounding the topic of professionalism. Other resources will also be shared for further understanding of this phenomenon. This book is intended to be especially useful to those in the early years of their teaching careers. However, even those educators who have been in the teaching profession for some time will still find information that will be helpful at all stages of one's career.

Courtesy of Andrea P. Beam and Russell L. Claxton. Copyright © Kendall Hunt Publishing Company.

WHAT IS PROFESSIONALISM?

While some sources define *professionalism* in vague terms, others seem to be more specific. The United States Department of Labor identifies it as, "a means [of] conducting oneself with responsibility, integrity, accountability, and excellence. It means communicating effectively and appropriately and always finding a way to be productive" (USDOL, 2016). While that definition is clearer than Oxford Dictionaries (2015), which states that to be a professional means that one displays "the competence or skill expected of a professional," it may be common belief that to be a professional means to behave and present oneself in an appropriate manner for a specific profession. For teachers and those entering the teaching profession, called "teacher candidates" from this point on, professionalism assumes a slightly distinctive perspective. Because "professionalism" is up for interpretation, and there are no specific books or pamphlets that walk a teacher candidate through all actions that should be exhibited, the sections contained in this text will describe and discuss what administrators and other leaders in the field consider to be appropriate in this realm of work. Professionalism, then, is one's conduct in the school building that displays collegiality, fairness, consistency, good communication skills, modest dress attire, and the artful craft of time management, which includes being productive throughout the workday and being on time for arrivals, departures, and meetings.

WHY IS PROFESSIONALISM IMPORTANT?

What a great question! Why *is* professionalism important? Scott (2015) suggests that those entering a specific field must demonstrate proper behavior for the long-term success of the business. This is no different than in the school environment. Teacher candidates must enter the classroom as a "rookie" with the understanding that teaching is a team effort and success can only be gained by the effective work of those around, such as other teachers, parents, students, and administrators. It is crucial that teacher candidates maintain polite interactions and relationships while presenting a positive attitude and showing pride by their appearance. Their appearance might encourage others to take pride in their work which, ultimately, improves overall performance. Administrators who behave professionally set an appropriate example by encouraging their staff to conduct themselves in a manner that supports school-wide success.

Because professionalism includes an educator's behavior, appearance, and ethics, anyone with high standards of professionalism is frequently perceived as being more credible and reliable than his or her co-workers. As a result, professional employees are frequently regarded as their school's leaders and potential leaders (Blandford, 2012).

LEADING THE WAY

During a teacher's first few months or even years on the job, it may seem like a challenge just keeping his or her "head above water," to complete daily tasks. It may take some time for a new teacher to feel confident managing their own classroom, and being a leader can be the farthest thing from their mind. It is important to point out, however, that as of the first day a teacher walks into their own classroom, they are a leader. Leading a group of students is an important role, but for many teachers, their influence on others will expand beyond the walls of their classrooms.

The primary objective of this book is to help individuals develop professional attributes that will improve their effectiveness as educators. However, it is also important to consider the impact those attributes may have on others. Effective teachers often move into leadership roles, formally or informally. Those roles may include serving on a committee, leading a department or grade level, or even moving into a formal leadership role as a school or district administrator. Even for teachers who have no desire to pursue a formal leadership position will have an influence on others and lead by example.

As you read this book, consider not only how your professionalism impacts your effectiveness, but also consider how it affects those around you. Furthermore, it may be beneficial to consider how you can lead others in the areas addressed in each chapter. You may find that your professionalism helps to promote a professional climate in your school or office.

ETHICAL CONSIDERATIONS

Ethical guidelines for any profession are vital in considering one's actions, interactions, and possible infractions. Most professions, including attorneys, doctors, and union workers have a specific set of guiding principles. Educators are no different. Today, more than ever, it is imperative to integrate ethics into our everyday routines. Within each chapter, the national Model Code of Ethics for Educators (MCEE) will be intertwined for a clear understanding of how ethics play a major role in our professions as teachers, teacher leaders, and administrators. It is important not only to review and consider the essential elements of each principle, but to go a bit deeper and actually unfold each guiding standard (see Appendix).

Ethical Considerations

Principle I: Responsibility to the Profession

The professional educator demonstrates responsibility to oneself as an ethical professional

As the message of ethics is delivered, aim to understand the overview of the MCEE. The Association of American Educators (AAE) (2016) discusses the main components as the following:

1. The professional educator strives to create a learning environment that nurtures to fulfillment the potential of all students.
2. The professional educator acts with conscientious effort to exemplify the highest ethical standards.
3. The professional educator responsibly accepts that every child has a right to an uninterrupted education free from strikes or any other work stoppage tactics (AAE, 2016, para. 2).

FAVORABLE PRACTICES

When moving into the teaching field, there are several "do's" to consider as candidates develop into professionals. Some favorable practices that teacher candidates can hone include, but are not limited to:

Maintain Boundaries. As a new teacher, be sure to maintain boundaries with everyone in contact such as students, parents, and other faculty members. While candidates might have great relationships with students and parents, it is important to remember that, while you are *friendly*, you are not *friends*. Do not cross lines with conversations, personal information, or inappropriate remarks. Always maintain your status as "teacher."

Strive for Improvement. While candidates are new in the field, it is important to always strive to perform optimally. This means improve in mannerisms, attire (i.e., dressing a step above the rest), and meeting all deadlines *before* the deadline.

Maintain Accountability. By maintaining accountability, this means the candidate is accountable to him or herself by ensuring correct information is relayed to parents and students. Teacher candidates should be mindful of the written correspondence that is filtered through emails, newsletters, websites, or other modes of communication. All information should be accurate and thoroughly proofread for common spelling or grammatical errors. By sending out inaccurate information with errors, it is not only a reflection on the teacher but on the administration, as well. Candidates represent the school at all times, regardless if they are working during school hours.

Encourage Respect. Respect is an important concept for everyone, but maybe more so for those in the field of education. There may be times when a parent or another individual portrays disrespect, but the teacher must maintain control of his or her emotions and not get absorbed in the negativity. To encourage respect is to remain positive and find the good in all situations, remain gossip-free, appreciate authority, and encourage constructive criticism.

Minimize Conflict. There are times when candidates will disagree with other professionals in the work environment, parents, or students; this is completely acceptable. What should not occur, however, is for the candidate to become argumentative in trying to prove a point or change another's opinion. Disagreeing on a particular topic actually enhances a discussion and allows problem-solving and brainstorming to transpire. If there is a situation where conflict may arise, allow the other person to share his or her concerns and actually *listen* to the concerns. Do not get emotionally caught up in the situation but hear what the other person is requesting. The role of the teacher is to deescalate the problem so that effective problem solving can occur.

Be Productive. Teachers have so many tasks to accomplish every day so it is extremely important to remain on task and minimize distractions. The more productive candidates become, the more effective they will also be for themselves, their administration, and their students.

Strive for Competence. It is evident that candidates are competent because they have a teaching license to prove their knowledge. At times, however, some teachers are placed in particular situations where they feel less than accomplished. It is those times when the professional needs to properly prepare, review, and practice to become more comfortable with the material, allowing for a job well done.

Demonstrate Reliability. Administration should be able to depend on their faculty to arrive to work on time (but candidates should arrive early—at least 30 minutes to properly prepare for the day), attend all invited meetings and contribute within those meetings, and meet all deadlines as requested. By consistently displaying this practice, other faculty will begin to see this behavior as dependable and leadership quality.

Practice Honesty. For some, honesty is an earned characteristic. For teachers to earn trust in all that they do and say, they must remain consistent in their words and actions, and those words must match the actions. How many times have we heard that "actions speak louder than words"? This is exactly where honesty plays a role in behavior. Teachers must tell the truth at all times, be upfront in position, and mirror their words.

Display Integrity. Vasicek (2010) defines integrity in more simple terms. He states that to display integrity means to, "do the right thing when nobody is watching" (p.1). Teachers must not only practice honesty but they must be *consistent* in their ideals and moral absolutes.

Remain Current. Teaching is a profession where professional development is imperative. Candidates must stay abreast of the latest research and best practices to remain current in their craft. While students are always changing, the manner in which they learn is ever-changing, too, so teachers must seek ways to reach the various learners on a consistently changing basis.

Stay Positive. All professions have their "ups and downs" but in the field of education, there are days when there are more "downs" than "ups." It is necessary for teachers to remain positive and display an upbeat attitude amidst the problems that will surely arise. Candidates should be problem solvers, not problem makers.

Support Others. As candidates enter the teaching field for the first time, there is a lot to learn. After a few years, though, the candidate may very well become a mentor. As the tide shifts, the teacher should take the time to train others in proper performance and strategies, allowing time for reflection as needed. As stated earlier, teaching is a team effort, and all are winners when working effectively together. **Remain Work-Focused.** The practice of leaving work at work and leaving personal business at home is essential for new teachers. Candidates should be mindful of their private lives and not carry any information into the work environment that could, potentially, have a negative impact on performance. As such, work duties, if at all possible, should also be left at work, so as not to disturb candidate's personal lives. Home and family are important too, so maintaining balance will allow for a productive and happy life.

COMMON MISTAKES

As professionalism continues to be discussed throughout this text, candidates will begin to notice the information tends to spiral, referring to some points in slightly different ways. While there are many favorable practices to be discussed, there are also, unfortunately, some "don'ts" that teacher candidates should steer clear. The list below is not comprehensive, but does provide a quick review of important reminders:

Do Not Be a Buddy. Everyone has the desire to be liked and we, by nature, want our students to like us. However, while we should strive to have a pleasant, likable personality, we do not want to fall into the trap of being our students' friend. There is a fine line between being a likable teacher and a student's "buddy." We should, at all times, ensure that we are not befriending our students, but, rather are mentoring, coaching, and instructing them. Many new teachers are told not to smile the entire first month of school. While this is very extreme and, certainly not necessary, it is important to establish and maintain appropriate boundaries and expectations with students.

Avoid the Teachers' Lounge Gossip. The teachers' lounge should be a place of encouragement, refreshment, and support; however, too often, the lounge appears to be a place where gossip, back-biting, and discouraging conversations take place. Do not engage in these discussions! Especially as a new teacher, you should be seeking out those who are positive, uplifting, and helpful, not those who drag you down and pull you into situations and discussions that are unnecessary or inappropriate.

Do Not Become Complacent. As a new teacher, your ideas will be new, fresh, and exciting! Over time, however, you may find that you have sunk into a comfortable role, not leaving much time for creativity in your work or lessons. It is during this time that you must break away from the mundane routine of following status quo and interject a newly devised plan to keep not only your students engaged, but to keep you engaged, too!

CONCLUSION

Teaching, while a very rewarding career, also has the potential to impact and influence our students exponentially. This influence goes beyond the content areas and spans character, actions, words, and thoughts. Students are always watching us and working to model the behaviors and actions that they observe. For this, we need to be extremely mindful of our impact through our behaviors. Additionally, we should exhibit respect for our administrators, colleagues, and students' parents, as this display of reverence is what we also seek. As you hone your craft, always remember the Golden Rule: Do unto others as you would have them do unto you! By displaying the elements of professionalism that are discussed and presented within this text, you will not only be effective in your new role, but also become a respected member of the educational profession. As teachers, we need to strive to exhibit attitudes and actions that we desire to see in our students and from our peers—practice what you preach and strive for excellence!

REFERENCES

Blandford, S. (2012). *Managing professional development in schools.* New York, NY: Routledge.

Scott, S. (2015). The importance of professionalism in business. Retrieved from http://smallbusiness.chron.com/importance-professionalism-business-2905.html

US Department of Labor (2016). Retrieved from https://www.dol.gov/odep/topics/youth/softskills/Professionalism.pdf

Vasicek, B. (2010). Scholastic: Integrity. Retrived from http://www.scholastic.com/teachers/classroom_solutions/2010/12/integrity

CHAPTER 2

INTEGRITY

James A. Swezey

"Stand with anybody that stands right. Stand with him while he is right and part with him when he goes wrong."

~ Abraham Lincoln, 1854

INTRODUCTION

Abraham Lincoln is always listed among our greatest presidents and it was his principled humility that anchored the core of his personal and professional integrity. It was not an accident that integrity was chosen to be the first content area addressed in this book after the introductory chapter because integrity is *the* most important characteristic of the professional educator. Every profession develops standards that guide and govern the vocation and those standards typically include some mention of integrity. Despite all the lawyer jokes that are circulated, the American Bar Association established standards to maintain the integrity of the profession. The American Medical Association established ethical standards for physicians. The preamble to the National Education Association's (NEA) Code of Ethics declares, "The educator accepts the responsibility to adhere to the highest ethical standards" (NEA, 2015, para. 2).

Courtesy of James A. Swezey. Copyright © Kendall Hunt Publishing Company.

Study after study consistently demonstrates that integrity is among the most important traits valued by others (Northouse, 2015). Integrity is something that can be gained or lost with every thought we contemplate, every decision we make, and every action we take. It can be carefully cultivated over an entire lifetime and yet lost in a single moment. Integrity is one of the most pondered of all human virtues, yet after thousands of years and the rise and fall of a myriad of views, we still struggle to grasp exactly what it is or is not.

All of the major religions of the world list integrity among their spiritual virtues. The Taoist text, *Tao Te Ching* (The Book of the Way and its Virtues), guides the observant to living an integrated life, linking all aspects in unity. The Buddhist Eight-fold Path directs the adherent towards right understanding, thought, speech, action, livelihood, effort, mindfulness, and concentration—all in an effort to lead a life of integrity. The *Qur'an* speaks often of the need for the Muslim's words to match his deeds. The Christian *Bible,* especially the Psalms and Proverbs, extol the virtues of the person of integrity.

Outside of religion, integrity has been written about and discussed by most of the world's foremost philosophers, including Confucius and Plato. A quote often attributed to Confucius claims, "The strength of a nation derives from the integrity of the home" (Virtue First Foundation, n.d.). Socrates is depicted by his student Plato as the epitome of both personal and intellectual integrity in Plato's classical work, *Phaedo*. When the leaders of Athens became jealous over the influence Socrates had on the young men of the city-state, they trumped up charges. He was tried and convicted of corrupting the youth and sentenced to death, but some of the leaders did not want him to die so they arranged for him to escape and live in exile. However, Socrates believed that leaving would make him a hypocrite and undermine all he had taught his followers, so he refused. Instead of escaping, he drank a fatal dose of hemlock as prescribed by Athenian law. His death was immortalized in Jacques-Louis David's 1787 oil painting entitled, *The Death of Socrates,* in which Socrates is depicted offering one last lesson for his students. As we examine integrity in this chapter, you might ask yourself, "What do I consider worth dying for?"

WHAT IS INTEGRITY?

Integrity is one of those ubiquitous words that is common, but difficult to define and yet people usually think they know it when they see it. It is commonly known as "practicing what you preach." Baltimore (1999) defined integrity as "the state or quality of being complete, undivided, [and] unbroken" (p. 260). Modern usage of the word integrity derives from the Latin *integer,* and common synonyms for integrity are intact, entire, whole, lacking nothing, and perfect. It implies a personal wholeness within and without. It usually refers to the general quality of a person's character. It is the steadfast commitment to maintain one's identity and sense of right and wrong. As a result, we speak of a person as being true to herself or as doing what is right, even when there is a substantial cost. The difficulty comes when different groups of people disagree over what is a healthy identity or what is right or wrong in any given situation. Teacher professionalism requires you to respect the identity of different people, even if you disagree with their lifestyle choices.

Integrity is also described using terms such as "the qualities of honesty and trustworthiness", "loyal, dependable, and transparent" (Northouse, 2015, p. 27). Integrity is "adherence to moral principles in all activities" (Nair, 1997, p. 1). Covey (1991) provided a sound depiction of integrity by describing what it is and is not:

> Integrity [includes] honestly matching words and feelings with thoughts and actions, with no desire other than for the good of others, without malice or desire to deceive, take advantage, manipulate, or control; constantly reviewing your intent as you strive for congruence. (p. 108)

Integrity of character does not mean perfection (Palmer, 1998). It is a heart orientation, a desire and willingness to pursue integrity, and when integrity is lost or violated, effort is made to restore it. Integrity is a commitment to one's own identity and the effort it takes to maintain wholeness. Teachers must begin their professional journeys by asking themselves questions such as, "Who am I?" and "What does it mean to be a teacher?" and "What am I willing to sacrifice to better serve my students?"

WHY IS INTEGRITY IMPORTANT?

My home state of California adopted standards for the teaching profession back in 2009. Most states have adopted similarly worded standards. Explaining the standards, the California Commission on Teacher Credentialing (CCTC) wrote,

> A growing body of research confirms that the quality of teaching is what matters most for students' development and learning in schools. Teaching is a professional endeavor, one in which effective practice is driven by an understanding of knowledge in the field and a commitment to all students and their families. (CCTC, 2009, p. 1)

The very first mark of an effective teacher is an "ethical concern for children and society" (p. 1). Ethics are essential to integrity, for what good are ethical standards if teachers do not have the integrity to embrace and implement them? Standard 6 is entitled, "Developing a Professional Teacher" and reflects the very heart of this book. Teachers are expected to "demonstrate professional responsibility, integrity, and ethical conduct" (CTCC, 2009, p. 15) both inside the classroom and within the local community.

It does not take much effort to search the Internet for stories of teachers who failed in their professional responsibilities either inside the classroom or in the community and lost their jobs as a result. In one of the largest school scandals, 178 teachers and administrators were found to have changed students' scores on a state test. Some of the teachers caught up in the 2009 Atlanta Public School scandal lost their jobs and their freedom, with some being sentenced to 20 years imprisonment for racketeering. There is a price to be paid when we demonstrate a lack of integrity. The actions of these teachers cost them and their students. Subsequent research has shown that many of students, whose test scores were changed by teachers, were struggling years later with English, language arts, and math (Burns, 2015). Who was the person with enough integrity to be among the first expose the scandal? Ryan Abbott, a four-year teacher at an elementary school whose principal opened an ethics investigation against him when he reported the cheating of a popular teacher (Judd, 2011). Ironically, having integrity is not without its own costs as well.

INTEGRITY IN RELATIONSHIPS

Educators navigate a complex web of personal and professional relationships inside and outside the classroom. Human relationships rely on the assumption of integrity between people. Most of us assume people are who they claim to be and will act in accordance with certain acceptable standards of behavior. Can you imagine sending a child into a classroom where you questioned the teacher's integrity? Now try to imagine that you are the teacher and it is your integrity that is being questioned. Among the most important relationships a teacher will develop are those with students, their parents, and fellow teachers.

The teacher-student relationship is at the core of the educator's calling. One of the most widely recognized treatises on this matter is found in Parker Palmer's (1998), *The Courage to Teach*. In it he explained, *"Good teaching cannot be reduced to technique; good teaching comes from the identity and integrity of the teacher"* (italics his, p. 10). He compared good teachers to weavers who can create a tapestry, entwining both their students and their subject matter into a beautiful pattern. Think back upon your own time as a student. Who were the teachers who had the greatest positive impact on your life and served as your role models? I am confident that they will be the ones with the clearest sense of identity as to what it meant to be a teacher and the greatest degree of integrity in their relationship with you and the subject matter they taught.

Ethical Considerations

Principle V: Responsible and Ethical Use of Technology

The professional educator uses technology in a responsible manner

Integrity with parents is becoming increasingly difficult as parents hold teachers with less regard and respect.

Most of us have probably seen some version of the popular two-panel cartoon that shows two contrasting frames. In the first, the date stamp is 1969 and the parents are holding a report card with an "F" emblazoned on it, scolding their son in front of the teacher demanding of him, "Explain these bad grades!" The second panel, usually dated "Today," shows the parents of a boy holding a report card demanding of the terrified teacher who is biting her fingernails, "Explain these bad grades!" All the while a smug young boy watches in glee. I experienced this contemptuous behavior and you will likely as well. How can teachers remain true to their identity when doing so seems to invite conflict? It begins and ends when identity is linked to integrity.

Fellow teachers are critical to the success of the novice teachers as they can serve as effective mentors and guides. Most new teachers are overwhelmed by their responsibilities and often feel unprepared. If these relationships are grounded upon integrity and mutual trust, they will serve as a lifeline when difficult circumstances arise. New teachers need an experienced mentor they can turn to when things do not turn out as planned. As you begin your career at a new school, you cannot help but wonder, "Who can I trust when I am not sure what to do with a disruptive student?" or "What should I do when I am afraid that my students are not prepared for the state's high-stakes testing?" or "What do I do about a parent who screamed at me in front of my class?" Integrity builds trust and trust allows for vulnerability.

INTEGRITY IN ASSESSMENT

We are all faced with challenges to our integrity, both great and small. I would even argue there are no small challenges to our integrity, because even the smallest lapse could lead to the unravelling of all our integrity. I face these challenges on a regular basis as will you.

Michael was a recent student of mine who failed to complete a few assignments for the course and was in danger of failing. The syllabus for this course explained that assignments would not be graded after two weeks past the due date. I had forewarned him and he communicated that he was committed to submitting his late work and to completing the course with excellence. Time went by and I did not hear from him again. I eventually received emails from him and his academic advisor stating that he was ready to submit the missing assignments. I wrote back relaying the information that it was too late because the two weeks had passed and that he should withdraw from the course. Michael wrote back that he was disappointed in himself, but understood. Later the next day, I was looking at my calendar and noticed that I had miscalculated the two week mark and Michael actually had until the end of the day to submit his late work. I had made a major mistake that would cost him thousands of dollars and delay his program. I hate to admit it, but my first thought was to just keep this information to myself. After all, I rationalized to myself, Michael had plenty of opportunities to submit his work and it was his procrastination that had created the problem in the first place. Besides, having to admit my error to Michael and his academic advisor would make me look bad and I did not want that. It only took a matter of seconds for me to come to the conclusion that my integrity would not allow me to cheat Michael in this way. He deserved better from me and it was not my character to hurt someone else for my own benefit. In the end, I made the call and worked hard to clean up the mess I had made.

Our integrity is constantly under threat of self-interest. Most of us are tempted to violate our personal integrity when we believe the cost of acting with integrity is outweighed by cost of being deceptive. What price are we willing to pay to be true to ourselves and our convictions?

Teachers will not only face internal pressures regarding student grades; there will be external pressures as well. What does integrity require when a student's work dictates a certain grade, but you understand that the grade will leave the student ineligible for participation in athletics, student government, or some other extra-curricular activity? What if the student is the child of a fellow teacher, or an administrator, or a school board member? It is not that far-fetched. In one well-publicized story, more than one third of teachers in Chicago Public Schools reported feeling pressured to change grades and give students higher marks (Greiner, 2009). Who did the mayor of Chicago blame? The teachers who felt the pressure, not those who applied it (Greiner, 2009). On the surface it might seem cut and dried to some. If the student earned a poor grade, that is the end of the story. But what if you know that this student comes from a terrible home life and the team or the activity is his only refuge away from home? What if he has done his best throughout the semester and, even with some earned extra credit, he is just a couple of points away from the grade he needs? What does integrity call for in this situation?

SKILLS FOR DEVELOPING INTEGRITY

Developing integrity begins with self-reflection. Among the uniquely human endowments is self-reflection leading to self-awareness and self-knowledge (Covey, 1991). Self-awareness is "a process in which individuals understand themselves, including their strengths and weaknesses, and the impact they have on others" (Northouse, 2016, p. 202). Palmer (1998) suggested an activity during which teachers spend time thinking about paradoxes. During this activity teachers are to think about two contrasting moments from the classroom: the first was a moment that went so well the teachers just knew they were born to teach and the second moment was a time when they regretted ever being born. This type of self-reflection can lead teachers to understand that

Leading the Way

Nowhere is leading by example more important than in the area of integrity. A lack of integrity not only sets a poor example, but it undermines ones authority and influence.

they can succeed one moment and fail in the next and it is okay. The activity then extends to the group and collectively the group sheds light on the situation and helps teachers identify their strengths and capacities. Teachers can then grow in their sense of identity and integrity. "When we are true to the light we have been given, when we keep our word consistently, when we are striving to harmonize our habit system with our value system, then our life is integrated" (Covey, 1991, p. 141).

One of the items upon which a new teacher should reflect is what it means to be a teacher. Integrity stems from one's own sense of identity as a person and from one's sense of vocation or calling. Equally successful teachers employ differing approaches, philosophies, and pedagogies within the classroom. Some teachers are effective because of their mastery of the subject matter, while others are effective because of their ability to connect with their students. Effective teaching, then, consistently flows out of a person's self-identity as a teacher (Palmer, 1998). According to Palmer (1998), you can lecture, use collaborative learning, or project-based assignments—it does not matter. You can be successful with any or all of these or you can fail using any or all of these. What matters is the integrity you bring to bear and whether it aligns with your authentic self. "Good teachers join self and subject and students in the fabric of life" (Palmer, 1998, p. 11). Successful, veteran teachers usually learn what works (and what does not) for them and master it, rather than feigning to adopt the latest teaching fad every few years. They have learned over time that what is old will eventually become new and what is new is likely quite old.

Integrity is grounded upon personal principles. Among my duties as a first-year teacher was student activities director, which required I teach and lead the student government class. I was hired as a history teacher, but the high school also needed an activities director and the principal made it a job requirement if I wanted to sign the contract. I found out later that nobody else wanted the job because it required so much uncompensated work outside of the classroom, but jobs were scarce in those days and I was young and was not afraid of a little hard work. Little did I know that this role would do more to shape my identity as a person and as an educator than almost any other. As I studied leadership to prepare for the student government class, I discovered the practice of actually writing down the principles that provided guidance for my life. Covey (1991) called these "true north principles" (p. 140). These principles had to be your "non-negotiables"—principles that you believed you could never violate without staining your integrity. It took quite a while to write my list and that year I had my student-leaders record their own lists. The students regularly cited it as one of the most important activities they had ever performed. More than 20 years later, I still have my original, typed list in my desk drawer and it still informs my integrity. What principles would go on your list?

Integrity requires an awareness of self-deception. In 2000, The Arbinger Institute published *Leadership and Self-Deception*, a book in story-telling form that addressed the human problem of self-deception. At its heart, the concept is rooted in the understanding that we are usually unable to accurately perceive our problems and that we are often the cause of our own problems because we are trapped within a box that limits our understanding. The book takes the reader on a journey through a variety of stories, case studies so to speak, that reveal how people encounter conflict without recognizing their own contributions to it. Teachers are capable of such self-deception and when I hear them complaining about administrators, students, and parents, I want to hand them this book so that it can serve as a mirror through which they can view their struggles in a new way and just maybe see their own role in causing the conflict. Sometimes seeing our role in a conflict requires a fresh perspective from a more seasoned colleague.

In order to build and maintain personal and professional integrity, find a mentor or an accountability partner (or both!). John Donne (1624) wrote in his oft quoted poem, "No man is an island, entire of itself, every man is a piece of the continent, a part of the main" (para. 2). Throughout most of my adult life, I've sought out mutual relationships through which I can grow personally and professionally. There have been countless individuals who invested in me in both large and small ways. I owe a tremendous debt of gratitude to those people who have helped me along my path. I have always sought out a person or two who would pour deeply and often into my life on a regular basis. Over the past eight years, it's been my friend, Don. We met almost every single week for an hour or more over the course of those years; literally, hundreds of times! We were both free to discuss any and every area of our lives and ask hard questions of each other. I knew that if I allowed my integrity to slip in my marriage, with my children, my work, or my faith, Don would hold me accountable and call me on it. Do you have such a mentor or friend?

FAVORABLE PRACTICES

We have all heard the saying, practice makes perfect. It is the same with personal integrity. Many of the favorable practices listed below reflect common sense, but it is surprising how often common sense gets in the way of integrity when there is a personal cost involved.

Practice What You Preach. There are few things worse than being labeled a hypocrite. The old parenting maxim from previous generations, "Do as I say, not as I do," no longer has any standing. This philosophy can no longer serve as a model for the parent or the teacher. Duplicity in your personal life will inevitably seep into your classroom. Establish a set of principles by which you live and stick to them!

Take Responsibility for Your Actions. Of all the complaints that I hear while working with teachers, this is the most common. Not only do students resist taking responsibility for their actions, parents model this behavior for them in the home and when they talk disrespectfully to the teacher in front of their child. No one is to blame for problems these days, except the teacher. But sadly, teachers also tend to avoid taking responsibility for their own actions. I hear them complain that they are overworked and underpaid (and I know it is often true). However, nobody forced them to sign the contract to become a teacher; they made that choice of their own volition. Take responsibility for your calling as a teacher and embrace the sacrifices it entails without complaining.

Keep Your Word. Integrity builds trust! As the father of three, few things have been more important to my philosophy of parenting than keeping my word. My children know that if I make a promise or a commitment, they can trust that I will do everything within my power to keep it. I have applied this same philosophy to my practice as a teacher. Some of the classes I teach are at a distance and so I often communicate with my students over the phone or online. Recently, I had an appointment to speak with a doctoral student about her dissertation and I have to confess that I got caught up in some other activities, did not have my cell phone with me, and completely forgot to call her. Hours later I retrieved my phone and saw that the student had called and left multiple messages (and emails) worried that something had happened to me because she knew that I always kept my commitments and she could never imagine me simply forgetting. After several embarrassed apologies, we were able to connect and move forward—remember integrity is not about perfection.

Be On Time. Punctuality used to be considered an important virtue. Pete Michaletos, my high school football coach, retired after 46 years of coaching the John F. Kennedy High School Titans as California's longest serving varsity football coach. One of his favorite sayings was, "You can't be great if you're late!" My time in the military taught me that if you are not 15 minutes early, you are late. President George Washington was notorious for his own punctuality and always expected it from others. He ate dinner every day promptly at 4:00 and if his invited guests were late, he would start without them. Being punctual reveals your integrity by demonstrating that you have self-discipline, keep your word, and that you are dependable. It also shows humility because it declares that the other person's time is as valuable as your own.

Admit Your Mistakes. For some reasons leaders, and teachers are leaders, do not like to admit their mistakes. Integrity is admitting our own faults before pointing out the faults of others. In a recent survey at Liberty University, students were asked if it was important that professors admit their mistakes. They scored it 6.62 on a 7 point scale! It was among the highest scores of all the survey items! When I was a high school history teacher, I used to give small amounts of extra credit points whenever students could point out a mistake I had made on their grades or a typo on a test or a handout. It helped keep me humble.

Walk Away. As you have read in this chapter, it is not uncommon for teachers to experience pressure to violate their personal and professional integrity. If you are new to teaching, you can count on it happening at some time in your career. Occasional pressure is one thing, but if you work at a school where integrity is not a virtue held in high esteem, walk away. I understand what this is asking. What value do you place on your own integrity? Is getting or keeping a particular job or position more important than maintaining your integrity?

COMMON MISTAKES

Integrity requires hard work and self-discipline. However, over time, age should afford us the wisdom of experience. Here are some of the common mistakes I have witnessed over my years as an educator.

Integrity and the Slippery Slope. It is rare that upstanding citizens see their world crumble with one decision that violates their integrity. It is far more likely that there were small, incremental decisions that led up to a tipping point where all was lost. Once on uneven ground, people lose their footing and once lost, balance is difficult to maintain without falling.

Integrity and Pride One aspect of military history that has always troubled me is the general reluctance of leaders to admit their mistakes. I have often read that it is because leaders perceive that to admit a mistake during war might be considered weakness or might cheapen the sacrifice of the men and women who died in battle. My theory is that pride, more often than not, keeps them from admitting their mistakes and, sadly, leads to the loss of more lives. There is an ancient Jewish story of Jephthah who had only one child, a daughter. After a great military victory, he made a rash vow to God that he would sacrifice the first thing to come out of his tent to greet him. It turned out to be his daughter who greeted him. Now, one would think that he would certainly sacrifice his integrity before sacrificing his daughter, but he did not. I do not know about others, but I would not have fulfilled my vow and accepted the consequences rather than allow my pride to pervert my integrity and harm another person. There are going to be times when pride gets in your way and your desire to be "right" becomes more important than the people around you who are hurt.

Integrity and Gossip. All of the world's religious and ethical systems teach that gossip is wrong. I learned early on in my career that one of the worst places for a new teacher to spend time is the teachers' lounge. If your school has a place where teachers congregate, I encourage you to spend time there only when necessary if it is a place where teachers gossip. They might bad-mouth the principal, parents, students, and even their fellow teachers and if you become associated with these malcontents, it will reflect badly on your own character, even if you do not join in.

Integrity and Rule-Followers. Rules are certainly important and need to be followed—in most cases. The fundamental question I ask you to consider is whether or not rules are more important than people. Were people made for rules or rules for people? In other words, are there exceptions to every rule and can exceptions be made when reason deems it appropriate?

The great leaders of various non-violent civil rights movements understood that rule-following is not always a sign of integrity. Sometimes the greatest symbols of integrity are those who are willing to break the rules and suffer the consequences.

Integrity and Zero Tolerance Policies. Zero tolerance policies were adopted because of a perception that too many exceptions to rules (see above) were being made and educators could not be trusted to use their discernment. When we have a kindergarten student being suspended for pointing his finger at someone like a gun and a teenager expelled for sharing an aspirin with a friend who had a headache, rational people must acknowledge that zero tolerance has gone too far and sanity must be restored. Integrity demands that we establish reasonable principles and enforce them using sound judgment.

Integrity and rationalization. If you anticipate an important decision will be needed in the future, make a commitment to your principles now! The closer the impending decision comes, the more likely you will experience the pressure and weight of the decision and the more likely you will succumb to that pressure by creating rationalizations as to why you should equivocate. The most common rationalization falls under the saying, "The means justified the ends." But wrong means rarely justify right ends.

CONCLUSION

In the chapter's opening quote, Abraham Lincoln had it right when he wrote that we must stand with those in the right, at least until they are no longer in the right. Whether the situation you face calls for you to stand or to walk away—it is important for you to understand that either action can require courage or integrity and it requires wisdom to know when which is best. Your career as a teacher will be inextricably linked to your personal and professional integrity and the judgment you use. Rest assured that your integrity will be tested on a regular basis. It may be tested by your students and their parents, your colleagues, or your school administration, but it will be tested. The key is to anticipate these challenges and to be prepared. So your homework assignment begins today. As a professional educator, what steps are you willing to take and what price are you willing to pay to develop and strengthen your integrity?

HITTING YOUR MARK

As posited by Palmer (1998), hitting your mark in regards to integrity is not about perfection. Working within schools is a messy business and your judgment will be put to the test every single day. Even if you make the right decision and follow the correct course of action 99.9% of the time, you will make mistakes and your integrity will be called into question.

These turbulent times are often like storms in life when we are tempted to lower our sails and allow strong winds to direct us against our charted course. Integrity is our compass, our moral bearing, which guides us during these storms. When difficult times arise and challenge your integrity, I encourage you to watch your compass, to stay the course, and even to hoist your sails so you can draw upon strong winds to your advantage! Hitting your mark requires you to do your very best, but also to stand ready to admit your mistakes when they occur. When all is said and done, there are few things more important than the ability to look yourself in the mirror and to know that you did your best. When you can do that, you know you will have hit the mark!

QUESTIONS FOR DISCUSSION

1. How do you define or describe integrity?
2. Why is integrity so important to all of our relationships?
3. When was there a time when someone violated their integrity towards you? How did you respond?
4. What has been the greatest test of your integrity?
5. What was an occasion where you had to admit a failure in your integrity? How did you weather that storm?

ACTIVITIES FOR ENRICHMENT

Debate: Assign two groups to each take a position. The first position is that there are occasions where it is okay to lie, cheat, or steal. The second position is that there are never occasions where it is okay to lie, cheat, or steal.

Weekly Log: Have participants keep a week long log of personal observations. These observations could include real-life activities, portrayals on television, or other media representations. Make a note every time the participant observes a situation where integrity is compromised. At the next meeting, discuss the observations and the participant's perceptions of the situations.

Personal Principles: Maintaining integrity occurs best when we can clearly articulate our principles before they are challenged. Assign participants the task of listing and describing their five most important principles. These would be principles they would work the hardest to maintain under any circumstances.

REFERENCES

Baltimore, J. P. D. (1999). *Public integrity.* London, England: John Hopkins University Press.

Burns, R. (2015, August 11). What has Atlanta Public Schools learned from the cheating scandal? *Atlanta Magazine.* Retrieved from http://www.atlantamagazine.com/news-culture-articles/what-has-atlanta-public-schools-learned-from-the-cheating-scandal/

Covey, S. (1991). *Principle-centered leadership.* New York, NY: Simon and Schuster.

Donne, J. (1624). Meditation XVII. In *Devotions upon emergent occasions, and several steps in my sickness.* Retrieved from http://www.online-literature.com/donne/409/

Greiner, A. (2009). Daley sends Inspector General after grade changers. *NBC Chicago.* Retrieved from http://www.nbcchicago.com/news/local/Daley-Sends-Inspector-General-After-Grade-Changers-56731332.html

Judd, A. (2011, January 24). Whistle-blowing teachers targeted. *The Atlanta Journal-Constitution.* Retrieved from http://www.myajc.com/news/news/local/whistle-blowing-teachers-targeted/nQpxt/

Lincoln, A. (October 16, 1854). A speech regarding the Kansas-Nebraska Act at Peoria Illinois. Retrieved from http://millercenter.org/president/speeches/speech-3503

Nair, K. (1997). *A higher standard of leadership: Lessons from the life of Gandhi.* San Francisco, CA: Berrett-Khoeler Publishers.

National Education Association. (2015). Preamble to the code of ethics. Retrieved from http://www.nea.org/home/30442.htm

Northouse, P. G. (2015). *Introduction to leadership: Concepts and practice* (3rd ed.).Thousand Oaks, CA: Sage Publications.

Northouse, P. G. (2016). *Leadership: Theory and practice* (7th ed.). Thousand Oaks, CA: Sage Publications.

Palmer, P. J. (1998). *The courage to teach: Exploring the inner landscape of a teacher's life.* San Francisco, CA: Jossey-Bass Inc., Publishers.

The Arbinger Institute. (2000). *Leadership and self-deception: Getting out of the box.* San Francisco, CA: Berrett-Koehler Publishers.

Virtue First Foundation. (n.d.). Integrity. Retrieved from http://virtuefirst.org/virtues/integrity/

CHAPTER **3**

COLLABORATION

Pamela P. Randall

"We may have all come on different ships, but we're all in the same boat now."

~ Martin Luther King Jr.

INTRODUCTION

Collaboration. What exactly does that word mean? The Oxford Dictionary (2016) states that it is, "United labor, co-operation; especially in literary, artistic or scientific work." Webster (2016) offers, "To work jointly with others or together especially in an intellectual endeavor." We might further add that collaboration should, especially when pulling from individual strengths, take the best of each of us and combine it in such a way that the desirable outcome is obtained. Evan Rosen, in his book, *The Culture of Collaboration* (2011) adds this twist to the definition: "Working together to create value while sharing virtual and physical space" (p. 7). The word "value" strengthens the concept that, collectively, what we create can have limitless, positive, possibilities!

Collaboration happens, or should, at many different levels in our daily jobs. Think about an average day in the life of a teacher. Teachers interact with peers, administration, support staff (i.e., bus drivers, cafeteria works, librarians), parents, and of course, students nearly

Courtesy of Pamela P. Randall. Copyright © Kendall Hunt Publishing Company.

every day! These are important relationships that must be cultivated, valued and nurtured so that productive collaboration can take place. Part of your job as an educator will be to teach social skills—skills that will help children learn to build friendships, recognize, and celebrate differences, and be productive citizens.

In the following sections, we will discuss, in detail, some of the typical collaborative settings in which you will be working.

WHY IS COLLABORATION IMPORTANT?

Collaboration is considered as one of the essential 21st century learning skills. The authors of *Communication and Collaboration* (n.d.) clarify by stating that teachers and students should be able to:

> demonstrate the ability to work effectively and respectfully with diverse teams, exercise flexibility and willingness to be helpful in making necessary compromises to accomplish a common goal and assume shared responsibility for collaborative work, and value the individual contributions made by each team member. (para 2)

The acquisition of these skills does not just happen; they must be taught, both in theory and in practice, in order to be mastered. It is also a relationship skill, meaning that we can read about it or study it, but ultimately we must actively participate in the skill in order to effectively implement. In a world that has become more digitally connected and yet more physically alone, this can be a challenge. What better way to teach the concept of collaboration than by watching teachers and other educational professionals model this behavior? In the following sections, we will touch upon some of the critical persons with whom you will be asked to collaborate in your new career path.

COLLABORATIVE RELATIONSHIPS

SUPERVISORS

Collaboration within schools can, and should, happen at multiple levels, including with administration, fellow teachers, support staff, and students. As a teacher your building level administrators most likely include principals, assistant principals, department chairs, grade level chairs, mentors, and perhaps other administrative designees. It is important that you build cooperative relationships with these persons. Many of the employees in these positions (if not all) have been in your position as a teacher. They understand the anxiety and pressure entailed. They are in a position to help guide and support you as you begin your new career. Spend time asking and listening to their advice and guidance and be willing to add your opinion and observations.

In my experience, most teachers come into the teaching profession ready to change the world. Please do not misunderstand—administrators love that quality! When you begin working in a new position you can bring with you with new techniques, theories, beliefs, and new blood. However, keep in mind that you are inserting yourself into a pre-existing culture, one in which you hope to become an integral part. As such, you must carefully listen to and reflect upon the guidance and advice your administrative staff will share with you. Many administrators will advise you to observe and collaborate with faculty in the building whom they respect and value. Conversely, they will often caution you to avoid other faculty members. Consider this wise advice. While you certainly will be judged on the results, both educational and emotional, you attain with your students, your ability to bond with and contribute to the cultural stability of the school will also be judged. Carefully choosing the teachers with whom you collaborate in your building will help you solidify your place in the school as a valued, trusted and respected teacher.

COLLEAGUES

In order for teachers to most effectively work together, they must first build relationships with one another. This means taking the time to talk to your fellow colleagues. The time spent building relationships will decrease anxiety when observing each other teach, increase comfortability to ask for help and input on difficult issues, and share lessons learned in a non-threatening and positive manner. Formal collaboration also insinuates that you will be professional when you meet, meaning that you will come prepared to share, ready to listen, and ready to contribute in a meaningful way.

Typical collaborative groups within schools include Professional Learning Communities (PLC), Grade Level groups, and Reading or Learning groups. Just as in any group structure, these clusters will only be as effective as their structure enables. In order to be most successful, any of the aforementioned collaborative groups must have a clear and motivated focus while meeting, have established goals and content to discuss, have shared voice/leadership and responsibilities, have an expectation of follow-up, and be accountable.

Professional Learning Communities (PLCs)

According to All Things PLC's (2015), PLC structures are defined as "an ongoing process in which educators work collaboratively in recurring cycles of collective inquiry and action research to achieve better results for the students they serve. Professional learning communities operate under the assumption that the key to improved learning for students is continuous job-embedded learning for educators" (para 1). As you can see from the description, not only is the value of collaborative grouping important here, but also the value of continuous learning on the part of the participants. Schools will often group teachers into PLC units when implementing a best practice pedagogical strategy, such as differentiated instruction or implementation of a new initiative. This purposeful grouping is usually accompanied by goals and objectives that are provided by the school or school system. Typically, meeting times, places, and agenda are also preset by administration. It is important to note that a PLC is not a program, rather it is a mechanism to group teachers into learning units that are faculty driven, and provide on-going and meaningful follow-up.

Grade Level Groups

Beyond formalized collaborative teacher groups, informal groupings are also common in high performing schools. Shared planning is an example of a strategy that is used by many teachers to help shoulder the responsibility and work load involved in creating and managing effective unit and lesson plans. Oftentimes, teachers will simply decide among themselves to meet as subject or grade level peers to develop common strategies, lessons or assessments. Research has again shown that this strategy is not only effective in helping with student achievement but also leads to higher retention of first year teachers (McClure, 2008).

Reading or Learning Groups

Reading or Learning groups are the least formal of the teacher groupings discussed thus far. These informal structures usually consist of teachers who are interested in a particular pedagogy, text, subject matter, or student. The groupings often cross grade levels. These teachers enjoy learning new things and also value the ability to talk, debate and bounce ideas off each other. Their meetings are often "by chance" and convenient, lacking the formal structure of PLC or grade level meetings; they meet to share, challenge and enrich each other. For instance, if a new pedagogical approach, such as differentiated instruction, has been introduced through a PLC, this informal grouping may take it upon themselves to research different resources, share about their experiences using the new approach, or offer to visit one another's classrooms to share feedback. Often, these groupings are created along pre-existing friendships and already-established relationships. These are the positive types of conversations that can happen around the copy machine during a teacher's planning period and are often very advantageous, both to the teacher and ultimately the student.

Support Staff Groups

Support staff are, unfortunately, sometimes overlooked as partners in our schools. However, personnel such as bus drivers, cafeteria workers, and custodians can be powerful allies in our vision to reach each student. Do not miss out on the opportunity to ask for their collaboration in helping to reach a child. Employees in these positions are often seen as less threatening to students, and can, therefore, interact and intercede with students when you cannot. Leverage the power they hold to your students' benefit. Allow them the power to positively influence your students and value the insight they can provide.

Service Provider Groups

Schools may also include the services of a guidance counselor, and perhaps social workers or other mental and physical health service providers. These professionals work with the extended family and can be a critical partner in helping you create intervention plans for your students. Social workers, for example, are uniquely trained to help in areas that present great challenges to learning, such as social development, human behavior, and family dynamics. In addition, they also often serve as a liaison between outside agencies and the school and classroom. Society places great expectations on teachers to provide a quality education for students. Remember, you are not in this alone. Take time to share your insights, observations, and thoughts with these professionals so that together you can keep the students' best interest at heart.

> **Ethical Considerations**
>
> Principle IV: Responsibility to the School Community
>
> *The professional educator promotes effective and appropriate relationships with colleagues*

STUDENTS

The most important area of collaboration is within your actual classroom. Despite the overwhelming amount of research that supports collaborative learning as an effective learning strategy, Robert Slavin (2014), states "teachers don't use cooperative learning regularly" (Gillies, 2014; Roseth, Johnson, & Johnson, 2008; Slavin, 1995, 2013; Webb, 2008, p. 22).

Students must be given the opportunity to practice collaboration. The Partnership for 21st Century Learning, (Communication and Collaboration, 2015), states that students should be able to "demonstrate ability to work effectively and respectfully with diverse teams, exercise flexibility and willingness to be helpful in making necessary compromises to accomplish a common goal, assume shared responsibility for collaborative work, and value the individual contributions made by each team member" (para. 3). Teachers must be able to facilitate this exchange of ideas in a structured and measurable setting for their students when they are working in groups. Expectations for collaborative work should provide clear expectations for each individual member, encourage higher-level thinking, and provide students with hands on experiences, resulting in measurable outcomes that are linked with state or national educational standards.

While some teachers are overwhelmed by the logistics of collaborative learning, there are notable experts in the area. Among these is Dr. Spencer Kagan. Dr. Kagan (2011), has written expansively on the value and structuring of collaborative learning in the classroom.

The acronym, PIES, which refers to his four principles of effective collaboration, "**P**ositive Interdependence, **I**ndividual Accountability, **E**qual Participation, and **S**imultaneous Interaction," serves as the organizing structure behind the vast collection of collaboration strategies he and his team have developed for teachers to use in their classroom. Resources such as these can help teachers effectively manage the logistics of collaborative learning in the daily classroom. Again, if you know that children must possess the necessary skills to work together in their future careers, then you must value and validate this by allowing them time to practice this skill in your classroom.

COMMUNITY

In order to maximize effectiveness in our teaching roles, we must build appropriate relationships with our colleagues, students, families, and communities. Time spent learning and collaborating with our students' families and communities can enhance our understandings, enrich our teaching and ultimately benefit all involved parties. From experience, it appears that effective collaboration outside the school walls helps ensure that students have support from all interested parties. This will, in turn, assist in their continued success and ability to contribute to the community as an adult. None of us exist in a vacuum. We live, function, and persist as members of a community, both in school and out. In order for our students to effectively transition into the community, teachers must be willing to open the door and collaborate with members of the community. This may be as simple as having an encouraging conversation with parents about their child at the grocery store, or as complex as volunteering in a community service group such as United Way. However you chose to become engaged with your community, it is critical that parents see you as someone who values the society and locality where you serve.

While there is a plethora of information to be found on how schools, and more importantly educators, can best collaborate with the community in which they work, The United States Department of Education (2014) provides perhaps the clearest summation of best practice guidelines in creating and maintaining effective collaboration between schools and communities. They state the following as extremely beneficial best practices:

- Make engagement a priority and establish an infrastructure;
- Communicate proactively with the community;
- Listen to the community and respond to its feedback;
- Offer meaningful opportunities to participate; and
- Turn community supporters into advocates

While some of the areas discussed above will fall within the purview of the administration of your school, there is certainly no reason that you cannot also become an active member of your community. Notice in particular, nearly all of the suggested guidelines hinge upon educators actively communicating with and listening to the members of the community. This two-way communication must then result in meaningful implementation of the ideas and feedback. Otherwise, each party is merely giving "lip service" to the idea of collaboration.

Margaret Wheatley (2006) speaks about connectedness and relational

> ### Leading the Way
>
> *Many teachers want to collaborate, but find scheduling common planning time to be a challenge. Leaders should try to facilitate collaboration by adjusting schedules, providing classroom coverage, or by effectively managing additional duties and responsibilities.*

dynamics. She says, "In this exquisitely connected world, it's never a question of 'critical mass.' It's always about critical connections" (p. 2). In order to create "connectedness," some schools rely on social workers or parent liaisons with the community. However, if we believe that meaningful relationships are the foundation of success, then we must also believe that the strongest relationships are those that are created in person—teachers reaching out to the community and the community being invited in as a valued partner. Strive to become the teacher that everyone sees at functions and activities in the community, the teacher that everyone wants to have in their class because it is obvious, based on the relationships they have forged, they care about their community.

FAMILIES

Family collaboration is a critical component in your teaching success. Research shows, in general, that there are many benefits for students and educators for this phenomenon to occur. According to the Virginia Department of Education (2002), the benefits include improved grades and test scores, positive attitudes toward schoolwork, positive behavior, higher rate of work completion, increased participation in classroom activities, and increased attendance. What are best practice strategies that can help facilitate this type of collaboration with families? The authors of Collaborative Family and School Relationships offer the following guidelines for best practices:

- **Family-school relationships should be focused on student progress and success**. The reason for educators and families to cooperate, coordinate, and collaborate is to enhance learning opportunities, educational progress, and school success for students.
- **Families are equal partners in attaining educational goals for students**. Educators view family-school relationships as essential for children's optimal academic, social, and emotional learning.

- **Both in- and out-of-school times are recognized as influencing students' school performance.**
  Decisions made at school affect home, and vice versa.
- **Sharing information about child behavior across settings is valued.**
  Each partner recognizes that he or she sees the child primarily in one setting and understands how the child is reacting in the other setting.
- **Collaboration has a positive impact on student learning.**
  Educators believe that home and school can accomplish more than either home or school can accomplish alone.
- **Families should be active partners in decision making.**
  Educators believe in the value of making decisions with parents. Educators believe in including parents when addressing concerns about student learning.
- **Problems are solved mutually and without blaming each other.**
  When students are experiencing school difficulties, school personnel and parents understand that two-way communication is necessary.
- **Problem solving is based on a positive, strength-based orientation.**
  School personnel view parents as resources for addressing educational concerns. Collaborative problem solving efforts help to foster optimism about what school personnel and families can accomplish by working together.
- **Family-school relationships are cultivated and sustained over time.**
  Families and educators work together within and across school years to address mutual concerns and provide mutual support for enhancing the learning progress of children and adolescents (Education, 2002, p. 18–19).

Just as it is critical for teachers to build relationships with peers in order to be successful in the classroom, it is likewise important to solidify these same relationships with the family members. In family-school partnerships, the input of both home and school is valued and the focus is on what both parents and educators can do to promote student learning. Successful school collaboration with families respect the goals for their children's education and work as active partners to help fulfill these goals.

FAVORABLE PRACTICES

It is clear that to be most effective it does indeed "take a village to raise a child." Education is a challenging vocation. However, we need not work in a vacuum. As educators, we must work to combine our collective wisdom, strengths, and abilities and learn to effectively collaborate for the benefit of our most precious resource—our students.

Value, encourage, and enable students to use the opportunity to collaborate effectively. If you need help organizing activities and developing procedures to enable this to happen effectively, make use of the Kagan strategies referenced earlier.

Invest in your community. Become an active participant in organizations and activities that celebrate and support the families you serve.

Take time to build positive relationships with the individuals with whom you work. As a teacher, positively model collaboration to your students by valuing your peers.

Remember that effective collaboration is a "learned" skill and will take time and patience to develop.

You are an integral part of the team. Take your place, contribute to and embrace your community.

COMMON MISTAKES

Teaching is a social activity. At its best, everyone connected to the children with whom we are working is involved. This team actively collaborates to make certain that we positively impact the development of our students. However, for various reasons, we often limit the opportunities to actively collaborate with all interested parties or actually prevent collaboration entirely. Below are some quick reminders of pitfalls to avoid when collaborating with other parties:

Do not put children in groups and expect that collaboration will "just happen."

Do not avoid classroom collaboration because of classroom management fears. If you have taken the time to teach grouping procedures and your expectations are clear and measurable, students will live up to your expectations.

Do not try it once and give up. It will take time for you and your students to master the protocols to ensure that the time spent collaborating is productive.

Do not avoid working with your peers and administration, even when you may not agree with them.

Do not miss opportunities to both invite and encourage the community to be active participants in the education of its children.

Do not fail to listen, validate and implement suggestions that parents and guardians have concerning their children.

CONCLUSION

As we have already discussed, collaboration does not come easily for some—be it students or teachers. For many teachers and students, it appears that collaboration has not been a part of their educational experience, or worse it may have been a negative experience. Whether it is pride, a sense of responsibility or stubbornness, we as human beings are sometimes reluctant to seek help or to actively engage in collaborative endeavors. The same challenges that can plague classroom settings can also hinder our willingness to collaborate. Such issues as the concern that one person will take over, a hesitation to share the workload, or difficulty finding common time to collaborative can all impede our progress. In addition, in my experience, effective collaborative lessons require the teacher to be highly organized and to have a well-versed understanding of their students, both educationally and socially.

As previously stated, research shows that teachers are more effective, students are more successful and, overall, school culture is improved if teachers effectively collaborate (Ronfeldt, 2015). Lily Jones (2014) while writing for *Tchers Voice*, reminds us that:

> the relationships you build with colleagues aren't just good for your mental well-being; they're also the foundation of collaboration that can result in increased student achievement. Just like building relationships with students lays the groundwork for academic success, building relationships with colleagues lays the groundwork for effective collaboration. (para 6)

Embrace your differences, stretch your possibilities and remember that, "in the long history of humankind (and animal kind, too) those who learned to collaborate and improvise most effectively have prevailed" (Charles Darwin on Collaboration, 2012, p. 1).

HITTING YOUR MARK

When the practice of collaborating is truly embraced at all levels of a school, success and positive social interactions happen and "Hitting Your Mark" becomes much more rewarding and enjoyable for everyone! The most effective schools develop a high degree of "relational trust" among the members. This trust can only be established if collaboration is practiced often and effectively. Successful collaboration results when we put the problem to be solved in the center, remove our egos, and find efficient and effective ways to work together in finding a common solution.

QUESTIONS FOR DISCUSSION

1. What community resources are available in your area that would be of benefit to the school systems? Are these resources utilized? If so, how? Could they be used a more productive manner? What would the likely outcome be?
2. Research various strategies to engage families and guardians. How would engaging family members benefit students? What hinders family and support members from being involved with students? How would you overcome these issues?
3. How do you plan to collaborate with other faculty and staff? Are there other individuals in the school whom you could also collaborate with to ensure success for students? (Think beyond instructional staff and administration). Why would active collaboration with other personal be beneficial to your students and you?
4. How will you make collaboration a meaningful part of your instructional day? What strategies will you utilize to ensure that students are working in meaningful groups and achieving at high levels?
5. Think – Pair – Share: What does the word collaboration mean to you? Have you ever worked in successful collaborative groups? Why do you think these groups were or were not successful?

ACTIVITIES FOR ENRICHMENT

Working with a team, create a presentation that details a collaboration plan for your future classroom. Included in the plan should be strategies and examples demonstrating best practice in action. At a minimum, the following groups should be considered: family, community, building level, and classroom teachers. Be specific, be creative, and think outside the box. Consider the challenges of implementing your ideas, as well as the benefits.

REFERENCES

All Things PLC. (2015). Retrieved from http://www.allthingsplc.info/about

Benefits of Parent and Community Engagement. (ND). Retrieved from IDRA: http://www.idra.org/IDRA_Newsletter/April_2010_Parent_and_Community_Engagement/Benefits_of_Parent_and_Community_Engagement/#sthash.l9uks05D.dpu

Communication and collaboration. (nd). Retrieved from P21 Partnership for 21st Century Learning: http://www.p21.org/about-us/p21-framework/261

Darwin, C. (2012, January 17). *Charles Darwin on collaboration.* Retrieved from The Future Organization: https://thefutureorganization.com/charles-darwin-collaboration/

Data-driven decision making. (2007, March 22). Retrieved from The Center for Comprehensive School Reform and Improvement: http://www.centerforcsri.org/index.php? option=com_content&task=view&id=85&Itemid=77

Dominguez, C. (2011, February 9). *Collaboration, what does it really mean?* Retrieved from http://blogs.cisco.com/news/collaboration-what-does-it-really-mean

Education, U. S. (2014, March). *Strategies for Community engagement in school turnaround.* Retrieved from Reform Support Network: http://www2.ed.gov/about/inits/ed/implementation-support-unit/tech-assist/strategies-for-community-engagement-in-school-turnaround.pdf

Education, V. D. (2002). *Collaborative Family and School Relationships.* Retrieved from Virginia Department of Education: http://www.doe.virginia.gov/support/student_family/family-school_relationships/collaborative_family-school_relationships.pdf

Johnson, B. (2011, March). *Making the Most Out of Teacher Collaboration.* Retrieved from Edutopia: http://www.edutopia.org/blog/teacher-collaboration-strategies-ben-johnson

Jones, L. (2014, July 18). *Tchers Voice.* Retrieved from Teaching Channel: https://www.teachingchannel.org/blog/2014/07/18/power-of-teacher-collaboration-nea/

Kagan, S. (2001, fall/winter). *Kagan publishing and professional development.* Retrieved from The "p" and "i" of PIES: Powerful principals for success: http://www.kaganonline.com/

McClure, C. (2008, September). *The benefits of teacher collaboration.* Retrieved from District Administration: http://www.districtadministration.com/article/benefits-teacher-collaboration

Merriam-Webster. (2016). Retrieved from http://www.merriam-webster.com/dictionary/collaborate

Oxford Dictionary. (2016). Retrieved from http://www.oxforddictionaries.com/us/definition/american_english/collaboration

Ronfeldt, M. F. (2015). Teacher collaboration in instructional teams and student achievement. *American Educational Research Journal 52(3)*, 475–514.

Slavin, R. (2014, October). *Making cooperative learning powerful.* Retrieved from Educational Leadership: http://www.ascd.org/publications/educational-leadership/oct14/vol72/num02/Making-Cooperative-Learning-Powerful.aspx

Virginia Department of Education, O. c. (2002). Collaborative family and school relationships for childrens' learning. 18-19. Retrieved from Virginia Depart of Education: Virginia Department of Education, Office of Student Services, Office of Special Education

CHAPTER **4**

APPROPRIATE RELATIONSHIPS

Allen R. Hackmann

"But once you are in that field, emotional intelligence emerges as a much stronger predictor of who will be most successful, because it is how we handle ourselves in our relationships that determines how well we do once we are in a given job."

~ Daniel Goleman

INTRODUCTION

Appropriate relationships can be defined a multitude of ways. As a new teacher, you will come in contact with countless people. For instance, teachers work directly with students every day, which prompts the relationship with their parents. We, as teachers, also associate with other colleagues, administrators, and the community as a whole. How, then, can any of those relationships be anything other than "appropriate?" This chapter will identify a variety of relationships one can expect to encounter as well as break down the favorable practices and common mistakes that teachers may face. One profound concept to always consider is that people are people and it is imperative that you take human nature into account as you are forming the many working relationships in which you will participate ("K", 2010).

Courtesy of Allen R. Hackmann. Copyright © Kendall Hunt Publishing Company.

WHAT ARE APPROPRIATE RELATIONSHIPS?

In education, there are multiple relationships that must be managed constantly. What, then, are considered "appropriate relationships?" In order to fully understand this premise, we must break down the words as they each provide mutual meaning. Cambridge Dictionaries (2016) defines "appropriate" as, "suitable or right for a particular situation or occasion." They also define "relationships" as "the way in which two or more people feel and behave towards each other." It would make sense, then, for a teacher, that appropriate relationships include interactions that are proper between two or more people.

Each relationship comes with its own set of rules and levels of appropriateness. As a result, appropriateness may be different depending on the parties involved in each type of relationship. Interactions with students, parents, colleagues, department heads, and administrators will all differ. One of the first and most important factors is recognizing those differences, which will be discussed throughout the remainder of this chapter.

HOW TO MAINTAIN APPROPRIATE RELATIONSHIPS

The over-arching theme of this text is professionalism. Understandably, this should be the foundation for maintaining mutually, respectful relationships. As a new teacher, you must take full control of your role in how you choose to interact with others. This is essential since others may not always behave in a professional manner. Do not participate in someone else's conflict and surely do not seek out others to participate in yours. For example, when listening quietly to someone vent, you must have the ability to discern when their "venting" is acceptable and when you need to speak up and let them know that they are putting you in an uncomfortable situation.

Before the specifics of each type of relationship are discussed, here are a few principles that are common among all constituents (Jaynes, n.d.):

Keep conversations professional in nature. Use language that your grandmother would approve. Stay away from off-color humor because you never know who is listening or how the words you use may come back to haunt you.

Take responsibility for your mistakes and successes. When you make a mistake that affects others, own it. Let people know what has transpired and give clear communication as to how it will be remedied in the future. Conversely, when celebration is in order, do not overdo it. Accept compliments graciously and make sure you give them appropriately as well. This principle goes all the way back to your playground days: nobody likes a sore loser or a sore winner.

Stay away from gossip. For the most part there should be no need to elaborate. However, one aspect of gossip must be considered because it can easily be overlooked. The phrase "guilty by association" describes this situation perfectly. If you idly stand by while others are airing dirty laundry you may be lumped into the group even if you are not actively participating. It is best to physically remove yourself from the situation. You may even consider using some sort of disclaimer statement that shows you do not agree with this type of banter. However you decide to separate yourself from the group, make sure you are very respectful. You do not want to be perceived as offensive or judgmental; you simply want to distance yourself from the current circumstances.

There is a fine line between venting and complaining. Since this line can be blurred, it is best to share frustrations with loved ones or confidants outside of the school system. Once again, it bears repeating that human nature can sometimes turn dark and you do not want your words to be used against you. Just because you say something in confidence does not mean it is going to remain in confidence. Supervisors and co-workers will want to hear about solutions to problems, so do not ever present a problem without also bringing a solution for remedy. Focusing on whom to blame or what is wrong with a given situation is unproductive. When you share an idea that could lead to solving a problem, be prepared to then let it go. Oftentimes, one of two things will happen when you have a great idea. First, you will be volunteering to lead the charge! This resembles the old cliché, "Be careful what you ask for because you might just get it." Second, and probably more frequently, your suggestion will be ignored. If this occurs—let it go. Never fear sharing a good idea, but conversely, do not assume others will see the same brilliance as you do. Share it, feel good about it, and be prepared to let it go.

RELATIONSHIPS WITHIN THE SCHOOL BUILDING

As mentioned numerous times thus far, relationships are expected and encouraged within the field of education. However, while trying to balance your role as "teacher," you must also balance your relationships. It is imperative that you understand the policy of your school division regarding various relationships in the school house, because your school policy will drive, in essence, your behavior with others. For example, some school policies may strongly discourage "inter office dating" ("K", 2010), while others make no mention. Others may have a written policy that teachers are not to "friend" their students on social media, while, again, other divisions may not address this. Another important fact that works with any connection in the school is the overwhelming importance of communication. Communication carries over into any effective relationship, and it can be used for good or for bad. Approach is everything.

RELATIONSHIPS WITH PARENTS

The relationships that you establish with parents will vary from child to child. Ideally, you should strive for each relationship to be professional and reciprocal. First, let's explore the term "reciprocal." Moore (2016) defines this term as, "Interdependent, complementary, correlative—these are synonyms for relationships that are connected, balanced, and interrelated. School/family relationships that mirror these characteristics help create environments where children feel relaxed and confident" (para. 2). Simply stated, the relationship between a teacher and a parent should be child-centered where both parties are striving to ensure student success. In a perfect world, there are 124 hours in a day and you would have unlimited energy allowing you to engage in weekly communication with every family listed on your class rosters. However, in reality, you will have to be very intentional and diligent if you wish to make parent/teacher communication a regular part of your teaching routine. Many school divisions will require you to make a minimum number of contacts per grading period, especially if students are struggling. From my experience, it is a good idea to make positive contacts with parents or guardians as part of your communication plan. Put yourself in the parent's shoes. How would you feel if every time the phone rang, and it was the school's number, it was bad news?

People are all very different, so be prepared to be flexible and establish relationships that both parties find comfortable. Some parents may be very comfortable with constant communication while others would look at it as an inconvenience. When first establishing parent/teacher relationships, take notes and ask questions to gauge how they wish to participate in the school-home relationship. It is also imperative that you support what you say with actions. Do not promise the cookie and deliver a crumb. We always have the best intentions, so if you say you are going to do something, you have to be intentional about following through.

Relationships should always be student-centered and professional. There are times when you will "click" with a particular parent or family and you may feel an urge to begin a more personal relationship. There are other scenarios where you may have a personal relationship with a family before you even teach their child (i.e., this will typically occur more frequently if you live in the same community that you teach). Nonetheless, if or when this happens, be clear and confident in the fact that you can separate the personal from professional in the relationship. In fact, over-communicate to the family that the teaching relationship will take precedence over the personal relationship. If the family believes you will be firm but fair with the child, you can avoid any misconceptions that favoritism will exist.

RELATIONSHIPS WITH STUDENTS

Now that the way you create appropriate relationships with parents has been established, it is extremely important to discuss the daily practice in working with your students. Above all, a teacher should always remain in a position of authority, gaining the trust and respect necessary to fulfill his or her duties. As a teacher, there will be times, depending on the grade level you teach, where you are only a few years older than those whom you will instruct. Therefore, it is essential that you do not cross boundaries, and that you maintain your role as teacher (not friend!) and the student maintain his or her role as your pupil.

There may be times, as mentioned above, that you already have a developed relationship outside of the school building. In those cases, you must be especially mindful not to show favoritism or allow misconduct that you would not otherwise allow from a new student in your class. It goes without saying that consensual sexual or emotionally-charged relationships are never allowed when you are in a supervisory (i.e., teacher) role with a student. This is the same for a student in your class or a student down the hall. If you are in a teaching position, you are not to engage in any type of behavior that could be misconstrued as anything other than a simple teacher-student relationship. There should be no exchanging of phone numbers, no "friending" on social media, and no emails to the student (unless the email is coming from a classroom generated account). Everything you do, as a teacher, will be scrutinized and evaluated by those around you, so be sure that you interact as in the public eye at all times. For example, when meeting with a student after school, never shut your door. Always leave your classroom door open so others walking by can see and hear the interaction, if need be.

Again, know what your school policy states regarding the teacher-student relationship. Some will have very specific rules about communication with students (i.e., either face-to-face or through technology), while others will not address the topic at all. Additionally, teachers will often accept coaching or sponsor positions within the school. During these times, it is natural to form a deeper relationship with the group of students you lead (either through a sport or club activity), but you must still maintain your professional position. This means, at the end of a track meet where you also serve as the coach, you do not take the athlete home because he or she does not have a ride. If you must take a student in your vehicle, you should ask another coach or adult to accompany. No matter how "good" you think your relationship is with a particular student, athlete, or family, all it takes is one accusation to ruin your good name.

Ethical Considerations

Principle II: Responsibility for Professional Competence

The professional educator acts in the best interest of all students

The University of Arizona (2013) has put together a simple list that teachers may appreciate as it serves as a guide to ensure we keep appropriate teacher/student relationships:

They are your students, not your friends. Depending on the grade level you teach and the stage of your career, this phenomenon will change over time. Just take the time to consider

Appropriate Relationships

that an 18 year-old senior in high school and a newly graduated 22 year-old first year teacher will have more in common than not.

Maintain a professional distance. Establish physical and emotional boundaries. As educators, we should value and love our students. Make sure this love is exhibited in appropriate ways. The headlines in today's news stories are cluttered with too many instances where teachers crossed lines and it cost them not only their career but their freedom in some cases.

Do not discuss the following with students: your social life, drugs, alcohol. Only when you are teaching from an appropriate curriculum should you engage in topics that are considered PG-13 or higher. Even when your intentions are noble, your words can be used against you.

Do not share the following with students: music, videos, photos, YouTube videos, or other non-school related websites. Keep your social life separate from your professional life. This can be trickier than one might think. Many school divisions are encouraging teachers to build relationships with their students. The push is to engage in student lives in order to build a rapport that will foster a positive learning environment. Showing up at a little league baseball game where some of your students are in the spotlight can go a long way in the classroom. This type of behavior is encouraged and recommended. However, it does not mean you should give them a snapshot into your personal life. Situations can get easily blurred and, once again, good intentions can put you in the hot seat.

Double check what you have on your answering phone message, your Facebook page, etc. Students and parents have access to these. Assume that people are looking at your social media. Here is a good rule to follow—if you do not want your principal or superintendent to see it, do not post it!

Have students call you by your formal name (i.e., Ms. Stowers), not your first name. Once again, limit opportunities for lines to be blurred in your relationships.

Do not socialize with students outside of school. This may seem to be redundant but you do not want your good intentions to be twisted and used against you.

Do not photograph students except for approved academic purposes. There can be legal ramifications to photographing people without proper permissions.

RELATIONSHIPS WITH COLLEAGUES

Another area of great importance as a teacher centers on relationships with colleagues. Teachers must be able to maintain professionalism at all times, even when others do not have the same standards. Some of your colleagues, while they also are educators, may not share your ethics or values. It is during these times that you must remain consistent and rise above any nonsense that may surface. There are countless ways that a teacher can maintain finesse;

one is ensuring that he or she practices honesty at all times. Earlier, it was mentioned that you should "own" things. This is never truer than when discussing events with colleagues. Whether you are discussing a student's grades, a situation with a parent, or sharing a frustrating moment—you should speak factually, leaving emotion out of the discussion. If you come from a place of honesty and truth, others will observe that you are a drama-free-zone type of teacher.

It is certain that you will build personal relationships with colleagues on top of your professional ones. This can be beneficial because it can foster higher performance in the workplace (Chacon, 2015). When this overlap occurs, you should be intentional about prioritizing the two relationships. It would be very unfortunate if you allowed a personal situation outside of school to affect your ability to work productively with colleagues. Being open and honest with co-workers who become friends is extremely important. As the friendship begins to grow it will give you comfort knowing that regardless of circumstances outside of the workplace you have prioritized your working relationship.

RELATIONSHIPS WITH ADMINISTRATION

This relationship can, possibly, be the most difficult of all the relationships you encounter as a teacher. Administration and teaching are two very different positions. All too frequently teachers misunderstand why administrators make certain decisions. When you look at a situation through the lens of a teacher, sometimes it just does not make sense. Keep an open mind and be confident that thought and purpose go into every decision from an administrator's perspective. There are several key factors that will ensure a healthy, balanced relationship between a teacher and administrator. Strive for good communication, a positive tone between parties, and always remain professional (TEDII, 2016). If you have forgotten what is considered "professional," please refer back to Chapter 1.

There are many factors that play into relationships between school leadership and the teachers they supervise. Some administrators can be very intimidating, but remember: you are a professional, an expert in your given area. Be confident that you can discuss your thoughts and ideas in a respectful manner. As previously stated, once you share an idea, be willing to let it go if administration does not mirror your enthusiasm. Do not get hung up on feeling like you have no voice. A teacher's responsibility lies in educating students, not running the school. Several factors play into building-level decisions. Administrators will appreciate your passion, especially when they feel you respect them as decision makers. Another important aspect of good communication regarding teachers and administrators is approaching them with solutions, not problems. If you see an area of concern, take the time to consider options and have a list of questions that may shed more light on the situation. Teachers who simply point out problems may eventually be ignored. Quality, open communication with your supervisors will enhance the workplace.

Support school administration; this will set the tone for the relationship. There will always be nay-sayers who will not take the necessary time to understand the complexity of how to run a school, much less, a school division. They tend to focus only on their circumstances. Even when confusing times are at hand, show support for your leaders. Do not talk behind their backs, do not engage in conversation when others are talking behind their backs, and follow through on requests. This type of support fosters trust, which leads to a healthy and happy working relationship. You want your leaders to help you to become a better employee. When it is clear that you support their position, then chances are they will be supportive of you as an individual teacher; this includes constructive criticism. Be willing to hear the feedback and make necessary changes. A positive tone should lead to a more positive work environment, even when the circumstances may be difficult. This is a key place where emotion should be eliminated. If you listen to your administrator's words from a neutral place, seeing the situation from his or her perspective, it will allow you to grow into the teacher you were always meant to become. Remember, we can all improve and should always strive for greatness.

Always try to maintain professional relationships, even if your leaders, on occasion, exhibit unprofessional behavior. This does not give you permission to follow suit. Regardless of any foul language, inappropriate comments, off-color humor, or anything else that may occur in front of you, your job is to remain professional. You can listen without participating. You can only control your own actions, so protect yourself.

Education should be a passion, and not everybody is called to this profession. This does not mean that it is easy. Yes, you should love what you do, but do not think it is an easy job. Nothing rewarding is ever easy, and teaching can be extremely rewarding. Where else can you work with one student and 20 years later have that student come back to thank you for the difference you have made in his or her life? Good communication and the proper tone of a professional relationship with administration (and others) will enhance your ability to be the most effective teacher possible.

RELATIONSHIPS WITH THE COMMUNITY

The final group needing coverage for building appropriate relationships is that of the community. Relationships within the community are very important because what you do on the "outside" could very well carry over into the "inside." Be mindful that while your teaching contract might list your work hours from 7:30 a.m. until 2:30 p.m., you are a teacher before 7:30 a.m. and after 3:30 p.m. How you present yourself in the public can have a rewarding or devastating outcome. For example, I remember going to school as an undergraduate student—I may have been about 20 years-old. I was eating dinner with my girlfriend and looked up to see my Abnormal Psychology professor sitting at the bar. Now, had he been sitting at the bar only eating dinner or having a beverage or two, I would probably think nothing of his actions. However, there was no food present, only drink after drink and his belligerent behavior from the excessive amount of alcohol that was consumed. Even though I was, technically, an adult, and he, technically, was "off the clock," his actions stuck with me the next time I had the class. I did not see my professor as a composed, respectable academic, but a drunk who could not control his behavior in a public venue. How you carry yourself and interact in the community can have lasting effects on your position in the classroom.

Another way to embed yourself into the community is by finding out personal habits or hobbies of your students and families. If you have a student who is especially talented with dance, go to a recital on the weekend to show your support. Likewise, if you have another student who excels at football, attend a game. You do not have to stay for the entire program or event, but your mere presence will speak volumes and, as a result, improve the teacher-student-parent relationship.

FAVORABLE PRACTICES

By now, it should be clear not only what are appropriate relationships, but also how to navigate through the different relationships, depending on the audience. There are a few take-a-ways that seem to spill over from one context to another. Tallia, Lanham, McDaniel, and Crabtree (2006) summarized a comprehensive list of successful characteristics in working relationships that carry nicely from the medical field into the educational field:

Trust. This concept is important in any working relationship, weather it is trust with students, or trust with the adults (i.e., parents, colleagues, administrators, or community). It allows each person to feel confident in you, as a new teacher, and know that what you say and do is for the betterment of the student. Remember that actions speak loudly, and if your actions do not mirror your words, a breakdown in trust can occur.

Diversity. Diversity is not mere race, but gender, age, ethnic background, religious preferences, or educational experience. It covers all aspects of those with whom you will come into contact. As a teacher, it is important to find out the strengths and weaknesses of each of your students so you can instruct them in the learning mode that will give optimal results. It is also important to understand the parents of your students so appropriate trust and communication can peak in the relationship. Understanding and appreciating the differences in your classroom will enable growth within you and your families.

Mindfulness. Being mindful enables you to remain current with best practices and approaches, getting the most out of your students. It is being open to new ideas and new strategies, without fearing ridicule or punishment. There will be times when a specific activity is successful with all students, and then the same activity causes frustration with another group of students. In times like this, do not throw out the activity, yet identify commonalities and tweak for the next use. Remember, what works once might not work again, and what does not work once might work the next time. Being mindful keeps you open to new plans and concepts.

Interrelatedness. As a teacher, this is a concept that you should welcome with open arms. Because you will work with a variety of people in your daily schedule, you must appreciate the interrelatedness that comes with the territory. When you are sensitive to your position and responsibilities, you are aware of how your actions affect those of whom you interact.

Respect. "Respectful interactions are considerate, honest and tactful. People who respect one another value each other's opinions and willingly change their minds in response to what others say. Respect is especially important in challenging situations, as it can help individuals focus on problem solving" (para. 8).

Varied Interaction. There are times when your relationships and interactions with others will be task-oriented, but other times it will be social in nature. As you move into your new position, understanding the difference can help you stay grounded. Tallia, et.al (2006) further discuss that, "Social relationships are personal and often based on activities that exist outside of work; task-related relationships are focused on professional issues" (para. 9). To be effective in your craft, you should try to encourage both types of interactions in your classroom.

> **Leading the Way**
>
> *Leading sometimes means addressing situations that may be uncomfortable. It is important for leaders to learn to tactfully address situations that potentially can become, or appear to be inappropriate. If the inappropriateness of a situation is unclear, it is best to discuss with an immediate supervisor.*

Effective Communication. We exchange information in a variety of ways as a teacher. Most of our correspondence comes through via email, or text messages. Still, other forms have carried through for decades: phone calls, letters home, or face-to-face interactions. It is important that you decide which method is most appropriate in given situations. For example, if you have an irate parent, you should not send an email or something impersonal, especially since it is extremely difficult to read tone in an email. For a parent who is upset, please pick up the phone or schedule a face-to-face conference. For more information on what is effective communication, continue reading to Chapter 5.

COMMON MISTAKES

Conversely, there are mistakes that educators, especially those new to the position, may find themselves practicing. Some errors that professionals find themselves engaging in are mentioned throughout this chapter. Below is a quick summary:

Using your work email for personal correspondence. Be very careful and realize that any email that you write to a colleague, parent, or friend can be used against you in court. It is critical to be professional and factual at all times, but especially when you are using your school system account.

Gossiping about your co-workers. Not only is this extremely unprofessional, but the gossip always seems to find its way back to the source. Do not engage in workplace drama. Be polite, work hard, do your job, and stay out of the teacher's lounge!

Wearing unprofessional dress. You are a teacher, so you should be identified as "teacher." Be sure to follow the dress code in your faculty handbook and, I would say, dress one step above the rest. Do not dress like the students, even if you are only a year or two older. You should have a certain presence about yourself that will set the tone for those of whom you work. Aside from dress, be sure that your hair (and facial hair, guys) is neat, your jewelry and attire is respectable, and your shoes match the type of wardrobe. For example, do not wear a suit and then slip on Converse (Walden, 2015).

CONCLUSION

This chapter has covered a variety of relationships and scenarios that you will inevitably encounter throughout your teaching career. If there is one take away from this chapter that can help guide you as you navigate through the trials tribulations of being an educator, let it be this—be professional. When professionalism remains the primary focus in your relationships related to your teaching career, you cover yourself with a layer of armor that will protect you in the most trying times. This is not to say that you will not find meaningful, deep relationships that can last a lifetime. You will. You are choosing a career where like-minded individuals have answered a calling to serve others. It is only a matter of time before some of your professional relationships will begin to foster into something new and rewarding. It is possible for you to allow these relationships to naturally develop while always keeping professionalism the primary focus. You are not judged by how you feel but rather by how you react when you feel less than your best. I often tell my students that being disrespected does not give you permission to be disrespectful. Take this to heart. One day one of your relationships is going to be tested. Behaving in a professional manner will garner you respect and admiration from others.

HITTING YOUR MARK

When it comes to relationships, "Hitting Your Mark" means being fearless in your interactions with others because you are always the consummate professional. There truly is a great deal of variety between the roles and responsibilities that come with the various relationships you will encounter. When professionalism guides your judgment, you can participate in relationships with confidence and security. Understand that others will challenge this notion regularly; some may even be your superiors or close friends. However, when you choose to remain professional, you protect yourself while earning respect from others.

QUESTIONS FOR DISCUSSION

1. Create a list of all of the people you will be in contact with related to your position in the school. (Be sure to include any people associated with extra responsibilities like clubs or sports).
2. Explain how you plan to get close to your students without getting too personal.
3. Two students get into a fight in your classroom. You have a personal relationship with one of the families. That night you get a call at home asking how the situation is being handled regarding the other child. How do you respond?
4. Using the four main relationships you will encounter—student, parent, colleague, and administrator—think of a situation that would cause you to become uncomfortable. Extend beyond this concept and explain how you would handle each situation.
5. After reading this chapter what impacted you the most? Explain how it changed your perspective regarding the relationships you will encounter?

ACTIVITIES FOR ENRICHMENT

Often, students will share a core group of teachers. Working in a small group (i.e., 2–3 classmates), create a yearly communication plan where all teachers share the responsibility of contacting each student's parent/s or guardian/s at least four times per year. (A guideline to follow would be 3 to 4 teachers sharing between 100 to 120 students)

REFERENCES

A Teaching and Educational Development Institute Initiative for the Queensland Higher Education Development Consortium. (2016). Establishing a relationship with your supervisor. Retrieved from http://www.uq.edu.au/student-services/phdwriting/phlink04.html

Cambridge Dictionaries Online. (2016). Appropriate. Retrieved from http://dictionary.cambridge.org/us/dictionary/english/appropriate

Chacon, B. (2015). 5 ways to build relationships with colleagues. Retrieved from http://www.careerealism.com/build-relationships-coworkers/

Flowing Wells School District Staff Development. (2013). Establishing appropriate relationships with students. Retrieved from https://www.coe.arizona.edu/program_reviews/establishing_relationships

"K". (2010). Appropriate work relationships. Retrieved from http://improvingyourworld.com/relationships/appropriate_work_relationships_006113.html

Jaynes, N. (n.d.). How to maintain appropriate relationships with management. Retrieved from http://careerplanning.about.com/video/How-to-Maintain-Appropriate-Relationships-With-Management.htm

Moore, K. (2016). Policies and practices: Establishing reciprocal relationships with families. *Early Childhood Today. Retrieved from* http://www.scholastic.com/teachers/article/policies-practices-establishing-reciprocal-relationships-families

Tallia, A., Lanham, H., McDaniel, R., & Crabtree, B. (2006). Seven characteristics of successful work relationships. *Family Practice Management, Vol. 13 (1)*, 47–50. Retrieved from http://www.aafp.org/fpm/2006/0100/p47.html

Walden, M. (2015). The most common workplace mistakes and how to avoid them. Infinity Consulting Solutions. Retrieved from http://www.infinity-cs.com/career-center/the-most-common-workplace-mistakes-and-how-to-avoid-them

CHAPTER 5

COMMUNICATION

Andrea P. Beam

> "Words are singularly the most powerful force available to humanity. We can choose to use this force constructively with words of encouragement, or destructively using words of despair. Words have energy and power with the ability to help, to heal, to hinder, to hurt, to harm, to humiliate and to humble."
>
> ~ Yehuda Berg

INTRODUCTION

Communication is the basis of all endeavors, especially in relation to education. Without proper communication, it is nearly impossible to hold a productive conversation with parents, other teachers, supervisors, or students. It is also quite necessary for teachers to become effective in communication as they lead their students because, without this interactive skill, it is difficult to assess student understanding—a task imperative in our 21st century schools. Several devices can be sought on how to effectively communicate; however, there are some simple remedies that prove helpful in any situation, even those where de-escalation is necessary (Beam & Pinkie, 2015).

Courtesy of Andrea P. Beam. Copyright © Kendall Hunt Publishing Company.

WHAT IS COMMUNICATION?

Communication is a concept that can change the whole focus of interaction with simple words or simple gestures. According to Merriam-Webster's Dictionary (2015), it is "the act or process of using words, sounds, signs, or behaviors to express or exchange information or to express your ideas, thoughts, feelings, etc., to someone else." As teacher candidates become familiar with their craft, this concept is of the utmost importance for everyday success, for it is used to intervene with potential problems that may arise, it is used to promote growth of students, and it is consistently used to exchange information with parents and other professionals. Communication can be verbal or nonverbal—each of which is especially effective in its own right.

WHY IS COMMUNICATION IMPORTANT?

When working closely with others, teachers should be mindful of their perception as well as the receiver's perception. Sometimes the one initiating a conversation might have the best intentions, but after relaying the information, he or she finds that the information was taken completely out of context. For this, perception is extremely important. The communicator needs to ensure that the message intended is the message relayed and that the receiver obtained the intended information. Without the two matching, the message could be completely lost. It is also good practice to engage in active listening. Not only is it important to be able to verbalize our thoughts and needs, but it is equally important to be able to listen to and understand what others are saying (either with words or body language). We must not ignore the language sent through our movements and facial expressions. This type of communication is just as important as articulation. As teachers speak to others, such as parents, administrators, students, or other faculty, they should be mindful of their body language. For example, what is their stance? Are their arms folded in a "closed off" mode? Are they leaning forward to show interest in the conversation? What is their facial expression? Are they paying attention, making good eye contact, and encouraging the exchange or are they rolling their eyes, looking at their watch/clock, or appearing dismissive? All of the noted actions speak loudly, whether intended or not intended, so candidates must monitor themselves at all times. There may be times when a conversation with someone turns from productive to quite unproductive or indifferent. The teacher, while practicing good communication skills, must be able to depersonalize in those situations. As candidates move into their first

Ethical Considerations

Principle I: Responsibility to the Profession

The professional educator fulfills the obligation to address and attempt to resolve ethical issues

few years of teaching, they will perfect their practice and become more successful when caught in unfavorable situations or conversations. They will learn to hear the words of the message and not take them personally, because, sometimes, others do tend to lash out at the messenger, not understanding that the message is not really a personal attack. Oftentimes, when this occurs, the teacher needs only to listen and acknowledge the upset. Then, and only then, will the two be able to move forward towards a productive outcome.

NON-VERBAL MODES OF COMMUNICATION

As mentioned, communication can be verbal or non-verbal. Some of the non-verbal cues have already been alluded to earlier, but now it is important to focus on other modes—possibly those not considered. For many teachers, their actions may speak quite loudly without ever uttering a word. Some modes of non-verbal communication used in the classroom environment include:

Space

For space, teachers should consider their interactions with others. Do they get really close in proximity to other students, parents, or other staff members? Some might interpret this "closeness" as endearing while others might interpret as threatening. Teachers must be able to "read" their audience and act accordingly. If it is obvious that they are too close, it is a simple fix by just stepping one or two feet backwards (Hansen, 2010).

Use of Furniture

What does the arrangement of furniture in a classroom reveal? Well, if the chairs and desks are arranged in separate "pods," it could send a message that group work is valued. However, if the teacher has the desks and chairs in clean rows facing the front of the classroom, it might portray that individuality is preferred, with all attention on the teacher, possibly devaluing the use of group work. There are other ways to express a certain "feel" in a classroom, too. Consider where the teacher has his or her desk placed; what about relaxing areas—are they available for students to read quietly and comfortably? How is the lighting in the classroom? Is there an abundance of natural light, or are the fluorescent lights used at all times? Does the teacher use lamps to soften the mood of the room? The use of furniture in the classroom speaks volumes (Faulk & Evanshen, 2013).

Eye Contact

Eye contact is an important part of personal communication. Do you look directly at the person to whom you are speaking or do you look past the person? Do you show interest by use of eye contact or is the contact overused to the point of making the recipient a bit uncomfortable? Too much or too little of anything is probably not a good idea; balance is the key (Hansen, 2010).

Movement

Consider how you move about in the room. Do you stay close to a podium at the front of the room, remain seated during instruction, or do you move about the room ensuring that everyone is on task? How is your movement during discussions and lectures? Do you "talk" with your hands where it becomes a distraction or is your energy noted in the movement of your body and expression? Affective teachers roam around the room and are excited about their content, so there probably is movement in their hands, body, and overall expression (White, 2012).

Level of Energy

A teacher's energy is contagious—If you are bored, guess what? Your students will be bored too. However, if your level is elevated, your energy is apparent, and your voice is appropriate, you have a hard time losing the interest of your students. The energy level that a teacher exudes will keep learning fun and engaging (Vijayan, Chakravarthi, & Philips, 2015).

Posture

We might not even notice the importance of this non-verbal mode of communication, but a teacher's posture is important in relaying information. Our posture shows our confidence and also our excitement about the information being shared (Rocca & McCroskey, 1999). When evaluating teachers that you might have had in the past, try to remember how your favorite teachers carried themselves. Did they hunch over or sit at every chance, or were they on the move and standing tall and strong? Did they convey an air of confidence and comfort or did they appear closed off, not wanting to be bothered? As effective teachers, we must always evaluate ourselves and strive to improve. Our goal, after all, is to reach all learners.

Attention to the Clock

This is a huge item to consider! Nothing says, "I am ready to get out of here" more than someone constantly watching the clock. While some teachers (or students) might simply be glancing—out of curiosity—to see the current time, it does give the assumption that time is dragging on and it is time to move on to another topic or idea. As a teacher, be careful of watching the clock. One thing that might be helpful is to have a watch or other device near your area of instruction so as you glance, it does not give the impression that you are moving too slowly through material. Another great idea is to have a clock on the wall at the back of the room. As a teacher, you are always moving about, anyway, so it would be easy to glance at the time inconspicuously.

Rate of Voice

Consider the rate, tone, and pitch of your voice while teaching. Are you talking too fast, too slow, too monotone, or too . . . all over the place? It is important to have a good tone in the classroom so those in the front and those seated in the back of the room can hear you clearly. Also, if you are writing on the board, never turn your back to the students. Not only does this muffle your voice, but you cannot see what is happening behind you. Be careful not to speak too quickly; some students take longer to process ideas, so be sure to provide appropriate "wait time" (Alban, 2012).

Positions of Feet and Legs While Sitting

This is a really interesting concept. Some research shows that the position of a person's feet and legs while sitting will show interest or disinterest. Reiman (2007) states that "the direction of our feet and the rest of our body indicate our interest" (p. 201). Because of this assumption, it is important to attend to the person to whom you are speaking so he or she can feel more comfortable during the interaction.

Gestures

The position of your body while seated is also important. Do you show interest by leaning forward in your chair? Do you smile while the other person is talking? Do you nod at appropriate times to show that you are engaged in the discussion? All of these gestures can show that you are interested in the other person, without using a single word (Hansen, 2010).

Clothing and Setting for the Interaction

The final non-verbal mode surrounds the idea of teacher dress. As a professional, it is common knowledge that appropriate dress is expected and encouraged. What, however, would be communicated if a teacher appeared at a conference wearing sweatpants or sloppy clothing? Could it give the impression that the teacher does not value the position or the meeting? Quite possibly. Because of this, a teacher's attire is extremely important in verbalizing the value of the profession—dress for the position that you are ultimately seeking. A teacher's clothing should be appropriate not only in accordance to school policy, but also for the many types of interactions that will be experienced throughout the school day with other staff, parents, students, community members, or school board employees. This appearance shows the value that the teacher places on the position by, again, not even saying a word.

SKILLS FOR COMMUNICATING

Everyone communicates, but how effective is your communication? Are you able to "say what you mean and mean what you say" (Preston, 2005)? Some teachers might believe they are quite skilled at engaging in conversation and retrieving information, but it is probably a good practice to hone already embedded skills to be even more successful. Five items to utilize that would equip a teacher for skilled communication are building rapport, being an active listener, learning appropriate assertion skills, learning effective conflict management skills, and integrating collaborative problem-solving skills (Valenzano, Braden, & Broeckelman-Post, 2013).

For rapport building, a teacher wants to ensure that positive relationships are established even before the school year begins. To do this, send home a friendly "welcome" card or letter to your student telling him or her how happy and eager you are to meet on the first day, make a simple call home to introduce yourself to the parents, or open your classroom so the parents and student can get acquainted with your expectations for the year. If candidates take the time to build positive relationships based on mutual trust and respect, it encourages others to want to work and meet the presented expectations.

The second item of discussion is learning to be an active listener. Teachers can be active listeners both verbally and non-verbally, and should actually practice both types during communication. Once rapport is established, it is necessary to show that the message being relayed is valued. Non-verbally, a teacher can nod, smile, or lean in to the conversation to show that he or she is hearing the conversation. Ensuring that you, are making good eye contact, using appropriate facial expressions and body language will all demonstrate your interest in the conversation. A teacher can actually invite additional information by asking questions, paraphrasing, or encouraging discussion. While engaging in active listening, it is important to deviate from judging or advice giving opportunities.

The final skill for effective communication incorporates the last three items to utilize and includes learning appropriate assertion skills, learning effective conflict management skills, and integrating collaborative problem-solving skills. There are several ways to communicate in uncomfortable situations, but it is crucial to do so in a manner that allows descent. Being assertive does not equate to being disrespectful, yet it gets your point across to the receiver. In situations that are less than desirable, teachers should focus on a plan of action to allow resolution to occur. The primary task is to figure out the problem. Oftentimes, if someone is upset, allowing that person to vent and share their displeasure is half of the battle. Both sides need to hear the issue at hand before the problem can be addressed. Once all parties are aware of the issue, they can (together) generate solutions and implement a plan to resolve the problem. It is extremely important for candidates to remain calm and listen during this time; never take anything personally. A good suggestion after a plan is developed is to follow up after a week or so to ensure that all parties are still satisfied. This will also strengthen the rapport in the relationship.

COMMUNICATION THROUGH TECHNOLOGY

Technology is both a blessing and a curse. Teachers rely on technology for an array of communicative tools, including email, newsletters, websites, and blogs. While the usage of technology has increased in our schools, our ability to walk across the hall to have an actual conversation has actually decreased—we email the person in the office next door! Because of the changes in practice, it is critical to check, double check, and triple check our conversations that are being launched across the web. What teachers might intend to send in an email might be the polar opposite of that which is read on the recipient's end, so be sure to always read your messages before you click the "send" button. If you receive an unfriendly email, it would be wise to not respond immediately. It is too easy to spout off a quick email without proofreading and have your intended tone read (or misread) loudly and clearly. If this happens, take a few hours or so to re-group, actually read the underlying message, and then respond in a professional manner (i.e., removing your emotions—again, not taking anything personally). Here are a few things that Strawbridge (2006) notes to keep in mind when sending emails:

> **Leading the Way**
>
> *Most teachers like to know the "why behind the what." When asking someone to make a change or complete a task, providing additional information or reasoning may improve cooperation and support.*

- When emailing a group, keep the addresses private by using the blind carbon copy (BCC) button.
- Use short sentences with spaces in-between paragraphs.
- Avoid abbreviations or popular contractions of text messaging.
- Keep writing style professional.
- Use a signature block and include information to help the recipient contact you.
- Re-read for grammar and spelling errors and never say anything in an email that you would not say in a crowded room.
- Do not deal with conflict or negative comments in an email. Bad news should be conveyed face-to-face.

FAVORABLE PRACTICES

There is an abundance of material discussing what makes up effective communication; however, effective communication might vary slightly from one profession to another. For educators, communication is one of the primary means of exchange and it is handled with and without words. Because of the array of methods, some practices yield better results than do others.

Active listening. In order to effectively communicate, teachers should be mindful of their perception as well as the receiver's perception. Active listening is a great strategy to employ. It allows the communicator to demonstrate understanding of the conversation by use of verbal and non-verbal cues. Some examples of active listening could be a simple head-nod, a smile, a person leaning into the conversation, or a repeat-back/summary of the discussion. All of these strategies show that the conversation is heard and understood. A really good task to assess personal communicative skills could be to evaluate yourself as you engage in a discussion with someone (i.e., spouse, co-worker, friend), and jot down typical habits that you find yourself repeating. When someone is talking to you, for instance, do you lean in, nod, smile at inopportune times, look at your watch, ask a lot of questions, or interrupt? If you find yourself performing any of these actions, it could open the door to examine your personal skills and provide work for growth.

Depersonalize situations. Another strategy that is very helpful in becoming a more effective communicator is the ability to depersonalize situations. Teachers and other staff members must converse with many individuals, but at the top of the list are students and their parents. In speaking with students and their parents, there will be many pleasant, productive conversations; however, on rare occasions, there will be unpleasant conversations. Either way, it is quite effective to avoid any negative comments or personal attacks that may follow in the discussion and take on a neutral stance, not taking anything personally.

Purposeful meetings. Teachers might also find that, when meeting with one or more counterparts, it is useful to have a purpose for the meeting. Never go into a meeting without an agenda—keep all meetings focused, timed, and paced. In addition to active listening and depersonalizing situations, find the main purpose for the meeting, find common goals, brainstorm solutions, and follow up to ensure that the goals, in fact, were productive. By following simple strategies, teachers can diminish potential problems that may arise.

Consider the mode. The form of communication you choose also says something about the content. Placing information on a web page, in a school newsletter, on a flyer, or in a group email indicates impersonal communication. However, these methods may be appropriate for mass communication, especially when forms or visual information is included. Sending a private message or making a direct phone call not only makes the communication more personal, but usually indicates that the information is a more important and specific.

COMMON MISTAKES

As with any position, some common practices are encouraged, while others are discouraged. With the topic of communication, it is no different. This chapter has highlighted effective practices for communication, but it would not be complete without a look at some of the common pitfalls. Most of the mistakes have been suggested throughout the discussion; here is a quoted recapitulation of the highlights discussed and reinforced by Marcus (2015):

We make assumptions. Most of us are guilty of this at times. We assume we know the way someone else thinks or feels and, therefore, we do not bother to fully explain or to ask questions to find out his or her opinion. We end up jumping to conclusions that can result in miscommunication, hurt feelings, and distrust.

We do not tailor our message to the recipient. One size does not fit all when it comes to communication. If you want your message to stick, it is important to understand what is important to the individual you are speaking with and tailor your message to that individual based on what you know about them. For instance, are they a direct no-nonsense type? Then make your message short and to the point. If they require justification and back up, be prepared with data and statistics to support your message.

We do not give timely responses or feedback. It is difficult for many of us to give feedback and constructive criticism, so we often procrastinate and think that if we wait, it will not be as difficult. Often, our procrastination makes it much more challenging when we finally get the courage to address issues. The feedback can also lose its impact if it is given too late.

We are not assertive. We hesitate to use assertive communication either because we do not understand its value or we do not have the confidence to state our opinion or reaction to something. When we can clearly state how we feel or what we think about an issue, it avoids a lot of wasted time and emotional energy. With assertive communication, you are focused on your reaction only and not casting any judgment or blame with another party. This often diffuses any potential disagreements.

We avoid confrontation. Confrontation is not necessarily a bad thing when handled properly. Because many of us have negative feelings about confrontation, we try to avoid it at all costs. This usually results in longer-range problems that can sometimes blow up unnecessarily.

We do not listen. Listening is paramount for good communication. If we are talking just to hear ourselves talk, that is a monologue not a conversation. Active listening requires a focused effort to hear what the other person is saying and perhaps what they are not saying.

We do not show respect for others. Nothing ends a conversation faster than a disparaging comment. Show respect by listening and acknowledging other people's opinions, even if you do not share those opinions. Respect is the foundation for open and direct communication.

We rely on email or tweets when face-to-face communication is appropriate. There are some conversations that must be held face to face. Sending an email or tweet to someone in hopes that they will understand your message and intent is not productive and can often lead to misunderstanding.

We do not think before we respond. How many times have we said something we later regretted because it was an emotional response and we did not give ourselves the time to calm down? Quick emotional reactions are usually a mistake. The purpose of the communication gets lost and what we end up remembering are the emotional consequences.

CONCLUSION

It has been said, "teaching is generally considered as only fifty percent knowledge and fifty percent interpersonal or communication skills" (Communications Skills World, 2013). Because the art of teaching is not simply knowing one's content, but also the craft of disseminating that information to all counterparts—all of whom might learn very differently—it is imperative that teachers utilize effective verbal and nonverbal communication skills. Several strategies have been shared that will encourage open lines of communication, including building rapport, being an active listener, being able to depersonalize uncomfortable situations, and being prepared for the unexpected.

Communication is a two-way street. It is important for the deliverer and it is extremely important for the recipient to be able to converse on various topics of interest. Both sides of a conversation need to have active participants who are willing to ask questions, solve problems proactively, and compromise as necessary. Only, then, will effective practice come to fruition and only then will candidates become teachers.

HITTING YOUR MARK

To be effective communicators, both verbally and nonverbally, it is essential to monitor one's own body language, words, and that of the recipient. Teachers and teacher leaders have a top priority to communicate with a whole host of individuals. Their students, students' parents, colleagues, and supervisors will all be carefully watching and listening as to how situations are handled and alleviated. It is a skill set learned with time and tenure and one that will provide, possibly, the most benefits as teachers balance their challenging schedules with the countless meetings that always follow. By learning effective communication early in your career, not only will you exemplify professionalism to those of whom you work, but you will demonstrate how teachers learn to hit the mark at every turn.

QUESTIONS FOR DISCUSSION

The following five discussion questions were taken from Chapter 10: Communication, from the text *Professionalism: Real Skills for Workplace Success*, published by Pearson Publications. http://wps.prenhall.com/chet_anderson_profession_1/77/19801/5069185.cw/-/5069195/index.html

1. Discuss the importance of good communication in the workplace.
2. Give examples of good communication and bad communication you have observed. What effect did they have on the situation?
3. Why is eye contact important?
4. Is it appropriate to send a "thank you" note or invitation via email? Why or why not?
5. Share a common form of body language that is often misinterpreted.

ACTIVITIES FOR ENRICHMENT

Toothpick Communicator. This activity emphasizes effective communication between the sender and receiver. You will need one volunteer from the class who considers him/herself to be quite effective with communication. Each student in the class receives 13 toothpicks. The volunteer will be given a model made from the 13 toothpicks and will be required to follow the rules in verbally communicating how to replicate the model. The rules of this activity are as follows:

- No questions can be asked
- Only verbal instructions will be given
- Instructions cannot be repeated

Time limit: 3 minutes

After 3 minutes, the volunteer will show the model to the rest of the class to see how well he/she communicated the procedures in replicating the model.

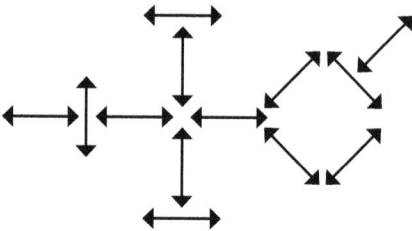

Active Listening Activity. This project is designed to provide systematic practice for your listening skills.

Select one person whom you have contact with each day.

Using the strategies you have learned, practice effective listening to the selected person for 5 consecutive days.

For each of the 5 consecutive days, critique your active listening and questioning ability. Complete a listening log for each day and include a "grand" log for all 5 days.

At the end of the 5 days, study all the data and reflect on your active listening ability. Write a grand summary including the following: Guidelines followed, correct mechanic and appearance, accurate summary of your data with insightful comments.

- What are your strengths? Give evidence (examples).
- What are your weaknesses? Give evidence (examples). How will you improve?
- What hindrances were noted? Give examples. How will you improve?
- What type of question did you ask most often? Give evidence.
- What did you learn about yourself? Give examples.
- What did you learn about your colleague? Give examples.
- What did you learn in general about active listening? Include facts and feelings.
- How will this experience change how you will communicate/listen?
- Other comments

This project should be typed and include (a) title page with name, title of the project, course number and date, (b) 5 completed listening logs, and (c) grand summary.

REFERENCES

Beam, A., & Pinkie, E. (2016). *Secondary curriculum in practice: Developing with an integrated approach.* Boston, MA: Pearson Publications.

Communication. (2015). Retrieved from http://www.merriam-webster.com/dictionary/communication

Communications Skills World. (2013). Retrieved from http://www.communicationskillsworld.com/communicationskillsforteachers.html

Marcus, B. (2011). 10 Common communication mistakes. Retrieved from http://womenssuccesscoaching.com/2011/02/10-common-communication-mistakes/

Reiman, T. (2007). *The power of body language: How to succeed in every business and social encounter.* New York, New York: Gallery Books.

Strawbridge, M. (2006). *Netiquette: Internet etiquette in the age of the blog.* Cambridgeshire, U.K.: Software Reference.

CHAPTER **6**

SOCIAL MEDIA

Chris Amos

"The power of social media is that it forces necessary change."

~ Erik Qualman

INTRODUCTION

Social Media—Most of us use it. We have accounts on various platforms such as Facebook, Twitter, Instagram, and others. For some, it is an entertaining and enjoyable medium. For others, however, it is a terrible vice that appears to make time move more quickly, yet enables even more efficient procrastination. While there are both positives and negatives to social media, the real question is, "Does social media have a place in education? Can it be of value to teachers and students?" It certainly has a use in our personal lives, but even in that setting it can be wrought with challenges and pitfalls. In this chapter, we are going to examine social media both in its role in the personal life of a teacher and its use in the classroom.

Courtesy of Chris Amos. Copyright © Kendall Hunt Publishing Company.

WHAT IS SOCIAL MEDIA?

Before engaging in a discussion regarding the uses and issues surrounding social media, we must first define it. Merriam-Webster's Dictionary (2015) defines social media as "forms of electronic communication through which users create online communities to share information, ideas, personal messages, and other content." Although the term social media did not enter our vernacular until the mid-2000s, social media has been in existence for much longer.

When looking at the definition of social media, it is easy to understand why there were nearly 100 major, active social networking platforms in existence in 2015 (Mehra, 2015). Also, while there may be close to 100 major social networking sites, there are hundreds more in existence that have not achieved the designation of "major." A 2013 study conducted by the Pew Research Center found that 73% of Americans use at least one social networking site (Mehra, 2015). Oftentimes, when you think about social networking, you simply think of the most common social networking platforms in use in your own social sphere (Facebook, Twitter, Instagram), however, there are countless others.

WHY IS SOCIAL MEDIA USED?

The whole point of social media is that it is, indeed, social. This may seem like a no-brainer but it deserves mentioning. You do not post pictures on Facebook or Instagram just so you have a place to look at your pictures. You are intending for your friends, family, and random Facebook friends (whom you do not actually know) to see your photos. Social media is really a cultural phenomenon. It is a way for people to document their lives and share the things that they feel are important in a way that civilization has never been able to before. We could spend chapters discussing the human psychology of why we post what we do to social media, but that is not the point. Nevertheless, it is important to understand that social media has uses in the world of education beyond just sharing your vacation photos.

Besides personal sharing, social media has also become a way for people to connect and find out information about other people. It is naive to think that your fellow teachers, administrators, and students have not attempted to look you up on social media. In today's society, if people want to know something about you, they will turn to social media instead of asking you directly. This trend actually has a name—Facebook stalking. Most of us have been guilty of Facebook stalking at some point in lives, sometimes out of nosiness and sometimes for legitimate reasons.

Because people turn so often to social media to find out things about others, it is important to make sure that your social media appropriately reflects who you are as a person, but more importantly, as a teacher. Most potential employers are looking up their job candidates on social media (Grasz, 2014). What you have on those accounts could mean the difference between being offered the position you are seeking or not.

PUBLIC VS PRIVATE VS NOTHING

The new great debate: Public vs Private. When it comes to social media, should you make your accounts available for everyone to see? Just friends of friends? Only those who have your email address? No one at all? The debate of public vs private is an ongoing one. Should you even have social media accounts? Should educators use social media in teaching? Let's explore these questions.

Professors oftentimes have this discussion with college students who will soon be, if they have not already started, applying for internships/practicums, student-teaching positions, and full-time teaching jobs. College students will ask if they really have to go in and delete all of their spring break photos or if they should go back through their Twitter account to see if they said anything offensive in the past. The basic questions is why can't you just go in and make your profile private and keep those administrators who are going to be interviewing you from seeing your accounts and seeing those compromising pictures that do not make you seem like an valid teaching candidate?

Here is the reality of situation—nothing posted online is ever truly private. Why are employers calling fewer references today than ever before? Because they often do not need to (Davidson, 2014). They can simply go to a teacher candidate's social media profile and find out everything they need to know about that person, and in reality, what they discover will be far more real and far more valuable than what most references would share. Even if you have the tightest filters and privacy settings on your account, your social media will still be scrutinized.

Regardless of whether you think this practice is fair, or violates your First Amendment Rights, it is occurring in thousands of interviews (Davidson, 2014; Grasz, 2104; Noguchi, 2014). What you create on social media is your personal brand. It is how friends, family, and others will come to view you. It is the reputation you are building. You may have the potential, the heart, and the drive to be the best teacher anyone has ever observed, but if your social media accounts are littered with inappropriate pictures, your chances of becoming a teacher could be threatened. Your online persona, your personal brand, can enable you to be

> **Ethical Considerations**
>
> Principle V: Responsible and Ethical Use of Technology
>
> *The professional educator ensures students' safety and well-being when using technology*

considered for tremendous positions, or it can keep you from ever stepping foot in a classroom.

You have to think beyond just future employers as well. Did you know that professors often look at your social media accounts, too? Whenever students come to me asking for a Letter of Recommendation or asking if I could make a phone call for them for a position somewhere, I often go to their social media accounts, first. What I know about a student from class may not the true character of the student. There have been countless times that I have looked at a student's social media account and decided they were just too immature for me to recommend them, in good conscience, for a position. I did not feel comfortable putting my good name on the line for a student who did not seem to have his or her act together. I have also seen students get turned down for scholarships because of the types of things on their social media accounts. It does not just come down to filters and setting your social media accounts to "private." There are programs that make it easy for people to get around privacy filters along with a number of other ways for people to get information about you on social media. Bottom Line: You have to be smart.

ADVANTAGES OF SOCIAL MEDIA

Now that we have opened with a word of caution and demonstrated the seriousness of social media, hopefully you are not ready to delete all of your accounts. There is value to social media and teachers are using it extensively within the classroom. Let us look at both the positives and negatives when it comes to social media in education.

NETWORKING

There is no argument that social media has value. The only question is whether the value outweighs the negatives. Social media is a great way to network. It is enables you to network with other teachers to share ideas and collaborate on projects, network with administrators and teachers to secure jobs (LinkedIn), and network with education professionals to help find solutions to educational issues and learn the latest and most effective techniques.

KEEPING IN TOUCH

One of the amazing outcomes that social media has provided is the ability to keep in touch with people. While this applies to networking, it also applies to former colleagues, former students, friends, and family. As a teacher, being able to know that your former students are succeeding without them having to come back and tell you is a blessing.

ENHANCING CURRICULUM

Beyond the traditional uses of social media, teachers have been discovering the benefits of integrating social media into the curriculum. Current and future generations of students are engaged in online media and social networking platforms; therefore, it makes sense that educators would utilize these platforms to enhance instruction.

A number of teachers have developed class Twitter Accounts or Instagram Accounts as a way to engage with students both inside and outside of the classroom. Teachers are able to post links to articles that are relevant to topics being covered in class or highlight the achievements of students through written posts or photographic means. Teachers are also developing class Wikis, which create an online classroom environment where announcements can be made, homework lists and schedules can be published, discussion boards can be utilized as well as many other uses. While Twitter, Instagram and Wikis are just a few examples of technological platforms that teachers are successfully employing, there are many others as well.

CONNECTING WITH PARENTS

Oftentimes, the interaction between parents and teachers is limited and occurs only in negative situations. While certainly this type of interaction with parents can be improved in other ways, social media does provide a possible solution. Having a social media platform that parents can follow and see what type of learning is taking place in the classroom, as well as see positive posts about their child's accomplishments (within FERPA regulations) can certainly foster a better parent-teacher interaction.

REMINDERS

Students forget things. Parents forget things. We all forget things; some of us more than others. What if there was a way to remind students to bring certain books for class, or that they need their lab goggles today, or that the class is meeting in a certain area? The great thing is that there are a lot of apps and social media platforms that allow this type of interaction between teachers and students. While email can sometimes work, students do not always check their email accounts, but they appear to always check their social media like Twitter and Facebook. These would be great locations to post reminders about upcoming assignments or due dates for projects. Also, apps like *Remind* allow teachers to send messages to students' phones without having to ever exchange phone numbers. Parents can also use this app and connect to the class to receive reminders and announcements as well.

SHARE PASSIONS

Social media allows teachers and other educators to indirectly generate conversations about the topics and issues of which they are most passionate. Social media accounts have spaces for bios and interests; students can see these, which may help generate discussions about important topics such as environmental issues or cyberbullying.

DISADVANTAGES OF SOCIAL MEDIA

While there are many advantages associated with social media, there can also be a significant amount of disadvantages. Extreme caution must be practiced among future and current educators to avoid the many dangers and pitfalls associated with social media.

VENTING

You should never use social media to vent. Frequently, people turn to social media to post passive-aggressive messages as a way of venting their frustration about a particular situation. This generally happens because we have access to social media at our fingertips—our phones. We do not take the time to walk away from a situation and decompress before we get on our phones and post something on social media that we should not because we are not in a clear frame of mind. While some people may feel that posting something on a private social media account is a harmless endeavor, nothing is ever truly private. This type of behavior can have extremely negative consequences, so it is imperative to walk away from a situation and gather ones emotions before addressing certain concerns. Remember, all it takes is one screenshot for your private rant to become very public knowledge.

DRESS

Most people are intelligent enough to know that the way they dress influences what people think about them. However, not many people think about the way that they dress when it comes to social media. As we established earlier, employers may go to social media to find out what they can about a job candidate. While showing up to an interview in a nice, work-appropriate dress or suit is great, if the majority of your pictures on social media show you wearing low-cut tops, an over-abundance of piercings or tattoos, or t-shirts depicting themes inappropriate for children, that potential future employer may form a negative opinion about you, which could eliminate you from the interviewing pool.

The issue of dress relates to how you are portraying yourself to students and parents. As stated earlier, your students and parents could look you up on social media. What type of image are you portraying? If you are wearing mini-skirts or cleavage-baring tops or showing a bunch of tattoos, what are your students being taught . . . that dressing in such a way is fine because our teacher dresses that way? Consider pictures with you in a bathing suit. Those may not seem like a big deal but your students will find these pictures. Let's say you are a 22-year-old new teacher fresh out of college teaching a high school class full of seniors. Some of those students will probably be 18 or even 19 years old. It will be hard enough for you to maintain a standard of separation by asserting yourself as a teacher and not as a friend. This challenge could be more complicated if your students are checking out photos of their teacher wearing revealing bathing suits. Overall, it could not only cause a lack of separation but also compromise your ability to be taken seriously by your students.

ALCOHOL

The minimum drinking age in the United States is 21 years old. There are no laws that say if you are over 21 you cannot drink. In fact, most schools are not going to tell you that you cannot drink. However, consider this—If you have pictures of yourself on social media drinking alcohol, what message are you sending to your students? The pictures of you at a party, drinking and having a good time are essentially sending the message to your students that alcohol is fun and that you condone drinking. If a teacher stands up in front of his or her students and tells them not drink and to avoid alcohol the students will see the teacher as a hypocrite. Even if your verbal message is that underage drinking is wrong, students are seeing your online photos and are receiving mixed messages. Most school administrators are not going to tolerate a teacher who posts or is tagged in photos that portray the teacher drinking as it creates a bad image for the school.

OLD PICTURES

We all have those old pictures that make us cringe when we see them. How in the world did we think those clothes or that hairstyle looked good?! However, beyond the potential embarrassment, there is additional danger here. There may be pictures lurking deep in your social media accounts that you completely forgot about that may display a youthful indiscretion—something that parents, students, or administrators may find. It is important to go into your social media accounts and go back as far as possible to make sure that only the things that you want to be on your account are there. This can be a time-consuming task if you have a particular social media account for an extended period of time, but still needs to be completed. You never know how far back and how deep students, parents, and administrators may dig. A good standard to use is, "Would I want my grandmother seeing this?" If not, you should probably take it down.

TAGGED PHOTOS/POSTS

Another area of concern with social media is your friends tagging you in photos or posts on various social media platforms. We have that one (or maybe three or four) whom we love but who has not quite come to grasp with maturity and being an adult. They have no idea that what they are tagging you in or posting on your wall or comments section could cause you to get in serious trouble. While you may not want certain items posted on your wall or account, if you allow friends to tag you without reviewing the tags, you could have negative items posted or tagged to you. It is a good idea to make sure that your settings prohibit items that people have tagged you in from showing up on your account until you have approved the post. In addition, be aware that even if you remove a tag, you may be tagged in other photos in the album, which will lead people to discover the untagged photos. Or, most commonly, people will look at your friends' accounts and can easily find you in untagged photos.

NOTHING IS TRULY PRIVATE

As was alluded to earlier, when it comes to social media, nothing is ever truly private. It is foolish to think that a private profile will ever fully protect you and the things you post online from possible circulation. Privacy filters can often lull people into a false sense of privacy and protection. If people are able to hack into government databases or Fortune 500 companies, then what makes you think your information is safe? In recent years, there have been several prominent security breaches involving online social interaction platforms. In November 2013, hackers successfully compromised 318,000 Facebook accounts, 70,000 Gmail, Google+, and YouTube accounts, 60,000 Yahoo accounts, 22,000 Twitter accounts, along with thousands of Pinterest and Tumblr user account's information being stolen. In early 2013 over 250,000 Twitter users account emails and passwords were stolen (Pagliery, 2013). Your social media accounts and your login information are not safe.

Most of us use the same email address and password for multiple accounts, so all it takes is one account to be compromised and all of your accounts are compromised. Even beyond the possibility of someone hacking into your account, most people are fairly repetitive and uncreative with their passwords. Your accounts may not even be hacked, but simply accessed by an unauthorized user. Along these same lines, how often do you accidently leave your phone somewhere or walk away from your laptop to work on something else and leave your social media accounts up on your browser window? There have been numerous examples of people who have had friends, co-workers, or students go onto someone's social media account that they have left open, post something that they think is funny, then someone sees the inappropriate post and suddenly it becomes a situation that can have very serious consequences for the person who actually owns the account. People have had their employment terminated over things someone else has posted on their account (Love, 2011).

In 2010, three students from Downers Grove North High School outside of Chicago were charged with hacking into their teacher's Facebook and email accounts where they began altering content, moving items around, and deleting emails (Bartosik, 2010). Later that year, Tufin Technologies, a cyber-security company based in Burlington, Massachusetts, conducted a survey of 1,000 New York City teenagers. The study found that 16% of the students surveyed admitted to attempting to hack social media or email accounts (Ash, 2010). While having a personal social media account hacked may not seem likely to happen in your perspective, you must understand how tech-savvy kids are now-a-days, and come to the realization that even if you do not leave your Facebook account open on your desk in the classroom, students may still be trying to access your social media accounts.

If you do choose to post something on social media, know that once you have posted something, it is out there forever. It does not matter if you delete a picture or post, it can still continue to exist in many forms and fashions. Electronic devices such as computers and cell phones keep track of actions that you perform, even after you delete the action. A skilled IT professional will be able to pull this ghost data off of your electronic device and retrieve "deleted" information.

If you happen to change electronic devices, understand that the social media platforms keep track of your information and the things that you post, even if you choose to delete them. You may not think this seems fair, but by using these social media platforms, you are consenting to this lack of privacy and allowing the various platforms to keep track of what you do on their sites. It is often included within the privacy agreement, which is generally part of a much longer User Agreement document that none of us actually read. We just click the "Agree" button and begin using that service.

SCREENSHOTS

While all of the previously mentioned scenarios are capable of happening and do happen, the most common way your private posts become public has not yet been discussed—screenshots. Most modern day electronic devices are capable of taking a screenshot. On a smartphone it only typically requires pressing two buttons simultaneously for a couple seconds. On a computer, you can quickly press the

Leading the Way

Teachers are often surprised to find that assuming a leadership role can affect how others interact with them socially. It can be difficult for leaders to navigate previously established friendships while fulfilling supervisory responsibilities. Relationships that can easily be overlooked by those established or maintained through social media. It is even more important to maintain a professional online presence for those in positions of authority.

"Print Screen" button. There are numerous ways to capture something on your device's screen and it makes no difference how the image is captured. It is now a permanent, lasting piece of evidence that can severely damage your career.

Even communication like text messages can be dangerous. Text messages are something that most people understand can be captured and distributed to others, but we often do not think about that. How well do you actually know the person you are sending the text to? To whom are they loyal? If you are complaining to a fellow teacher about a school administrator, do you know for sure that the teacher would never show the text to that administrator? If you need to vent, it is best to do it in person with no paper trail. Venting or gossip that takes place in form of email, text message, or any other easily recordable medium is never a good idea.

Applications like Snapchat are not foolproof, either. While an app that allows you send messages and pictures that have viewing time-limits and delete themselves may seem like a great solution, these types of apps just lull you into a false sense of security. At least apps like Snapchat alert the sender when their Snap has been screenshotted but that does not do anything to prevent the receiver from keeping the screenshot. Extremely tricky people will use a different phone to take a picture of the screen so the sender never has any idea that their private message has been captured and digitized.

CYBERBULLYING

As teachers we know the dangers of bullying. Kids can be cruel. We remember bullying incidents from our own schooling: kids would be picked on in the hallways or at recess, students would get beat up, or rumors would be spread by other students. As teachers, we try to prevent bullying as much as we can both within and around the schools, but bullying has changed a lot in the last several decades. It is no longer confined to the ball fields or the playgrounds but is taking place in the cyber world. Text messages and social media accounts are the newest arenas for bullying; it is called "cyberbullying."

People who cyberbully often hide behind this cloak of anonymity or a sense of fearlessness since the other person cannot just step up and immediately confront them face-to-face. For this reason, cyberbullying has reached levels never seen before. Students are posting mean comments on Twitter, creating fake profiles on Facebook, and posting embarrassing photos to Instagram. In 2013, the Youth Risk Behavior Surveillance Survey found that 15% of high school students (grades 9–12) were a victim of cyberbullying the previous year (CDC, 2015). The number of cyberbullying victims is likely even higher, but with rapidly evolving technology and cyberbullying being so new, current surveys and research are limited.

Why is cyberbullying relevant when discussing teachers using social media? The answer is simple: because teachers can use social media to spot cyberbullying and help prevent it from continuing. Children who are victims of cyberbullying are more likely to use alcohol and drugs, skip school, experience in-person bullying, earn poor grades, have lower self-esteem, and have more health problems (Cyberbullying, n.d.). Teachers who are engaged in social media, on the contrary, can be a part of the solution by helping to identify and stop cyberbullying from reoccurring.

However, the reverse is also true. Teachers who are on social media are also at risk for becoming a victim of cyberbullying. While you may not be worried about your third grader bullying you on Twitter, you should be aware of the potential for that third grader's parent(s) to attempt cyberbullying.

A recent study from Great Britain found that in 2015, 40% of teachers surveyed had been abused online by their students' parents. The most alarming part is the sharp increase from 2014 when 27% of teachers reported online abuse from parents (NASUWT, 2015). Teachers are being subjected to disparaging comments about their appearance, competence as a teacher and even more shockingly, sexist, racist, and homophobic slurs. The study also found that 34% of students had taken photos or videos without the teacher's consent and 62% had posted offensive comments about their teacher online. In addition, 15% of teachers reported having been threatened or subjected to threatening behavior from a parent. Teachers interviewed shared stories of pictures taken by students or parents that included vulgar language being posted to social media or having fake profiles made on social media accounts using the teacher's name. These postings were highly offensive items used in an attempt to have the teacher terminated (NASUWT, 2015). Teachers must be aware of the dangers of being cyberbullied and know what recourse they have if they are victims of cyberbullying.

FAVORABLE PRACTICES

While we have spent a large portion of this chapter discussing the pitfalls of social media use as a teacher, there are also substantial benefits. As a teacher, if you decide to utilize social media, you should keep some final key points in mind. Remember the benefits and uses of social media. Some advantages are networking; keeping connected to friends, family, former students, and parents; enhancing your curriculum; and being able to share your passions. These are all wonderful things, if you keep up with the best social media platforms for accomplishing each of these.

It is important to stay on top of social media trends. Social media is constantly evolving and new social media platforms are emerging every year. All of your students may be using Twitter one year and then none of your students are using it the following year. Why is it important for you to stay on top of social media trends even if you are not using it in the classroom or for personal use? The simple answer is that even if you do not use social media, your students are and it is where they are getting information and learning about anything and everything. Very few students are reading books, newspapers, or scholarly sources; you are lucky if they are even using credible sources at all (Rideout, 2014). The current social media trend is apps (Hensel, 2016). It seems that the anatomy books are going to need to be updated soon, because the cell phone is quickly becoming an addition to the skeletal structure of kids' hands. They are seemingly never without them. Kids, even adults, are never far from their phones. Social media is moving away from traditional computer content and user interfaces, to platforms that work almost exclusively on a smartphone. Platforms like Instagram are not designed to be used on a computer, but rather a smartphone.

Because social media is where students are gathering their information for personal and educational use, teachers need to take advantage of these social media platforms. Teachers should be mindful in discovering the things that are learned, how they are learned, and examining ways to embed social media in the learning process to better capture their students' attention. I firmly believe that as educators, we must meet the students at their level. The days of a chalkboard and slide projector are long gone; we must stay current with trends so as to better understand our students' needs in becoming more effective educators.

COMMON MISTAKES

If you are connected with a student on a professional social media, you should never send private messages to the student. You may be thinking, "What's so wrong with sending an encouraging Facebook message to a student?" While your intentions may be clean and well-meaning, if there are ever any questions asked or doubts raised about a possible inappropriate relationship with a student, those messages could be taken the wrong way. Plus, sending private messages just seems suspicious. This especially goes for messages being exchanged about non-school activity or anything to do with a student's private life.

Teachers should know the dangers that simple accusations may have on their professional reputation. There need not be any proof either, because the accusation alone can have a severely negative impact on a budding career. If accusations can kill careers by themselves, why take a chance? Put yourself in a parent's shoes. If you knew your son or daughter was sending private messages back and forth with a teacher, would you feel a little uncomfortable about the situation? Maybe you would want to investigate? You have to be extremely cautious. If you would not say it publically in front of others or your school administration, then chances are you should not say it at all. All comments and messages should be posted publically to avoid any appearances of wrongdoing.

This type of danger with social media is even more amplified for high school teachers. Most first year high school teachers are only a couple years older than some of their students. The separation at this stage has to be even greater. Teachers cannot put themselves in any compromising positions. New teachers have to consider things not just from their perspective, but from other perspectives, as well.

CONCLUSION

Social media can be a wonderful tool or a career-ending minefield. As an educator, it is really what you make of it. If you adhere to the best practices of social media while taking precaution not to stumble into any of the pitfalls, your students and you can benefit immensely. Do not be afraid of social media. It has tremendous value and can actually make your job much more efficient. It is important to keep in mind that the suggestions and warnings in this chapter are not just for those seeking their first teaching position. Veteran teachers and even school leaders must be mindful of their social media presence and what it says to their students, parents, leaders, and communities.

HITTING YOUR MARK

How many times per day do you access social media? Have you ever thought of its implications on your career or its ability to make you a better teacher? Social media can do both of those things. Teachers must be cognizant of the new role that social media plays in the life of students and in the classroom environment. Social media can be used in a myriad of ways to your advantage as a teacher. Shift your mindset from thinking about social media as something that is done only for personal enjoyment to a medium that you can utilize in enhancing student learning in innovative ways.

QUESTIONS FOR DISCUSSION

1. Do you think teachers and teaching candidates should keep their social media accounts private? Should teachers allow students to connect with them social media? Parents?
2. What are some ways that social media can be used to facilitate learning outside of the classroom? How can you integrate social media into your in-classroom activities?

3. How can you team up with other teachers at your school to create opportunities for students to use social media platforms across different academic subjects and from year to year?
4. What social media accounts does your school currently have? What is the purpose of the accounts? Is the information on these accounts well organized and posted in a timely manner for students and parents? What suggestions would make to your school's administrator regarding how they could improve the school's social media accounts?
5. How can you use social media to create an inclusive environment where students can learn proper online behavior as well as ways to build up their peers?

ACTIVITIES FOR ENRICHMENT

If you are a teaching candidate, review your social media accounts. Check for photos and posts that may demonstrate questionable behaviors or create negative perceptions to school administration. Go all the way back to the very beginning of your accounts. Also, check for pages you may have liked or followed that may have changed names in recent years and may involve causes or activities that you do not support.

Develop a social media policy for your classroom. Create standards for communication, discuss how students should interact with each other, and establish a process that students can safely report cyberbullying if they are a victim or see it occurring.

Create a Wiki or use some other type of platform to build an online hub for your classroom. Set up pages to make announcements, list homework assignments, and provide links to resources to enhance learning. Use this space not just for students, but parents as well.

REFERENCES

Ash, K. (2010, June 14). Tech-savvy students hack into school computers: Schools work to prevent security breaches. *Education Week - Digital Directions.* Retrieved from http://www.edweek.org/dd/articles/2010/06/16/03hackers.h03.html

Bartosik, M. (2010, April 2). Social media harassment: Former student may have had lingering animosity toward her former softball coach. *NBC Chicago.* Retrieved from http://www.nbcchicago.com/news/local/Students-Harassed-Teacher-with-Facebook-89779492.html

Centers for Disease Control and Prevention (CDC). (2015, December 2). Youth risk behavior survey data and documentation. Retrieved from http://www.cdc.gov/healthyyouth/data/yrbs/data.htm

Davidson, J. (2014, October 16). The 7 social media mistakes most likely to cost you a job. *Time*. Retrieved from http://time.com/money/3510967/jobvite-social-media-profiles-job-applicants/

Grasz, J. (2014, June 26). Number of employers passing on applicants due to social media posts continues to rise, according to new CareerBuilder survey. Retrieved from http://www.careerbuilder.com/share/aboutus/pressreleasesdetail.aspx?sd=6%2F26%2F2014&id=pr829&ed=12%2F31%2F2014

Hensel, A. (2016, January 4). 3 biggest social media trends to know for 2016. Retrieved from http://www.inc.com/anna-hensel/what-to-watch-2016-social-media-trends.html

Love, D. (2011, May 11). 17 people who were fired for using Facebook. Retrieved from http://www.businessinsider.com/facebook-fired-2011-5?op=1

Mehra, G. (2015, April 14). 91 leading social networks worldwide. *PracticalEcommerce*. Retrieved from http://www.practicalecommerce.com/articles/86264-91-Leading-Social-Networks-Worldwide

Noguchi, Y. (2014, April 15). Can't ask that? Some job interviewers go to social media instead. Retrieved from http://www.npr.org/sections/alltechconsidered/2014/04/11/301791749/cant-ask-that-some-job-interviewers-go-to-social-media-instead

Pagliery, J. (2013, December 4). 2 million Facebook, Gmail and Twitter passwords stolen in massive hack. *CNN*. Retrieved from http://money.cnn.com/2013/12/04/technology/security/passwords-stolen/

Rideout, V. (2014, May 12). Children, teens and reading. A Common Sense Media research brief. *Common Sense Media*. Retrieved from https://www.commonsensemedia.org/research/children-teens-and-reading

Social Media. (2015). Retrieved from http://www.merriam-webster.com/dictionary/socialmedia

The National Association of Schoolmasters Union of Women Teachers – The Teachers' Union (NASUWT). (2015). Pupils using social media to bully teachers. Retrieved from http://www.nasuwt.org.uk/Whatsnew/NASUWTNews/PressReleases/PupilsUsingSocialMediaToBullyTeachers

U.S. Department of Health & Human Services – Stopbullying.gov. (n.d.). Effects of cyberbullying. Retrieved from http://www.stopbullying.gov/cyberbullying/what-is-it/index.html

PART 2

GETTING THE JOB

CHAPTER **7**

RESUMES AND PORTFOLIOS

Russell G. Yocum

"Credentials are like potential energy, the compliments of a name on paper, in documents, word of mouth, but faith is like kinetic energy, the motion and the force that which is witnessed. Hence in the end it is the faith rather than the credentials that really takes you places."

~ Criss Jami

INTRODUCTION

Perhaps the most critical step between earning your education degree and landing your first job as a teacher is developing a resume that will get you noticed so that you will secure an interview. Even after obtaining that first teaching position, effectively communicating your experience and preparation can improve your chances of being considered for advancement opportunities. In this chapter, sample cover letters, resumes, and portfolios are presented along with discussion of each and tips for couching non-educational work experience in terms that translate to commensurate skills in educational settings. Finally, references will be listed that you will find helpful as you use the material in this chapter to refine your own resumes and portfolios.

Courtesy of Russell G. Yocum. Copyright © Kendall Hunt Publishing Company.

COVER LETTERS

You have earned your teaching degree and a professional teaching certification for your state. You may have even acquired some valuable experience to prepare you for the position you are seeking. You have put together an amazing resume . . . that never gets seen because you lack an attention-grabbing cover letter. An "effective cover letter specifically and concisely points out the most relevant skill sets mentioned in your resume and relates them to the stated needs/qualifications of the position" (Parker, 1999, p. 59). Dissecting this phrase proves useful. "[S]pecifically and consisely point[ing] out the most relevant skill sets mentioned in your resume" (Parker, 1999, p. 59) presupposes that you have a resume that highlights skills needed for the job. Additionally, the phrase "relates them to the stated needs/qualifications of the position" (Parker, 1999, p. 59) means that this cover letter should not be a generic, one-size-fits-all cover letter, but it should be tailored to a specific job opening. Armed with this information, we are now ready to discuss each of the elements of a cover letter in detail and then have a look at a sample cover letter.

DATE AND SUBJECT LINE

Place the date at the top right margin of your cover letter. You will want to save an electronic version of your cover letter, but remember to manually update the date each time you modify and send your cover letter (in print or electronically) to a new prospective employer. Below the date, you should place the address of the organization to which you are applying for an interview. Directly below that, it is helpful to provide a subject line. The principal that you are hoping will hire you may have multiple job openings for which he or she will be interviewing applicants. Use the subject line to specify which position you are seeking.

SALUTATION

Avoid using some iteration of "To Whom It May Concern" or "Dear Sir or Ma'am." Do a little bit of research and find out the name of the principal with whom you hope to interview.

BODY

The next element of your cover letter is the body. This is the place where you will "[S]pecifically and consisely point . . . out the most relevant skill sets mentioned in your resume" (Parker, 1999, p. 59). The key words here are "specifically," "consisely," and "relevant" (Parker, 1999, p. 59). Be specific. State the job you want and list those relevant skills that make you qualified for the job. Be consise. You want to have a one-page cover letter that the principal can read without having to flip back and forth between multiple pages. List only the relevant skills that translate to the teaching job you are trying to acquire. If you worked at a landscaping company, you do not need to tell your prospective principal about the perfect length and type of grass for the lawn on the school football field, but you might mention the translatable skills sets from this job that may include being able to follow instructions, work with little to no supervision, and paying attention to detail. If you worked at a toy store, the principal does not need to know about your skill for stocking shelves or running a cash register, but the fact that you learned to quickly establish rapport and communicate with children and parents who came in to the store would be relevant.

CLOSING AND SIGNATURE BLOCK

Now that you have briefly presented the related skills that qualify you for the job at hand, you should have a closing statement and then your signature block. In case your cover letter becomes separated from your resume, and to make it easier for potential employers to contact you, be sure to remember to include your contact information (address, phone number, and email) in your signature block. Refer to the sample cover letter below (Figure 1) to see how all of the aforementioned elements come together.

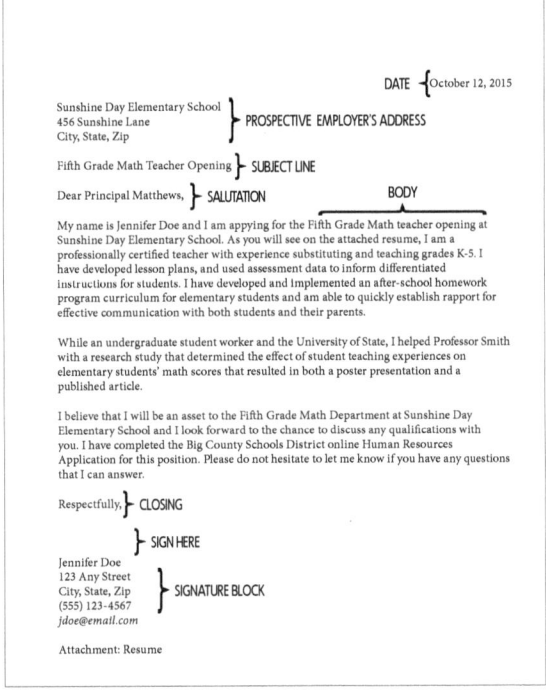

FIGURE 7.1. *Sample Cover Letter*

RESUMES

Now that we have discussed how to prepare a cover letter to get your resume noticed by a principal, we will detail the sections of a resume and look at a sample. If you include jobs from outside the educational setting on your resume, make sure that you do so in a way that shows how the skills you obtained from that job will translate to the educational sector. Try to make all of the elements of your resume fit on one to two pages.

HEADING

Your resume should include a heading that contains your name and contact information.

EDUCATIONAL BACKGROUND

On this portion of your resume, list the degrees you have earned, the university, the date awarded, and your major. Note any degrees that you are also currently pursuing.

TEACHING/ADMINISTRATIVE EXPERIENCE

Use this section to list any teaching and administrative experience. Be sure to list your student teaching and other relevant experience, at least until you have established yourself in your own classroom (part-time babysitting, working in daycare centers, and doing substitute teaching will all help). Again, include non-educational jobs if you can that demonstate skills that will also apply to education.

PROFESSIONAL LICENSURE

List your state's professional teaching certification information.

PROFESSIONAL RECOGNITION

Provide details for any awards you have won.

SCHOLARLY ACTIVITY: PUBLICATIONS AND PRESENTATIONS

Include a list of any publications and presentations that you have authored or co-authored. If you have not yet obtained any publications or presentations, consider working with a faculty member at your college or university to begin getting some material for these sections of your resume. Most new teachers have not yet had the opportunity to present at conferences or be published. If this (or any other) section has no information, simply do not include it, as opposed to including it and stating "none" or "not applicable."

SERVICE: PROFESSIONAL AND COMMUNITY

Principals will be pleased to know that you are willing to work to serve your students and community beyond your contractual obligations. Provide some information on volunteer service you have done in both the educational and community settings.

PROFESSIONAL MEMBERSHIPS

Most universities' teacher education departments will require you to have a membership in one or more professional organizations related to the education field. List your memberships in this section.

Refer to Figures 2 and 3 to see how all of these elements look on a sample professional resume.

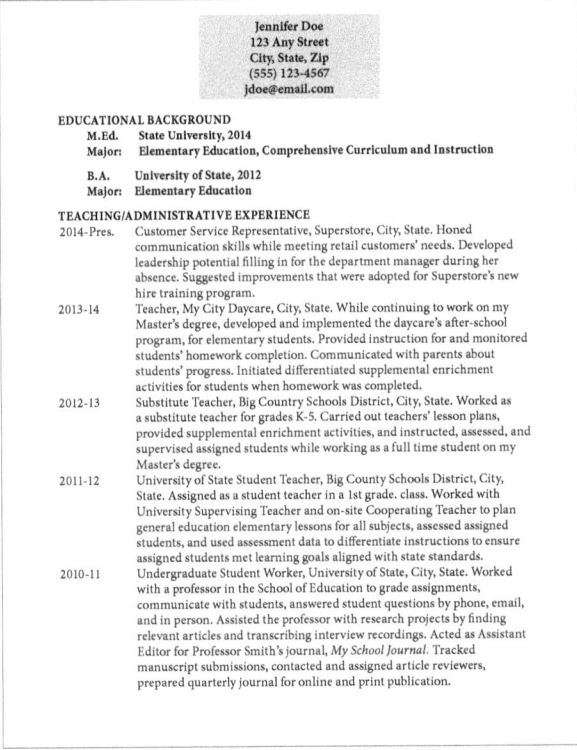

FIGURE 7.2 *Sample Resume, Page 1*

PROFESSIONAL LICENSURE
MyState Professional Educator's Certificate (#1234567, Valid through 6-30-20)
-Elementary Education (K-6), SOL (K-12)

TEACHING/ADMINISTRATIVE EXPERIENCE
2010   Undergraduate Student Worker of the Month (November, 2010), University of State, City, State. Recognized for my diligence as an Undergraduate Student Work for Professor Smith

SCHOLARLY ACTIVITY: PUBLICATIONS
Smith, P., & Doe, J. (2010) Making education count: Effects of student teaching experiences on elementary students' math scores. *My Education Journal, 1*(1), 1-12.

SCHOLARLY ACTIVITY: PRESENTATIONS
University of State Research Symposium, 2010, Smith P., & Doe, J., Poster session, "Making Education Count: Effects of Student Teaching Experiences on Elementary Students' Math Scores." June 13, 2010.

SERVICE: PROFESSIONAL
2010-11   Assistant Editor: *My School Journal*
2010-11   Secretary: University of State Council for Exceptional Children chapter *Education*

SERVICE: COMMUNITY
2010-Pres.   Volunteer Activity Director, Big County Senior Citizens' Center, City, State

PROFESSIONAL MEMBERSHIPS
Association of Christian Schools International
Council of Exceptional Children

FIGURE 7.3 *Sample Resume, Page 2*

PORTFOLIOS

While the resume provides potential employers with your educational and work related experience, along with highlighting your achievements, the portfolio is more expansive. Portfolios are much more visually and artifact based and provide potential employers with a better chance of getting to know what really makes up your professional identity (Higgins, Nairn, & Siglo, 2009).

If you graduate from a traditional teacher preparation program at a university, it is likely that you will be required to develop and maintain a portfolio that you will submit during your student teaching experience. If you are an alternative certification career changer, your school district will probably require you to maintain a portfolio during your "rookie" teaching years. While there is not a uniform format of paper versus electronic (Chuang, 2010; Oakly,

Pegrum, & Johnston, 2014) or an all inclusive list of contents for portfolios, a good portfolio will contain the following: a professional photograph, an accounting of the number of hours of direct instruction and observation hours, your resume, copies of any degrees and certifications earned, sample lesson plans you have developed, samples of students' work stemming from those lesson plans, samples of how you have assessed students' performance, and how you have used that assessment data to inform instruction. You may also conisder including pictures of yourself working with students on a specific activity (be sure to obscure students' faces unless the school had permission on file for their image to be shared), photos of bulletin boards you created, or photographs showing how you have set up a classroom.

Ethical Considerations

Principle II: Responsibility for Professional Competence

The professional educator demonstrates responsible use of data, materials, research, and assessment

---

FAVORABLE PRACTICES

To strike a balanced combination between the best types of resumes for business and academia, McNeilly and Barr (1997) conducted research on what human resource specialists and college recruiters expect to see on resumes. The most favorable business resumes contain educational qualifications, work experience, honor, awards, and information about any extracurricular activities (McNeilly & Barr, 1997). College recruiters felt that academic major, grade point averages, and a list of all colleges attended were necessary (McNeilly & Barr, 1997). Interestingly,

> [t]he results of both . . . suggest that recruiters want to see all work experience, not just the experience that is relevant to the current job opportunity . . . This information provides employers with evidence of loyalty, stability, and commitment and predicts future performance on the job. (McNeilly & Barr, 1997, p. 359)

The most favorable resumes and portfolios then, will contain all of the information described in this chapter, but in a way that also highlights the positive character traits of "loyalty, stability, and commitment" (McNeilly & Barr, 1997, p. 359). Additionally, do your homework about your prospective employer. For example, find out whether the employer expects to see hardcopies or prefers electronic submission of a resume or portfolio—give prospective employers what they want!

Be prepared to provide additional details of items and experience listed on your resume, but also be ready to speak about your anti-resume. Employers who are impressed by the achievements and successes you provide on your resume and portfolio may also be curious about how you handle setbacks and failures, for these reveal as much about your character as do your accolades (Furst, 1995).

COMMON MISTAKES

You have 6–15 seconds to get your resume noticed (TheMuse, 2014), so you want to catch a recruiter or prospective employer's eye. There is a fine line between getting your resume noticed and coming across as, well, just plain weird! You might be tempted to add pretty colors or graphics or to deviate from the standard resume format. Don't! Employers are more interested in a resume that lists the qualifications they are looking for over a resume that is pretty (TheMuse, 2014).

Finally, Smith (2015) lists the top three mistakes that will get your resume thrown away: You do not meet the minimum qualifications for the job, you are seeking any job and your cover letter and resume are too generic (as mentioned earlier, your cover letter should include the principal and school name and the position for which you are applying), and you are missing attention to detail (mistakes, typos, changes in font style and size, etc.).

Do the opposite to combat these mistakes that will land your resume in the trash instead of on the principal's desk! **If you have just graduated from your teacher licensure program, have no graduate degree, and little teaching experience beyond your student teaching hours, do not apply for an instructional coach position that requires a master's degree and five years' teaching experience.**

While you want to list all relevant education, work experience, and accomplishments, do not turn in the exact same cover letter and resume to entirely different schools/school districts. A parochial school in the Bible belt is obviously looking for a different kind of teacher than a public school in New York City. Showcase your qualifications, education, experience, and accomplishments in a way that shows you can be a good fit for the "culture" of the school to which you are applying (Smith, 2015, para. 7). This means you will need to have many slightly different versions of your cover letter and resume by the time you finish!

Show attention to detail. Avoid using fancy fonts, huge font sizes, or crazy colors to get noticed. Read, reread, and reread your cover letter, resume, and portfolio again and again before submitting them. Then have peers read, reread, and reread them again. You want to catch any mistakes before your materials are sent. Imagine applying to teach high school English and literature with a resume that has a tiny spelling or grammar error.

CONCLUSION

With the information in this chapter, you can write a cover letter, resume, and portfolio that should get you and your qualifications noticed. However, there is no substitute for experience. Begin joining professional organizations. Do some community service. Rack up some hours volunteering or substituting at a school nearby (maybe even one where you would like to work). Work with professors whom you respect to try to get some presentations and publications. Writing a good resume is work, but the real work is gaining the relevant experience to put on a resume that will get you the job you seek.

> ### Leading the Way
> *If you are interested in future leadership opportunities, the time to gain leadership experience is now. Whether you are preparing for your first full-time teaching position, or you already have several years of experience, take advantage of opportunities to lead. Leading a club, a committee, a sport, or an activity can help you develop and list your leadership skills.*

HITTING YOUR MARK

Hitting your mark is not something that is done by accident. You must be intentional and work hard to achieve your goals. There is an oft-quoted adage that states "if you aim at nothing, you'll hit it every time." Do not be aimless. If you are not currently in the classroom, set your sights on how to get the experience needed to have the right kind of resume and portfolio that will get you hired. If you are already in the classroom, do not rest on your laurels. Prepare yourself for the next step, whether that is tenure, chairing a curriculum committee or grade level, or becoming an administrator. Complete one or more of the activities below to make sure that you are in the best position to hit your mark!

QUESTIONS FOR DISCUSSION

1. Considering the ideas presented in this chapter, what are some aspects of your resume' that might need some work before your next interview?
2. Consider your most meaningful accomplishments related to teaching and/or working with children. Do you have experiences that can be documented in a resume or portfolio?
3. What can you do over the next year to enhance your resume, cover letter, and portfolio?

ACTIVITIES FOR ENRICHMENT

Draft a cover letter, resume, or portfolio (or all three) for what you would consider to be your dream position in education. Have a peer or classmate review and provide feedback comments. Edit and repeat until both you and your reviewer believe that you've hit your mark!

Contact a principal or assistant principal in your area and ask if you can schedule a mock interview for practice. Be sure to let your mock interviewer know if you are trying to prepare for a first teaching position, a position as a veteran teacher, or if you are seeking an administrative position. Take notes or ask your interviewer's permission to record the mock interview. After the interview, ask the interviewer about your strengths and opportunities for improvement. Transcribe the interviewer's questions, your answers, and the feedback you received. Write a reflection about how you might answer differently for your next interview.

Think-Pair-Share. Reflect upon this chapter's content, then pair up with a classmate or peer to discuss. What is the most meaningful thing that each of you learned from this chapter? How can you use this chapter's information to hit your mark? Share your thoughts with the class or with your professional learning community.

What other information do you still need to hit your mark? Consider what else you would like to learn about drafting job-winning cover letters, resumes, and portfolios. What else do you need to know and do to get your dream job? Ask your instructor, a trusted peer, or supervisor if they can help you fill in the blanks.

Network! Even if you are not currently planning to obtain a new position, it is always smart to be prepared. Familiarize yourself with online job search engines and prepare resumes for networking sites like Monster.com or LinkedIn.com.

REFERENCES

Chuang, H. (2010). Weblog-based electronic portfolios for student teachers in Taiwan. *Education Tech Research Dev, 58*, 211–227.

Furst, L. (1995). Young scholars might take some consolation from the 'anti-vitae' of their elders. *The Chronicle of Higher Education, 41*(18), B3.

Higgins, J., Nairn, K., & Sligo, J. (2009). Alternative ways of expressing and reading identity. *Ethnography and Education, 4*(1), 83–99.

Jami, C. (2015). *Killosophy*. Seattle, WA: CreateSpace Independent Publishing.

Oakly, G., Pegrum, M., & Johnston, S. (2014). Introducing e-portfolios to pre-service teachers as tools for reflection and growth: Lessons learnt. *Asia-Pacific Journal of Teacher Education, 42*(1), 36–50.

McNeilly, K., & Barr, T. (1997). Convincing the recruiter: A comparison of resume formats. *Journal of Education for Business, 72*(6), 359–363.

Parker, L. (1999). An effective resume and cover letter for the new millennium. *Black Collegian, 30*(1). 56–59.

Smith, A. (2015). 3 things that will get your resume thrown in the trash. *TheMuse*. Retrieved from https://www.themuse.com/advice/3-things-that-will-get-your-resume-thrown-in-the-trash on December 11, 2015.

TheMuse. (2014). How to get your resume noticed in the blink of an eye. *Forbes/Leadership*. Retrieved from http://www.forbes.com/sites/dailymuse/2014/07/23/how-to-get-your-resume-noticed-in-the-blink-of-an-eye/ on December 11, 2015.

CHAPTER **8**

PROFESSIONAL DRESS

Kristina DeWitt and Russell G. Yocum

"No matter how you feel . . . Get up. Dress up. Show up. And never give up."

~ Anonymous

INTRODUCTION

As one walks around any college campus, a myriad of fashionable statements in clothing and personal expression can be seen. Many types of boots, booties, leggings, and chunky tops for women, and hats, skinny and modern jeans for men, can be seen around academic environments. Somewhere in the near future, all of these college students will transition to jobs and careers, finding new possibilities in wardrobes and personal images. Educators are no different. The days of lazy, relaxed fashion with attitudes and body language of "hurry-to-class" instantaneously change when student teaching begins. Is it possible to employ the dress needed in a professional arena and be accepted, valued, and respected as a professional educator? Let's see how simplicity and modesty not only help educators look outwardly professional, but also alter the overall demeanor and projection of confidence and respect which should exhude from the proper intrinsic values.

Courtesy of Kristina DeWitt and Russell G. Yocum. Copyright © Kendall Hunt Publishing Company.

WHAT IS PROFESSIONAL DRESS?

Although 56% of all public schools have a student dress code, most schools do not define appropriate dress for teachers and many administrators believe teachers take advantage of the lack of formal policy (Association of American Educators, 2012). It is not easy to define professional dress, because what constitutes appropriate or inappropriate attire can vary depending upon the district, school, grade level, and content area.

Some districts and schools have begun to put some favorable practices and common mistakes for professional dress in writing. A school district in Arizona now bans teachers from wearing:

> rubber-sole flip-flops, visible undergarments, any visible cleavage, bare midriffs, clothes that are deemed too tight, too loose or transparent, bare shoulders, short skirts and exercise pants. Administrators in the district also suggested guidelines for natural hair color, limiting piercings, and covering tattoos—all of which can come across as unprofessional. (Association of American Educators, 2012, para. 3)

Similarly, a Kansas school district prohibits "cutoff shorts, pajama pants and flip[-]flops" (Association of American Educators, 2012, para. 4). And while t-shirts and athletic wear may be perfectly appropriate for physical education teachers, school administrators in Milwaukee deem those unprofessional for the classroom (Association of American Educators, 2012).

In the case *Jacobellis v. Ohio* to establish a threshold for obscenity, United States Supreme Court Justice Potter Stewart famously stated,

> I shall not today attempt to further define the kinds of material I understand to be embraced within that shorthand description, and perhaps I could never succeed in intelligibly doing so. But I know it when I see it . . . (Jacobellis v. Ohio, 378 U.S. 184, 1964)

This same kind of common sense should apply to a definition of professional dress. Even if your district or school does not codify professional dress and inappropriate attire in writing, you can use your common sense to see how other faculty and staff dress in your district, school, grade level, or content area and challenge yourself to view that average as the minimum acceptable look for professionalism. The bottom line is, if your appearance could be construed as distracting, it is not professional.

WHY IS PROFESSIONAL DRESS IMPORTANT?

In a discussion regarding this topic with a colleague, it was evident that professional dress needed to be redefined for our new teachers:

> People do not dress professionally at my school. Some women and men look like they are just too tired to come to work while others look like they actually slept in their clothes. My administrator wears a suit and tie every day, but no one seems to take the hint from him.

Why do some teachers not see professional dress as part of their own success? Is being casual worth the negative connotations that reflects upon our attitudes and demeanor? Is being a role model for students only part of what a teacher says and does? These are all tough questions so let's break it down to the basics.

In a National Education Association (NEA) article on dress code, Graham (2014) states that:

> It's true that being taken seriously as a teacher necessitates that one look professionally ready for the classroom, but what exactly does "professional attire" for educators look like? In a world where "business casual" can refer to a wide variety of attire, how should a teacher —who, it should be noted, often assumes other school responsibililties such as lunch duty, afterschool duty, and a bevy of other impromptu roles that require mobility and comfort—be "professionally" dressed? Dressing too casually sends off a blasé vibe to students and fellow faculty that might undermine their ability to teach from a position of respect and authority. (para. 11–12)

If your adminstration wears a coat and tie, the standard is already set for the male teachers in that building to also wear a coat and tie. Teacher candidates should "raise the bar" and begin their teaching career understanding what constitutes professional attire. "'It's important to dress the part,' says Sherell Lanoix, a fourth grade teacher in Los Angeles, California. 'Students, parents, and administrators take you more seriously when you come to work dressed as a professional'" (Graham, 2014, para 10).

What does this look like to a teacher possibly living on a budget? Some women may feel uncomfortable with dressier clothes because of their body type. There seems to be a trend that spandex black knit pants are dress pants. While it may be appropriate to wear these pants under a dress or long blouse, are they pants or tights? This is a generational question for many female teachers. A school needs to begin with setting a standard, not a fashion trend.

A standard in dress does not necessarily mean a dress code standard. Some school districts do opt to adopt a specific dress code, but what is proposed here is setting a standard of dress. Teachers are professionals, teachers are role models for children, and teachers are community liaisons. Consequently, teachers need to consider how they dress and what the image portrays more seriously than the statement, "I need to be comfortable on my feet." We are not advocating here that a new teacher needs to buy a specific brand of clothing or stand in high heels all day with preschoolers. What we are saying is how you look as a teacher directly impacts how people relate to you. "'Teachers were coming to school in Birkenstocks (sandals) and running shorts, and then complaining they were not being treated as professionals,' said Donna Hines . . . 'The committee felt that was inappropriate dress for work'" (Education World, 2012, para. 30).

DRESSING FOR SUCCESS

The statement a successful teacher should consider when advocating for professional dress should connect to a positive, professional one. Standards in dress help maintain respect, establish credibility, and depict oneself as an authority figure. We will break each of these down to examine favorable practices for dressing for success in a 21st century school environment.

MAINTAINING RESPECT

Respect is a multidimensional topic in teaching. Teachers need respect from students and students need respect from teachers. In order to create a positive sense of respect, a teacher needs to be the first to show it. My first impression of a teacher naturally gravitates to how the teacher looks and carries himself or herself. An effective teacher should dress appropriately as a professional educator to model success to students and parents. Your own respect in the classroom begins with your appearance as a teacher who strives to be a positive role model for each student. Making a good impression is the best solution. Smile, offer a firm handshake, look your students in the eyes, and dress appropriately. They will notice a sense of professionalism about you and respond accordingly.

Ethical Considerations

Principle III: Responsibility to Students

The professional educator respects the rights and dignity of students

---

ESTABLISHING CREDIBILITY

Making a good impression during parent-teacher conferences or open house nights may help to foster a more positive and productive relationship with parents toward helping their children excel in your classroom.

Your credibility starts with the first impression. Consider situational context. When you go to a fast food restaurant, you expect to receive a fast food experience, quick service, substandard quality of food, and employees dressed in a standard uniform. As unimpressive as it may be, the experience meets expectations. However, when you go to a fine dining establishment with white starched and pressed napkins, you anticipate a different experience. The expectation includes a custom menu, gourmet meal, and a stellar wait staff. The meal is best when the experience meets pre-established ideals of fine dining. Do you want parents to equate you and your classroom with fast food or fine dining?

For teachers, establishing credibility begins at the job interview and continues through to every day on the job and at appearances out in the community. A credible teacher knows how to teach, collaborate, and maintain the professional role at all times. Whether in the school, community center, or local sporting event, a teacher is only seen as a professional if the students and parents view the role model in that manner. There is something to be said for the adage "actions speak louder than words"; so does your attire!

DEPICTING ONESELF AS AN AUTHORITY FIGURE

Establishing yourself as an authority figure by following the dress code policy and the established rules of the school will help instill a sense of integrity in your interactions with each student. All new teachers need to start off with the innate desire that their role as teachers will always be that of authority figures and role models for all students. Take charge, be the leader and example in your classroom. Your students desire to see you as a positive authority figure, one that looks and plays the part—the whole package!

When student teachers struggle with establishing themselves as the authority figure, the following example proves helpful. If you go to court, how do you expect to see the judge? Do you expect to see him or her dressed in a black robe, sitting in a central position behind a wooden bench or sitting on the attorney's table, legs crossed and drinking a latte? The authority comes not only from the actions, but also the appearance!

FAVORABLE PRACTICES

Teachers should try to dress conservatively and professionally from their first day on the job through their last. Dressing for success is a crucial part of the profession since first impressions are key in any environment. Students deserve to see their teachers look and behave in a professional manner. Regardless of the students' age, it is our duty to be a role model in our classrooms. Whether we know we are being watched or not, students are watching us. What signals and messages are you sending your students? What example are you setting? Lead by example (in actions and attire) even if the teacher down the hall does not. The norm for attire can vary depending upon the type of school (public, private, or parochial) and even within school depending on grade level and content (pre-school teachers and physical education teachers may need to dress more comfortably). The best rule of thumb is to guage the average dress for your particular setting and challenge yourself to always dress a bit better than would be expected of you.

Favorable dress practices for men.

- Conservative dress styles are appropriate.
- Dress slacks, not jeans.
- Collared shirts.
- Coat and tie (if expected by your administration), a sport coat can dress up any casual outfit.
- Shirts should always be tucked in (unless you are outside as a physical education teacher).
- Body piercings and tattoos should not be visible.
- Shined or polished shoes.
- All belts should be worn appropriately.
- Polo shirts for casual meetings and events, but not the norm.
- Wash and wear. If it is "dry clean" or "hand wash only" you do not want it. Wrinkle-free fabrics are also a plus.
- Cologne should be used sparingly.

Favorable dress practices for women.

- Dresses that are structured and well-fitting but not too tight. Be aware of how far from the knee the hemline is (short becomes even shorter when sitting, reaching, bending, kneeling, and teaching in front of a class or at a small group table).
- Skirts—Make sure the length is comfortable and appropriate for the amount of movement you do. This is dependent on your grade level. Consider wearing bike shorts underneath, so when the kids crawl under your legs, they cannot announce the color of your underwear.
- Spandex pants and leggings are too revealing. Wear nice cotton or polyester blend slacks that are not too tight.
- Oxfords, ankle boots, and loafers are all good shoe choices, if you cannot or do not want to wear heels. Low heels and wedges are also acceptable, but stay under 3" as you will be on your feet all day. Avoid tennis shoes, UGGs, Toms, and anything resembling a flip-flop.
- Midriff skin or revealing cleavage should never show. Use camisole tops underneath clothing.

- Make up should be subtle and natural looking.
- Hair should be a natural looking color (no pink, purple, blue, or teal—stick to natural colors like shades of blonde, brunette, or natural shades of red and auburn).
- Wear your hair conservatively styled (messy buns look like you overslept).
- Perfume should be used sparingly.
- Make sure your clothes fit you well; go to a tailor if needed. Do not buy clothes in the junior miss section so you can look like a teenager. Nothing makes you look less authoritative than ill-fitting clothes.
- Jewelry should be tasteful and conservative. Body piercings and tattoos should not be visible.

COMMON MISTAKES

Dress down day emerged as a motivational technique to allow teachers and staff to show support for events like spirit day or a jeans day. Oftentimes, the events coincide with those of fundraising opportunities such as Breast Cancer Awareness or Autism Speaks. The idea was simple and reflected a sense of team unity within the school. Students observed teachers support the athletic teams and clubs. All of this was an excellent team-building tool for administrators, at least at first glance. These rare instances were treats for the faculty and staff, but soon evolved into any excuse for a dress down day. There are now "bad weather" days, "I don't feel so good" days, "benchmark testing" days, and "find a reason to wear jeans" days. The idea of dress down days started as a positive initiative, like many things in education; however, teachers need to represent their profession in the best manner possible. "Dressing down" in attire evokes an attitude of "dressing down" that portrays a sense of casualness, relaxation, and inactivity. Except for mandatory fundraising events, physical activities, or extra-curriculars that require casual dress, it would be wise to seriously consider opting out of optional dress down days or casual Fridays.

As teachers, we need to rethink our own professional demeanor. We need to advocate for our profession and our students to show that we take pride in how we look, perform, and execute our job. No teacher should be frowned upon for lack of dress or lack of skills. It is our responsibility to take our profession to the next level. If we want to be taken seriously by society, then we need to take ourselves seriously. Consider the "future truth."

Leading the Way

Leaders must set their own appearance standards above what they expect from those they lead. For example, a male leader who wears khakis and a polo each day will probably not inspire his male teachers to wear a tie, but if his standard dress is a coat and tie, his male teachers might be more willing to wear a tie.

Do not dress for the job you have, but the next one you want. Believe in what you want to be in the future, envision yourself in that position, and begin embodying the characteristics of that future truth today. If you want to be a principal, then dress like a principal. If you want to be the superintendent in the future, dress like a superintendent now. Is dress down day really worth the impact it has on our teachers' attitudes and lack of urgency? It is the students who ultimately suffer when we change into this casual mind set.

CONCLUSION

Why is professional dress important to you as a teacher? Honestly, it is all about your image as a professional. From the first day on the job, through the years of service that follow, you—the teacher—are being judged each day you are in the school. Make a great impression. Be professional in appearance. Know what makes you show confidence and portray a sense of urgency in all duties, big and small. You have a chance to change the lives of children. Take yourself seriously in the sense that being professional is what you are all about.

HITTING YOUR MARK

You wake up to get ready for work. If you are deciding what to wear at the last minute, you may need to adjust to hit the right mark. Consider planning your professional work attire the night before, or even prepare a week's worth of attire at a time. Be as deliberate about your attire as you would be about your lesson planning. If you are not yet employed in a classroom, make it your aim to put together a professional wardrobe. Veteran teachers should observe their administrators' attire and begin to assemble a similar wardrobe. It is always a good idea to dress for the next higher position. Consider the activities listed below to prepare yourself to hit your mark!

QUESTIONS FOR DISCUSSION

1. Think about a teacher you have had who dressed in a less than professional manner. What was your perception of that teacher at the time?
2. Now think about a teacher who dressed in an exceptionally professional manner and how your perception of them might have been affected by their appearance.
3. What professional appearance habits can/should you develop early in your career?

ACTIVITIES FOR ENRICHMENT

With your class, peers, or professional learning community, plan a "fashion show." Put together a professional ensemble that you would wear to work and/or prepare professional attire that you would use if you had your supervisor's job. Wear your choice to your next meeting and be prepared to give each other constructive criticism.

Dressing nicely for work is not cheap, but it also does not have to break the bank. Plan a field trip with classmates or peers to local consignment shops, thrift stores, or yard sales. See if you can find suitable professional attire that will help you hit the mark. Put together an outfit that is store bought and one that you found second-hand and see if your peers can tell which is which.

Think-Pair-Share. Consider the chapter content, then team with a peer or classmate for discussion. What does each of you consider the most important element from this chapter? What will you do with the information you have learned from this chapter to hit your mark? Share your reflections with your class or professional learning community.

What else would you like to learn to enable you to hit your mark? Are there wardrobe choices that you are unsure about? If you have to ask yourself whether a wardrobe election is appropriate for work or not, then the answer is usually "not." If you consider yourself fashion-challenged, ask a supervisor, peer, or instructor for tips.

This chapter has provided you with lists, ideas, do's and don'ts. If you try to go grocery shopping without a list, you are likely to forget something you need and buy lots of things you do not need. Be just as intentional when it comes to making professional attire shopping decisions. Using the information from this chapter, make yourself a cheat sheet/shopping list for work clothing. Go window shopping and see what kinds of attire and prices would help you hit your mark, then budget the average amount to buy one new outfit each month.

REFERENCES

Aegis Law Library. (1964). *Jacobellis v. Ohio*, 378 U.S. 184. *Aegis Law Library*. Retrieved from http://www.aegis.com/law/SCt/Decisions/1964/378US184.html on February 14, 2016.

Association of American Educators. (2012). Teacher dress codes. *Association of American Educators*. Retrieved from http://www.aaeteachers.org/index.php/blog/802-teacher-dress-codes on February 14, 2016.

Education World. (2012). Dressing (teachers) for success. *Education World.* Retrieved from http://www.educationworld.com/a_admin/admin/admin422_a.shtml on February 14, 2016.

Graham, E. (2014). Do teachers need dress codes to know what to wear at school? *NEA Today.* Retrieved from http://neatoday.org/2014/06/02/do-teachers-need-dress-codes-to-know-what-to-wear-at-school/ on February 14, 2016.

CHAPTER 9

INTERVIEWING SKILLS

Russell L. Claxton

"You never get a second chance to make a good first impression"

~ Will Rogers

INTRODUCTION

It is not uncommon to have anxiety about a job interview. This can be true of a teacher candidate applying for that first teaching position, or an experienced teacher applying for a new position. This chapter will provide some tips on preparing to interview for a teaching position, and hopefully reduce some of the anxiety you may feel prior to interviewing. Do not just go into an interview cold; take the time to prepare as best you can. If you are prepared, you do not have to stress out; you can just be yourself.

The first thing you need to know is that not all interviews are the same. Find out as much as you can about the interview process at the school or district where you are interviewing. In order to mentally prepare for the interview, it is important to know if you will be meeting with an individual or if your interview will be a panel (group) interview. Additionally, if you are expected to bring a portfolio, be prepared to present it if requested. Some interviews may even include the candidate teaching an actual lesson. The more you can find out about the interview prior to your arrival, the less likely you will be caught off guard during the interview process.

Courtesy of Russell L. Claxton. Copyright © Kendall Hunt Publishing Company.

Also, be aware that there can be different interview levels and phases. For example, a large district may conduct preliminary interviews at the district level. This initial interview can help the district identify the most qualified candidates to include in an applicant pool. Administrators can then choose from the pool of applicants when a position becomes available at a specific school (The Hiring Process, 2015).

An ideal interview should be a "two way street" (Dorsey, 2004). In other words, the interviewer is trying to determine if you are a good fit for a position, but you should also use the interview process to determine if the position is a good fit for you. It is common for a teaching candidate to take the first offer they get, and that may be wise. However, if you have multiple options, the interview process can be a great opportunity to determine your best option.

PRIOR TO INTERVIEW

KNOW THE LOCATION

Research the school and community. It is so much easier today walking into an interview with a wealth of information about school community than in the past. Much of the information you should know prior to an interview is available online. Some of the issues you can become familiar with may include the following:

- The socioeconomic breakdown of the student population (Title I, Free and Reduced Lunch, etc.)
- The school's standardized test scores
- The number of students enrolled in each grade
- The number of teachers
- Percentage of students with special needs served
- Programs offered

These are just a few of the pieces of information that will help you sound more knowledgeable about the school. Do not just look at the formal information provided by the school or school district. Although the school website can be helpful, it is often presented from a public relations standpoint. Social media can be very helpful in finding more informal information about a school and community (Cannata, 2011). Searching some of the popular social media sites for parent, student, group, or news comments can be enlightening.

In a private religious school interview, be prepared to discuss your religious beliefs and to get a little more personal. If the school is affiliated with a particular religion or church, it is important to have a sound understanding of the school's doctrine and beliefs. It is also important to know what is expected of faculty in regard

Ethical Considerations

Principle IV: Responsibility to the School Community

The professional educator understands the problematic nature of multiple relationships

to religious beliefs. For example, a private Christian school may expect applicants to be Christians, and may ask substantial questions to determine sincerity. Although reviewing issues of doctrine before an interview may be helpful, I do not suggest trying to fake it in this area. If you do not hold the same religious beliefs as the school in which you are applying, you may want to seriously consider if this school would be a good fit for you. There are many private schools with no religious affiliation, and many that are only loosely connected to a given religious denomination. Some private schools may consider hiring teachers of varying religious backgrounds, while others may not, but it is always best to be honest up front. Most parochial and private religious schools prefer to hire teachers who believe, and will teach, the same values as the school and/or affiliated church.

Talk to those in the community. This may be a challenge if you are in town only long enough to interview. It could also be difficult in a small town where asking questions to people you do not know can seem suspicious. However, if you are visiting a restaurant or business and have a chance to chat with some of the local residents, asking a simple question such as, "What are the schools like around here?" can potentially result in some enlightening comments. Even if you are interviewing in a community with which you are familiar, asking specific questions about the schools can help you understand the community's perceptions.

Know current issues. This is one of the most important areas to study. Find out the strengths and weaknesses of the school and district. If the school has been struggling with poor test scores, you might want to talk about how you believe you can help improve student performance. If it is a high-performing school, you may want to emphasize the high expectations you have for your students. If it is a school that has been experiencing significant discipline problems, you may want to emphasize your classroom management skills, and so on. I am not suggesting that you go into an interview claiming to be an expert in every area, but you do not want to miss out on an opportunity to express how your skills and experiences can help the school meet their goals and address their most important issues.

Get to the area early. Arriving late to an interview can cause significant anxiety and start the interview off on a bad note. Even worse, it could cost you the interview opportunity, and ultimately the job. A common recommendation is to get to the interview 10 minutes early, but I suggest getting to the area much earlier than that. The 10 minute rule applies to your arrival in the office, but if you plan on leaving your home at a time that will get you to the interview 10 minutes early, you leave very little room for error. An automobile accident ahead of you, a flat tire, or unexpected construction can easily cause more than a 10-minute delay. A better strategy might be to arrive half an hour early and sit in the parking lot reviewing your notes. You might arrive an hour early and sit at a restaurant a mile from the school. Once you are in close proximity of the interview location, you can alleviate the anxiety of arriving late and take advantage of the extra time to collect your thoughts.

Make a practice run. You may already know that you cannot always depend on your Global Positioning System (GPS) or Internet map. Even if your directions are correct, a detour or road construction can throw you off schedule. If the location of the interview is one with which you are unfamiliar, visit the location the day before, or days prior to the interview if possible. Make sure you know the correct building, where to park, and where to enter the building. These may seem like minor details, but having to figure them out at the last minute can cause unnecessary stress.

Lay out your clothing the night before. This is not intended to be fashion advice, but many of us have had the unpleasant experience of getting dressed for a big interview and realizing there is a big stain on our favorite interviewing outfit, or that we left our best suit at the dry cleaners. Feeling good about how you look will often increase your confidence going into an interview. If possible, it may be a good idea to invest in some professional attire, even if your normal style is more casual. It is better to be overdressed than underdressed, and a professional outfit or suit will pay for itself after a few interviews. If you do not have a strong sense of fashion, it never hurts to get a second opinion.

When planning your attire, I suggest avoiding extremes. The definition of "extreme" may vary based on the school or the interviewer. If you are not sure what an interviewer might find extreme, you may want to talk to a veteran teacher, administrator, or college professor for opinions. Extremes in clothing, makeup, piercings, and even cologne/perfume are just a few examples of areas to consider (Dorsey, 2004).

Conduct a practice interview. If you do not have much interviewing experience, the thought of applying and interviewing for a new position can be intimidating. Take advantage of interviewing opportunities along the way. Practice interviewing skills when you apply for summer or part-time jobs. Many colleges, and even community organizations, offer mock interview opportunities. If you cannot find one of these practice opportunities, have a friend or family member interview you with a list of scripted questions. Have them look for potential distracting tendencies you may have such as use of repetitive words or phrases such as "umm," "you know," "like," or slang words (Dorsey, 2004). Another helpful tool is to record your mock interview. This will help you to see how you may appear to an interviewer. You may be surprised what you can learn from a practice interview.

FAVORABLE PRACTICES

Most interviews revolve around two things, being prepared and being yourself. Although all interviews and interviewers are different, there are a number of practices that can improve your chances of a successful interview, while others can derail the process very quickly.

Know about the job. Try to find out what you do not know. This includes learning the state standards, the student population, the community, etc. Is the job in a different grade than your experience? Is the community different from those with which you are familiar? Are you applying to a state with different standards?

Know your qualifications. An interviewer can often tell if you are trying to make yourself out to be someone you are not. As an applicant, you are not expected to know everything. Do not be afraid to admit that you do not have the answer to a question, but you can still emphasize your willingness to learn. Knowing your qualifications gives you the opportunity to highlight your strengths as a teacher.

Know the possible interview questions. Although no two interviews are the same, there are many questions, or at least topics, that are common to most teacher interviews. Below are some examples of common teacher interview questions and some generalized responses:

Q: Tell us about yourself.

A: Focus on your strengths and positive experiences, especially those that would be beneficial in the position for which you are applying. Keep non job-related personal information to a minimum, unless you are asked specifically.

Q: Why did you choose to go into teaching?

A: This is where you might want to speak from the heart. Chances are, you have been asked this question before. Again, stick to the positives. Avoid speaking negatively about other career options.

Q: Why do you want to work here?

A: Mention what specifically you like about the particular school or district. This is where knowing something about the school will come in handy. Talk about the job as if it were your dream job, not as if it were your last resort.

Q: Tell me about your experience working with children.

A: Your experiences as a teacher or during student teaching would most likely be included in this answer, but almost any experience can be included. As a new teaching candidate, summer camps, volunteering, even babysitting can be meaningful answers.

Again, focus on your positive experiences. Using real-life stories may help make a solid and lasting impression which will help you stand out from the other candidates.

Q: What would your classroom look like?

A: Being organized and structured are valuable qualities for a teacher. Talk about your processes, organization, classroom management, and overall classroom environment. You can mention how you would differentiate your instruction and value every individual student.

Q: What is your personal educational philosophy?

A: This is another question that you have probably answered in your course work. You may want to combine the philosophical with the practical, and make sure your answers are student centered.

Q: What is your classroom management philosophy?

A: You will probably want to mention terms such as a firm, fair, and consistent. Talk about how you would be proactive, how you would deal with disruptive students, and the importance of communicating with parents. If you have learned any unique or exceptional classroom management techniques, this would be a good time to mention them. Again, giving real examples of your experience with classroom management may help set you apart from other candidates. If you developed a classroom management system or strategy in your student teaching, this may be beneficial to mention. If you handled a particularly challenging situation discuss the incident, how it was handled, and the outcome.

Q: How do you address different learning styles?

A: There are many ways you can answer this question and you have probably learned a lot about differentiation in your course work. Looking back at your class notes and textbooks can be valuable resources. The main focus here is that you will have high expectations and will attempt to meet the needs and learning styles of every child in your classroom.

Q: Tell me about a success you have experienced in the classroom.

A: The answer to this question will come from your teaching or student teaching experience. Did you teach a unit, a lesson, or even just have a great day in the classroom where everything seemed to come together and the students were "getting it"? You may even want to mention an experience you had with one student where you really felt like you made a difference. If it was an experience that made you feel good as a teacher, it would probably be a good answer to this question.

Q: What is your knowledge/experience in working with students with special needs?

A: Most teaching assignments today, especially those in a public school, are going to include some interaction with special education services and programs. Even if your experiences have been limited, make sure you express a willingness to work with students who have special needs.

Q: How do you know your students are learning (assessment)?

A: This is another question where you can refer back to your lessons on differentiation. Make it clear that you understand the importance of a variety of assessment tools. This is a good place to mention concepts such as Blooms taxonomy or formative versus summative evaluation, just to name a few.

Q: How would you deal with a difficult student, parent, co-worker, or situation?

A: Your answer should include positive communication, proactive steps, empathy, and patience. The interviewer is probably looking for an answer that indicates that you can work through interpersonal problems and get along with others.

Q: How would you communicate with parents?

A: You should communicate with parents early and often. Discuss the importance of making positive contact with a parent or guardian and not just communicating when there is a problem. Your first communication should be positive, so contacting parents before the school year starts with a phone call or postcard could start your relationships on a positive note. Also, mention the need for more positive communication than negative, thus frequent communication is essential.

Q: How would you collaborate with other teachers?

A: Understand that a collaborative work environment is an important part of teaching. Express a willingness to work on committees, teaching teams, collaborative teaching assignments, etc. Emphasize your willingness to work as a team player.

Q: How would you use technology in the classroom?

A: Describe your knowledge of current technology, but also express flexibility based on technology resources available. For example: you can discuss how you have used a Smart Board, but do not suggest that you have to have one in your classroom.

Q: What are your strengths and/or weaknesses?

A: Most teaching candidates are aware of their strengths and find it easy to answer that part of the question. Identifying a weakness that will not hurt your chances of getting the job can be much more difficult, but it would also be perceived as a negative to state that you cannot identify a weakness. Try to come up with a weakness that is fixable, and/or has some positive attributes. Some possibilities might be that you are overly competitive, a perfectionist, too talkative, or are new to the position and have much to learn. If you identify a weakness, try to also address how you are working to improve in that area.

Q: Recall a mistake you have made and how you handled the situation.

A: A good answer here would be a work situation where you made an honest mistake, but took full responsibility and made it right. Emphasize that you learned the lesson that helped you not to make the same mistake again. Be careful not to get too personal here.

Q: What are your long-term or short-term goals?

A: Your short-term goals will most likely include success in your first year teaching. Your long-term goals might include pursuing leadership opportunities within the school, supporting other teachers, advanced degrees, or even personal goals.

Q: Possible content specific questions.

A: Brush up on the specific content of the position for which you are applying. For an elementary position, you would need to be prepared to discuss general content and pedagogy, whereas an interview for a secondary position might include specific questions about how you will teach a specific subject. It is possible, even probable, that as a secondary applicant you may be asked to interview with a teacher or leader in the department in which you wish to teach.

Q: Tell me about your teacher preparation program.

A: Discuss the most valuable experience you had in your program. What were some of the other valuable experiences you had that prepared you for your first classroom? If you had a lot of negative experiences in your program, keep them to yourself. If you are asked about your worst boss or professor, focus on the take away, and do not use this occasion to criticize him/her. This question will be less likely as you gain teaching experience.

Q: Do you have any questions for me?

A: Come up with some questions in advance that are unlikely to be answered during the interview. It is best to have several just in case. Some general categories might include asking about the strengths/successes of the school, or even some of the challenges. You could ask about the most important attribute the principal is looking for in a candidate, or a specific program you would like to know more about. Your question(s) here can indicate that you have a sincere interest in the school, students, and community.

There are many other common themes such as lesson plans, homework, reading, etc. (Sample questions, 2015). You can make your own list of common interview questions by conducting a basic Internet search. If you are prepared to answer the most common questions, chances are you will be prepared to answer other questions that are similar or cover the same topics.

Look professional. The concept of professional appearance has changed significantly in recent decades. However, it is important for applicants to understand that many of the administrators responsible for hiring teachers are from a generation that still values traditional business attire. Although professional business attire varies to some degree based on the location, it is usually appropriate to dress more formally for an interview than will be required of you as an employee. If you are unsure, is better to be overdressed than to be underdressed. Even if wearing a suit or other business attire is not your style, dressing up portrays a higher level of interest and professionalism. Choose conservative colors such as black, navy, or charcoal. Avoid bright colors.

When speaking to groups of undergraduate teaching candidates, I often receive questions about less conventional appearance issues such as piercings, tattoos, unusual hairstyles, etc. I would not try to give fashion advice, nor would I try to address these as moral issues. My only recommendation would be to lean toward a more conservative look when preparing for an interview. It may be that once you are employed some schools may allow you a little more freedom of expression than others, but during the interview is probably not the best time to try to make a statement about your unique sense of fashion. I once heard a teacher candidate state, "If they don't like how I look, I don't want to work for them anyway." This statement may be correct if the candidate's look is more important than that particular job.

Be personable. Not everyone can be Mr. or Ms. Charisma. Good teachers come in all different personality types. Some personality traits, however, can be learned and practiced. Even if you are very nervous entering an interview, a smile can do wonders to convince someone that you have a warm and friendly personality. Manners can also be considered an indication of your personality. Although the norms for manners can vary regionally, it is usually to the interviewee's benefit to use terms such as "please" and "thank you," "yes, sir" and "no, ma'am". You can also practice focusing on the positive.

Have additional information available (portfolio, references and letters, certificate, etc.). You may not know going into an interview if the administrator will want to see any additional information, but it is a good idea to have it available just in case. It is a good strategy to put together a portfolio that contains examples of experiences and successes, as well as documents such as a resume and teaching certificate. You can offer to share that information with the administrator during the interview, or offer to leave it with them to review later. It is preferable that you have multiple copies, as asking an administrator to return the portfolio to you later could come across as being unprofessional. Even if the administrator chooses not to review your portfolio, it is still an indication of your preparation.

Be aware of body language. You are probably aware that body language is a significant part of communication; be aware of yours and that of the interviewer (Dorsey, 2004). Try to avoid nervous habits or negative gestures that may indicate you are not comfortable with the interview. Additionally, watch the interviewer for body language that may indicate interest or approval, or dissatisfaction. Reading these signs can give you an indication of topics to emphasize, or topics to avoid discussing further.

Ask good questions. It is common for an administrator to ask you if you have any questions for them, typically near the end of the interview. It is wise to have a few questions planned, especially those that are unlikely to be answered during the interview process. Be flexible with your questions, as you do not want to ask a question that was just answered. Because this is such a common part of an interview, not being prepared with a question could be perceived as a negative. Asking questions about the strengths and weaknesses of the school, what the administrator is looking for in a candidate, or questions about a specific program are all possibilities. It is usually best to avoid questions about pay and benefits during the initial interview.

COMMON MISTAKES

Being late. As mentioned above, being late for an interview most likely will hurt your chances of getting the job. Some interviewers are more understanding than others, but most will perceive tardiness as inconsiderate or unprofessional, even if it is inadvertent.

Making demands. There may be a number of things you would like to have in your new position. Your own classroom, a Smart Board, or a particular teaching assignment are possible preferences you may have, but an initial job interview is not the time to start making your requests. If an administrator asks you a question such as what subject or grade would you like to teach, it is fine to express your preferences. However, this is also good time to express your willingness to be flexible and be a team player. You may describe how you can effectively use technology during instruction, but also explain how you can be an effective teacher even if you do not have access to the latest gadgets. Making demands, or even stating too many preferences, may indicate to an interviewer that you will be high maintenance or discontent if you do not get what you want. Administrators constantly have to make decisions based on limited resources, so letting them know that you will make the most of whatever you are given is usually the best strategy.

> **Leading the Way**
>
> *Interviewing for a leadership position is not that different from interviewing for a teaching position. Know as much as you can about the position you are applying for and speak from the heart. Your potential to learn the position can be as important as your qualifications.*

Speaking poorly of other employers or jobs, or making negative comments. You may have had a negative experience in your previous job or student teaching. Even if your comments are truthful, a job interview is not the time to vent. Speaking negatively about another employer can cause an interviewer to question your attitude and loyalty. Focus on the positives and what you learned, even in difficult circumstances. Even general negative comments about the weather, traffic, difficulty finding the building, etc., should be avoided as you are trying to present an overall positive attitude.

Sharing much more than is asked. If you tend to be a little talkative, you may need to be mindful of your propensity to ramble or get off-track. It is fine to throw out pieces of information about yourself or your experiences that may not be a direct response to a question, but a job interview is also a good time to practice being a listener. Avoid going into too much detail about personal issues or details that are not related to your qualifications, unless you are responding to a specific question.

Trying to take control of the interview. The interviewer should be in charge of the interview and will usually provide direction regarding the interview process. Follow his or her lead and do not try to reroute the interview. An interview is a good time to talk about your leadership skills, but do not try to show them by being too aggressive or overbearing.

Making commitments you do not intend to keep. If you make a commitment in order to improve your chances of getting a job, plan on keeping that commitment. This is an issue of personal integrity and it will most likely affect your future in that position. For example, if you express your willingness to coach a sport or sponsor a club, plan on following through. Willingness to participate in an extracurricular activity can improve your chances of getting hired over another candidate, but if it is later determined that you were insincere, it will most likely cause you problems with that administrator.

Lying. Failing to be honest during the application process may very well cause you employment problems in the future. This includes what you put in writing and what you say during the interview. If it is determined that you are not being honest during the interview, your name will most likely be removed from consideration. Furthermore, if you are hired and it is later determined that you were not being honest during the application process, it is still possible, and even likely, that you can be fired at that point. It is relatively easy for an administrator to verify most information and the truth usually comes out. Do not exaggerate your qualifications, or try to cover up past mistakes if you are asked in the interview or on the application. Even if you have to share information that is embarrassing or negative, it is best to be honest from the very beginning.

Keeping your cell phone on. Having your cell phone ring, or even vibrate, can be distracting and even rude. Turn it off, or better yet, leave it in the car. That call or text message can wait.

AFTER THE INTERVIEW

Once you have completed the interview, you should sense a feeling of relief knowing that the most difficult part of the application process is over, even though it may be days or weeks before a decision is made. Hopefully, the topic of the hiring timeline was discussed during the interview and you can leave with an idea of when and how you will be notified of the decision. However, this may not always be the case. If there are a large number of candidates being considered, multiple positions, district level interviews, or if the interview is for a position that has not yet been approved or finalized, the process could be lengthy.

Do not be surprised if you walk out of the interview feeling like you have blown it. It is common for applicants to second-guess themselves after having some time to collect their thoughts. You will most likely remember questions that you wish you had answered differently. Consider how you can improve your answers in future interviews, but beyond that, do not spend much time worrying about how the interview went. Most interviewers understand that applicants are often a little nervous, and in most cases any minor mistakes you may have made were not as significant as they may have felt. In other words, the interview probably went better than you thought it did.

Follow-Up. It is a common professional courtesy to send a handwritten note shortly after the interview thanking the interviewer. You may get an answer about the job very quickly, or it may take weeks before the process is completed. Regardless, a quick note to say "thank you, I enjoyed learning about your school, I hope to hear from you soon," and other similar statements can be a positive reflection on you. You may even have the letter written and prepared in advance so you can write the name of the interviewer on the card, stick a stamp on it, and send it in the mail right away. If the opportunity presents itself, try to get the business card of each interviewer and send a hand written card to each interviewer (personalized, if possible). It is typically not a good idea to follow-up with a phone call, and although not necessarily inappropriate, an email is not as personal as a handwritten note.

Although it may be difficult, in most cases it is best to just wait to be contacted about the job after you have sent a thank you note. However, if the interviewer expressly encourages you to follow-up, or if you are faced with multiple job offers, most administrators would understand a follow-up call asking if a decision has been made. This can be a tricky situation and the best course of action just depends on the circumstances.

Do not look at a "no" as a failure. Look at each job interview as a learning experience. When the interview goes well, make notes regarding your interview strengths. However, even if the interview was a disaster, reflect on what went wrong and how you can make improvements for your next interview. It is probable that you will get more comfortable with the process with each interview experience.

It can be a positive experience to go on a job interview, even if you are not sure if you would be interested in the job. You may become more interested in the position once you learn about it, or the interview may confirm that the job is not the right fit for you. Either way, you have gained some experience by going to the interview. Remember that the first teaching job is often the hardest one to get. After you get your first teaching position and establish yourself as an effective teacher then you can consider other opportunities as you grow into your career.

CONCLUSION

This chapter is intended to provide you with some basic interview preparation strategies. I encourage you to take the time to research additional strategies, especially as you get closer to your interview. There are many educator websites that provide information specific to teachers, and even major employment websites such as *monster.com, educationworld.com, forbes.com, and teach.org,* just to name a few. Terms such as "teacher interview tips," "common teacher interview questions," or even just "teacher interviews" in any of the major search engines will provide numerous websites with helpful information.

HITTING YOUR MARK

Like so many other areas of education, your interviewing skills can be practiced, developed, and improved upon. The problem is, most people are not involved in formal interviews on a regular basis, so getting realistic experience can be a challenge. Whether you are preparing for your first real interview, or you have had many, there is much you can do to prepare for your next interview. Below are a few activities to get you thinking.

QUESTIONS FOR DISCUSSION

Consider the following scenarios and how you might respond:

- You are invited to interview for a position on a day that you already have other plans.
- You interview for two positions during the same week. You consider one of the jobs your "dream job," while the other is significantly less appealing. The principle of the lesser job calls and offers you the position before you have received an answer from your preferred school.
- An interviewer asks for your references, but you do not want your current administrators to know you are applying for another job or you are concerned you will not receive a positive recommendation.

ACTIVITIES FOR ENRICHMENT

Search popular education sites, or do a general search of questions typically asked in a teacher interview. Note questions that appear on multiple sites as there is a probability you will see these type of questions in an actual interview. List at least 10 questions that would be helpful to have when preparing for an interview.

From the list of teacher interview questions above, identify the three that you believe would be the most difficult for you to answer. Prepare written answers for each of the three most challenging questions.

Conduct a practice interview. If the interviewer is a friend or relative who is not an educator, provide them with a list of commonly asked questions. If the interviewer is a practicing teacher or administrator, you may want to allow them to choose the questions. Videotaping the interview will allow you to review your strengths and weaknesses.

Make an interview checklist. What information about the school and community should you study before the interview? What should you take to the interview (resume, portfolio, etc.)? Do you have appropriate interviewing attire? What follow-up activities are important after interviewing? Add any other important reminders and review this checklist several days prior to an interview.

REFERENCES

Cannata, Marisa (2011). The role of social networks in the teacher job search process. *The Elementary School Journal*. Volume 11, Number 3.

Dorsey, Jason (2004). *Graduate to your perfect job*. Golden Ladder Productions, Austin, TX.

The Hiring Process, (October 2015). Education World http://www.educationworld.com/a_curr/columnists/mcdonald/mcdonald033.shtml

Sample interview questions for teachers (2015). University of Delaware. https://www.udel.edu/CSC/pdf/InterviewTeach.pdf

CHAPTER 10

WHAT ADMINISTRATORS LOOK FOR WHEN HIRING TEACHERS

Russell L. Claxton

"I am convinced that nothing we do is more important than the hiring and developing of people..."

~ Larry Bossidy

INTRODUCTION

Although there are many factors that have an impact on a child's education, a quality teacher is one of the most important. Some research even suggests that a quality teacher has more impact on student success than most other outside factors (Darling-Hammond, 1999). For this reason, it is critical that school leaders prioritize the hiring and development of quality teachers. Unfortunately, identifying exactly what makes an outstanding teacher is not an exact science.

After years of experience as a public school principal, and hundreds of teacher interviews, I have developed a pretty good picture of what I believe to be an outstanding teacher candidate. I have also participated in many group or panel interviews where my evaluation of the candidate varied from that of the other interviewers. So, what does that mean to a teacher preparing for a job interview? It means that the definition of quality teacher can vary from one administrator to the next. It also means that the ideal candidate for one position might

Courtesy of Russell L. Claxton. Copyright © Kendall Hunt Publishing Company.

not be the ideal candidate for another. Although there is no one universal list of qualifications that all school administrators are seeking, there are many qualifications that will consistently improve teaching candidates' chances of becoming employed.

QUALIFICATIONS

What are some of the qualifications that most administrators are looking for in a teacher? These qualifications can be broken down into two categories: formal and informal. Formal qualifications are those tangible qualifications that are quantifiable, and can often be put down on paper. These are the qualifications that you will find as standard requirements of most administrators. Informal qualifications are often more difficult to define. The definition and importance of these qualifications vary from one administrator to the next, and may be more accurately defined as characteristics than as qualifications.

FORMAL QUALIFICATIONS

A well-written resume. Most of your formal qualifications, and some of your informal, should be listed on your resume. This is a candidate's chance to make a good first impression. There are a few qualifications that should be on every resume: job experience, education, specific skills, and training. Having the required qualifications is important, but how these are presented in your resume can help determine if you get a chance to discuss your qualifications in person. There is no one best way to write a resume, but a resume for a teaching position might look different from an effective resume in other professions, so assistance in writing your first professional resume can be helpful (see chapter 7 for additional information on writing resumes). There are plenty of online resume building websites that often include templates. It is also helpful to have an educator who has already been through the process review your resume and provide honest feedback. I suggest starting with what is sometimes called a "living resume" long before the job interview. A living resume is just a document that you update on a regular basis. You begin with a base resume and add to it every time you complete a significant event or experience that you can add to the document. This process helps ensure that you always have a current resume prepared, and also helps you identify areas where you may need to gain some experience.

References. References are a standard part of the application process. Unfortunately, it is an aspect that is often taken for granted by applicants. During the teacher selection process, administrators often want to know more about an applicant than what they can find out during an interview. The people you choose as references can say a lot about your potential as an educator. Some applications require specific references, such as your supervising teacher. Others may ask you for previous employers or personal acquaintances, but you will often have some flexibility regarding the references that you choose.

Listing references that barely know you, or have only known you for a brief time, is not only ineffective, but can even be considered a negative. That is why it is important to begin developing positive professional relationships as early as possible. Those that you interact with during your student teaching are obvious potential references. A poor relationship with your supervising teacher or administrator during your student teaching not only results in an unpleasant student teaching experience, but can also result in a squandered opportunity to obtain a meaningful and positive reference.

Ethical Considerations

Principle III: Responsibility to Students

The professional educator demonstrates an ethic of care

Do not underestimate the value of a positive relationship with your boss during a summer job, the leader of a volunteer organization, or the instructors in your degree program. Any of these people can represent a potential reference. Also, be aware that an administrator may seek references that you did not list on your application. As much as it is within your power to do so, build positive relationships with those around you, especially those you interact with in a professional setting.

Evaluations. Evaluations from previous employment can be helpful, although usually not as meaningful as a good reference. Your teaching or student teaching evaluations will most likely be a requirement, but evaluations from other related jobs or experiences could be a useful addition to your resume if you are given an opportunity to provide supplemental material. The reason that evaluations are not as meaningful is that many employees receive satisfactory evaluations by default. In many cases, especially in education, outstanding educators and mediocre educators alike can receive a similar "satisfactory" evaluation. A satisfactory or acceptable evaluation is not always perceived as an indicator of an outstanding employee, but only as an indicator that someone is not an unsatisfactory employee. In other words, a good evaluation is expected and a bad evaluation is unacceptable.

Degree. Having a college degree is usually a basic requirement to obtain a teaching position. However, the college or university from which that degree is earned is usually of less importance. That is not to say that an administrator will not prefer a degree from one university to that of another, but as long as the university from which you earned your degree is accredited, the specific college or university is of less importance than many other factors. Furthermore, private or out-of-state colleges can cost thousands more than public in-state colleges, and private college graduates, on average, graduate with thousands of dollars more debt than public college graduates (Woodruff, 2014). My point is not that the specific degree program is not important, only that it may be unnecessary to spend the additional thousands of dollars that it might cost to attend an expensive university, when the less expensive option may have been sufficient.

There are times when the university from which you graduate matters. For example, a degree from a respected Christian university may give you an advantage if you are applying for a teaching position at a Christian school. Another example might be favoritism shown toward graduates of a particular university when applying for a position in close proximity to that university. The key here is to place more emphasis on your experiences and personal qualities than on the location and prestige of your college or university.

Licensure. Your teaching license can actually be as important as your degree. Your license indicates that you have a college degree, but just as importantly identifies what grades and content you will be able to teach. In many school settings, outstanding qualifications mean very little if you do not have the necessary endorsements on your license. In most states, administrators have a list of what credentials are required to teach each course and grade level.

If you are in the early stages of your preparation program, it is important that you consider which grades and subjects you are interested in teaching, and weigh that with the teaching needs in the location(s) where you would like to work. Understand that not all teaching credentials are equally marketable. However, it is usually possible to add endorsements to your original license after you complete your program. When considering the teaching content area that you are going to pursue, it is best to consider marketability (what are the needs in this teaching field) along with your teaching preference (what and where would I enjoy teaching). It is not uncommon for a teacher candidate to desire to work in a specific grade, location, or even school, but it is important to keep in mind that this will limit your employment opportunities. Obtaining licensure in a high needs area such as math, science, special education, or English as a Second Language (ESL), as well as flexibility in geographic location, can significantly improve your marketability (Teacher Shortage Areas, 2015).

Most states offer license reciprocity, often with few or no additional requirements beyond completing the necessary paperwork, but it can still be helpful if you know what you want to teach and where, as early in your program as possible. You may be the most qualified candidate applying for a position, and the principal may even want to hire you, but if you do not have the correct credentials for the position, you will probably not be considered.

Private schools do not have the same licensure requirements as public schools, although they may still choose to hold candidates to the same standards. It is possible that a private school could hire a candidate that they believe is qualified for the position, even if they do not have the specific content area listed on their state issued teaching license. Many private schools can even hire candidates who have not obtained a teaching license, although this has become less common in recent years.

Content knowledge. Content knowledge includes some level of expertise in the content area that you will be teaching, as well as pedagogy and classroom management. Just as being an athlete does not necessarily make someone a good coach, completing courses in a particular content area does not necessarily make someone a good teacher. However, having a thorough understanding of the content you will be teaching is usually a basic expectation. Teaching candidates should be able to express their understanding of their subject matter and how they can effectively teach the content at an age appropriate level.

Experience—Formal or Informal (sub, volunteer, practicum hours). Experience is something that newer teachers often lack, but it should not be absent from your resume. Most administrators understand that every outstanding veteran teacher started out as a novice teacher at some point. For this reason, your student teaching and any practicum opportunities are critical until you have full-time teaching experience. It is important that you consider every opportunity to step into the school building as a time to learn and to build a reputation. Do not look at your student teaching experience as just another requirement to complete your program. This may be your best opportunity to prove your potential as a capable educator. Your student teaching can result in experiences that allow you to describe how you performed in a classroom setting. Furthermore, look for occasions to obtain additional experiences during student teaching placement. Volunteering to assist with athletics, clubs, fine arts, or general supervision are just a few ways you can gain additional experiences while student teaching. If you are already a classroom teacher, but are not in your "dream job," do not wait until you are in a better position to give your best. The job you do in a situation that may not be ideal can still have a significant impact on your future opportunities.

There are many other ways you can gain valuable experience beyond the classroom setting. Summer camps, recreational sports leagues, community centers, Young Men's Christian Association (YMCA)/Young Women's Christian Association (YWCA), and various other organizations may offer volunteer or paid positions working with children of all ages. These opportunities not only help to confirm your interest and ability to effectively work with children, but they can also provide you with insight regarding your personal strengths and weaknesses. Almost any occasion to work with children, especially in the age group you are interested in teaching, can be considered a valuable learning opportunity. When asked in an interview to describe your experiences working with children, it is better to have several informal experiences than none at all.

Informal qualification (the intangibles). If you were to conduct an Internet search on the qualities of a great teacher, many of the qualities you would consistently see would fall under informal teacher qualities, or what I refer to as intangibles. These qualifications are more difficult to identify, as you may not learn them in your coursework or include them on your resume, but they are critically important, nonetheless.

Personality. To some degree, your personality is determined before you walk into your first interview. There is no one personality type that makes an effective educator, although there are some personal traits that most educators should possess to some degree. For example, most administrators want to see a teacher who is friendly, caring, and personable, although not every teacher is expected to express these traits in the same manner. Many of us have met teachers who were very stern and serious, yet were effective educators. Likewise, we may remember teachers who were more effective because they were funny and outgoing. The good news is that teachers of different personality types can all be effective if they are aware of their weaknesses and make the most of their strengths.

Although there is not a list of personality traits that all teachers should have, there are many that can be important assets. Some aspects of your personality may seem natural, while others may seem forced, but many personality traits can be developed or changed over time. Being friendly to your students when they walk in the classroom, adding some occasional humor to your lesson, and being firm when necessary, are examples of personal characteristics that can be developed and practiced. Furthermore, personal characteristics displayed by a kindergarten teacher may be different from those characteristics that are important for teacher of high school seniors. Do not accept your weaknesses as "just how I am," as our personalities can be improved, but also learn to use your personality strengths to the best of your ability.

Passion. Regardless what age or subject area you hope to teach, administrators want to see teachers who are passionate about teaching, learning, and children. Likewise, students like to see teachers who are passionate about what they are doing. The fact that you have chosen teaching as a profession may indicate, to some degree, a passion for education. The most desirable candidates are those who express an exceptional enthusiasm that could fuel their ability to be an outstanding educator. This is a trait that is hard to fabricate, but when it is sincere it is obvious to everyone around.

Attitude. Much like your personality, your attitude is developed over many years often before you even decided you wanted to be a teacher. However, to a greater degree than your personality, your attitude can and most likely will change over time. Many of you have heard instructors warn you to avoid teachers with negative attitudes when you are in a school building. I would also add to that a warning to make sure you do not become a negative teacher. Teaching is a difficult job and teachers have to regularly deal with difficult situations and people. Dwelling on the negative aspects of teaching can make the job much more difficult for you and for those around you. Much of your attitude is a choice, but making improvements often includes self-reflection and a concerted effort to look for the positive in the people and situations around.

It is important that you are aware of the attitudes that you convey to an administrator when applying for a position. When interviewing, or even having conversations with other educators, avoid negative comments about other schools or teachers, even if the statements are accurate. Likewise, avoid focusing on things you do not like to do, the challenges of dealing with students or parents, or difficult working conditions. Instead, focus on the positive aspects of previous jobs, personal interaction, and things that you enjoy. Administrators will be much more confident in your potential to meet the daily challenges of being a teacher when they perceive that you approach your life and career in a positive manner. Mendler (2012) even suggests that attitudes are more important than strategies in many situations.

Leadership. Being an educational leader is not just for school administrators. Even if you do not consider yourself a leader prior to your first teaching job, once you step into your first classroom, you become a leader. I have met a number of teachers who are uncomfortable taking a leadership role among other adults, but when they step into their own classrooms they have no problem taking control. In addition to leading their own classrooms, many teachers desire to broaden their influence by taking on leadership responsibilities within their schools, while other educators pursue more formal leadership roles as department leaders, school administrators, or district level leaders.

Not every teacher will pursue a formal leadership role in the school, but every teacher is a leader. Some lead by position or title; others lead through their words and actions. Many school administrators like to develop teachers who have potential to fill formal leadership positions, but almost all administrators want teachers who are going to lead by example. Prior to seeking your first teaching position, seek opportunities to take leadership roles at your job, club, student organization, or even in your college classes.

Flexibility. Administrators are looking for teachers who will, not those who will not. Take opportunities to express your willingness to be flexible. Most schools are rapidly changing environments and effective teachers need to be able to go with the flow. Make it clear that you are a team player and you are willing to do whatever is needed to benefit students. Avoid making demands or listing requirements you may have for your classroom. It is not inappropriate to identify your teaching preferences if asked, but make sure the focus is on what you are willing to do, not what you are unwilling to do. Many school leaders feel that they are being asked to do more with less, so hiring flexible teachers is a necessity.

Student centered. Being student centered is not only a good strategy for getting hired, it is a good strategy for making decisions in an educational setting. In my years as an educational leader, there were many times when a decision had to be made, but the best course of action was unclear. Often, the decision became clear when I asked the question, "What is best for students?" Most administrators understand that new teachers are going to make some mistakes along the way. An administrator will be more prone to trust you when they can trust that your decisions will be based on doing what is best for your students. This concept can be especially helpful to a new teacher with limited experience. When being asked questions about which you have limited knowledge or experience, focusing your answer on your desire to do what is best for students can be a good start.

Above and beyond. I mentioned earlier in this chapter the importance of giving your best effort in student teaching. As a principal, I was always amazed to see student teachers or new teachers who came in a few minutes before school started, completed only the required tasks, and left shortly after the students. Although they were technically fulfilling their responsibilities as a student teacher, they rarely showed any additional effort. This is not the kind of teacher that most administrators want to hire. School leaders often must make the most out of limited faculty and staff; therefore, they want to hire teachers who are going to give a little extra effort. Granted, some principals can take this to the extreme and expect teachers to put in excess hours at the school, but many just want to know that a teacher is going to go above and beyond the minimum requirements. For most teachers, a workweek is more than 40 hours. This does not mean that you cannot have a life, but you should be productive when you are at work, and be prepared to put in some extra hours at work or at home when necessary.

FAVORABLE PRACTICES

As mentioned earlier in this chapter, there are very few absolutes regarding what an administrator is looking for in an applicant. However, there are some do's and do not's that will consistently affect your chances of getting a teaching job. Here are just a few:

Know that you are preparing now for your future job. Do not wait to start addressing some of the issues discussed in this chapter. Start gaining experience, looking for opportunities, building skills, and acquiring knowledge that will be beneficial to you in your next job. If you have already begun doing this, then do not stop. It is much better to have to pick and choose which qualifications you are going to emphasize than to have very few options.

Know what you want to do. As early as possible, decide what you want out of the teaching profession. This will allow you to gain experience and focus on skills that will be most beneficial to you. Although you can always change your mind, it is beneficial to know if you want to teach elementary or secondary, in a rural or urban setting, in public or private school, or eventually pursue leadership opportunities. If you are not sure where you are being led, make opportunities to visit various educational, community, or church settings. The end of your student teaching is not a good time to realize that the teaching field you have chosen is not a good fit for you.

Be persistent. You may not get every job you apply for, and you may even interview more than once for a job at the same school. For most teachers, getting the first job is the most difficult. After getting that first job, looking to upgrade is usually much easier. Do not get discouraged if you are not selected for a position that you desire, as disappointments can often be learning experiences, and there may be something even better down the road.

Keep your online profile professional. Understand that almost anything that has ever been posted online by you, or about you, has the potential to be seen by a future employer. Even if you have made an effort to keep your online profile "private," your information is most likely available to a tech-savvy interviewer. Fair or not, teachers are often held to a higher standard in regard to morality and professionalism. Avoid putting any pictures, comments, or information online that you would not want seen by a future employer.

COMMON MISTAKES

Waiting until it is time to interview to consider your experience. Consider any activities you are involved in that might be relevant in a future interview. Write down the details of potential job-related activities as you go. Avoid being reactive in an interview by preparing to talk about your experience, skills, and qualifications.

Being too narrow in your goals. It is great to have an idea of what your "dream job" might look like, but be open to opportunities that might not seem as perfect. You may want to return to your hometown and teach where you went to school. That is a great goal, but if that is the only option you are considering, your employment opportunities will be limited. You can significantly improve your chances of finding a job if you are open to opportunities that might be a little out of your comfort zone. You might even end up enjoying a job that you had not considered before.

Being too aggressive. I mentioned earlier that it is important to be persistent, but it is also important to avoid being too aggressive. Multiple attempts to contact a building level administrator can be perceived as pushy, especially when the application process is not being followed. The application process can vary from school to school, or district to district, so familiarize yourself with the application process before applying for a specific job.

> ### Leading the Way
> *Do not wait until you are ready to apply for a leadership position to consider your leadership qualifications. Start taking advantage of leadership opportunities, no matter how small, as soon as possible.*

HOW QUALIFIED SHOULD YOU BE?

Most teaching jobs require specific qualifications. Minimum requirements usually include a college degree and teaching license. However, teaching candidates often pursue advanced degrees and training to improve their marketability. It may be difficult to decide when and if you want to pursue an additional degree.

DO PRINCIPALS WANT TO HIRE TEACHERS RIGHT OUT OF COLLEGE OR THOSE WITH EXPERIENCE?

Having a diverse faculty includes having a combination of veteran teachers with years of experience, and new teachers with fresh ideas and recent training. This is not to say that veteran teachers do not have fresh ideas, or that first-year teachers cannot be outstanding educators. It does mean, however, that there is some value in having a combination of both groups represented in the makeup of a school's faculty.

So, what does this mean for you as a teacher candidate applying for a job? It means that either can work for you, or against you. A principal may be trying to bring in some new teachers to offset a more veteran staff, or they may be trying to bring in veteran teachers to provide experience and leadership among a very young staff. It may even be that a principal favors one group over the other as a matter of personal preference. The good news is it is projected that almost 300,000 new teachers will be hired each year for the next few years (Public and Private, 2013).

The point here is that every veteran teacher was at one point a first-year teacher. It is also a fact that every year new teachers are hired at schools across the country. Although there is no guarantee that a first-year teacher will be considered for any particular job opening, overall attrition will ensure that many positions will be filled by new teachers. If you are wise in your job search, you can find job openings where your experience, or lack there of, will be considered and you just need to convince the interviewer that you are the best applicant available.

SHOULD I GET AN ADVANCED DEGREE?

New teachers will often ask if it is a good idea to earn a graduate degree early in their teaching career. This is a great question because having a graduate degree when applying for a teaching job could be a positive or negative. For example: if you are applying for a teaching position in a very small district, or even in a private school where salary is based on a set scale, having a Master's degree could cause you to be a "more expensive" candidate. Having an additional degree would mean they would be required to pay more in a place where every dollar is carefully spent.

Not all districts have to be so conscientious about hiring someone with an additional degree. Many larger districts and even some private schools only consider the average cost of hiring a new teacher and can pursue the most qualified candidate regardless how many degrees they have. In this case, having a master's degree may give the candidate an advantage over a new teacher with only a bachelor's degree. Some schools and districts place an emphasis on hiring teachers with advanced degrees as it can improve the perception of teachers in the community.

In general, earning an advanced degree is a good investment for a teacher, and since most states provide some salary increase for additional degrees, the sooner it is earned the better. That is why close to 50% of teachers have a master's degree or higher (Chingos, 2014). When making a decision about whether to pursue a graduate degree prior to obtaining your first teaching position, you may want to consider the following:

- What is expected in the school or district where you are planning to apply?
- Are you more likely to be able to meet the financial obligations of graduate school at the current time or in the future?
- Will you be more motivated to complete a graduate degree after obtaining your first teaching job?
- Do you have the time now, or will you have the time as a new teacher to complete coursework at the graduate level?

NETWORK

When speaking to teacher candidates about getting a teaching job, I often suggest that they be related to someone in the school system. Although this is usually said in jest, there is actually some good advice underneath that statement. The advice is to take advantage of established relationships. Friends, relatives, former co-workers, and educators you met while earning your degree can all be resources to help you get an interview, and possibly even a job. Most people understand the challenge of obtaining their desired position and would be glad to help you connect, especially if you have built a positive relationship.

CONCLUSION

In some ways, asking what an administrator is looking for in an applicant is like asking what is an administrator's favorite food. Each administrator is different and has different priorities, values, and expectations for their teachers. However, there are common traits that many, even most, administrators will agree are important and valuable. These "common" traits are no secret, and a teacher candidate will most likely hear them numerous times throughout their career, read them in books or articles, or hear them emphasized by current educators. Some of the less common traits, many of those mentioned in this chapter as informal or intangible traits, are the ones that can help you stand out when there is a deep pool of applicants. Although completing a teaching degree, or working as a new teacher can keep you very busy, I encourage you to take advantage of as many opportunities as possible to gain experience, learn skills, and develop your personal philosophy of education. Each experience and learning opportunity, no matter how small, helps prepare you for that next interview, and ultimately your first or next teaching position.

HITTING YOUR MARK

Getting that first teaching position is a great first step in your career as an educator, but what comes next? Even if you are content with your current position, it is important to consider your long-term goals and start planning your next steps sooner rather than later. The following activities will help you as you consider the possibilities.

QUESTIONS FOR DISCUSSION

1. Of the formal and informal qualifications that principals are looking for in a teacher, which ones do you believe are, or potentially could be, your strengths?
2. Of the formal and informal qualifications that principals are looking for in a teacher, which ones do you believe are, or potentially could be, weaknesses when applying for your next job?
3. What are some strategies you can consider to make yourself more qualified for a future interview?

ACTIVITIES FOR ENRICHMENT

Make a list of job categories in the field of education that you would consider somewhere down the road. Consider positions within your school, at the district level, at the state level, or even with outside educational organizations. List all jobs that sound appealing, even if you are not sure if you will ever be qualified or interested.

Of the positions that you list, select two or three that sound the most appealing. Search job postings (these can usually be found at school/district websites, recruitment websites, or in educational periodicals) for those or similar positions and make notes of the qualifications, education, and experience required for each position.

Review the job descriptions for any of the positions that you listed above. Consider which duties/responsibilities you will enjoy, and those you might consider unpleasant. Does reviewing the job description make you more or less interested in that particular position?

Make a list of your short (1–3 years), medium (4–6 years), and long-term (7–10 years) employment goals. Under each category, make a list of the steps you will need to take and an estimated time frame for completing these goals. Examples may include professional development, leadership experience, or an additional college degree.

REFERENCES

Chingos, Matthew (2014). Who profits from the master's degree pay bump for teachers? SERIES: The Brown Center Chalkboard | Number 69 of 115. Retrieved from: http://www.brookings.edu/research/papers/2014/06/05-masters-degree-pay-bump-chingos

Mendler, A. (2012). *When Teaching Gets Tough: Smart ways to reclaim your game.* ASCD, Alexandria, VA.

Public and private elementary and secondary teachers, enrollment, pupil/teacher ratios, and new teacher hires: Selected years, fall 1955 through fall 2023 (2013). *Digest of Educational Statistics.* Table 208.20. Retrieved from: http://nces.ed.gov/programs/digest/d13/tables/dt13_208.20.asp

Teacher Shortage Areas Nationwide Listing 1990–1991 through 2015–2016 (March 2015). U.S Department of Education Office of Postsecondary Education. Retrieved from: https://www2.ed.gov/about/offices/list/ope/pol/tsa.doc

Woodruff, Mandi. (Jan., 2014). Is public or private college a better investment? *Business Insider.* Retrieved from: http://www.businessinsider.com/public-and-private-college-costs-2014-1

PART 3

KEEPING THE JOB

CHAPTER 11

COMMITMENT TO JOB, STUDENTS, AND PROFESSION

Susan D. James

"So be sure when you step, step with care and great tact. And remember that life's A Great Balancing Act. And will you succeed? Yes! You will, indeed! (98 and ¾ percent guaranteed). Kid, you'll move mountains"

~ Dr. Seuss

INTRODUCTION

A great educator is constantly reflecting on the art of teaching, unearthing epiphanies that drive and inspire instruction. To my surprise, the one discovery that has impacted my teaching the most came late in my career. Dr. Shelbie Witte from Florida State University reshaped my thinking regarding the vital choice of becoming a professional educator. As Witte Skyped with teachers participating in a National Writing Project, she shared a lecture from Lorenz about The Butterfly Effect in education. He found that small change in initial conditions had created a significantly different outcome. Lorenz's image provides an extraordinary analogy for how small actions in teaching can have tremendously powerful effects. Sometimes, these effects are spawned not from our intended actions, but from the way we present ourselves as professionals in our field.

Courtesy of Susan D. James. Copyright © Kendall Hunt Publishing Company.

As educators, we should remember that teaching, while challenging, is the one career in which individuals' daily actions make a big difference. With this awesome responsibility comes the balancing act of being committed to the job, students, and profession. When considering that our actions impact not just the young people seated in our classroom, but the offspring they will someday have, as well as individuals they come in contact with daily, the magnitude of the importance of our job is clear. This thought alone should inspire educators to consider the importance of commitment to the world's most noble vocation.

COMMITMENT TO THE JOB

While traveling to a conference, I began to reflect on my years as an educator in order to prepare to write this chapter. I found myself on a plane seated next to a high school girl. Our discussion was a reminder of several key principles in becoming an effective teacher. First, we must not forget to listen to our students. The young lady validated what I already know to be true: students want their teachers to be professional role models. They want to connect with their teacher and classmates and feel that they are the teacher's priority. They want to be heard and understood. Our discussion clearly revealed that the young lady felt that her English teacher did not fit the profile of a professional teacher who was committed to her work, students, or parents, as she relayed stories of assignments that lacked relevancy to her life, her lack of "choice" in reading, and assignments that are would prepare her for the "real world." Additionally, her mother spoke of her lack of connection to the teacher and her frustration with finding reading material that would inspire her daughter to read. This conversation allowed me to focus on what is important for current practitioners to remember daily.

DRESS UP AND SHOW UP

In our society of "Dress Down Fridays," it is important not to lose sight that educators are with their students, oftentimes, more than the students are with their families. We are the face of our profession, and with that comes the awesome responsibility of dressing up and showing up. Always considering that this may be THE day your students will always remember can be a strong reinforcement of the footprint you will leave with each individual.

We need to remember that first impressions do matter. Dressing up includes not only professional dress and a cleanly appearance, but also "dressing up" how we communicate (both in speech and writing) with students and the adults in our school community. Watching us relate to our administrators respectfully, seeing how we collaborate with other teachers, and witnessing how we interact with the entire school family will impact how students will conduct themselves in the world of work. A rule of thumb could be this: if conducting business around the one person we respect most in life, what would our actions demonstrate? These students are the future; they are tomorrow's work force. This alone should guide our actions.

Dressing up is not the only component of professionalism to the job, but showing up is critical, as well. Being on time to school (or in some instances, early to school, since some leaders might suggest that being on time is actually considered late), committing to professional development opportunities, and attending students' outside events are all important. For the first 13 years of their schooling, we are the adult models for our students in demonstrating work environment behavior. We teach them, either negatively or positively, how to present themselves, interact with others, and think critically.

I have watched as my words and actions have been imitated through my students. It can be seen in big instances, such as in the students' career choices. Due to her work in my class, one of my students went on to become a poet who not only teaches high school, but fights for educational change. Danielle, now a teacher in Los Angeles, was one face in a sea of confused eighth grade faces in my classroom who were alerted that a plane had struck the Pentagon during the 9/11 attacks. Residing by Dulles Airport, the plane flew over our school before finally striking its target. Witnessing how I handled the crisis and dealt with my own grief, my students took to writing with me as their model. That experience has shaped Danielle, as well as many others in that class, as writing became a vehicle for expression and a coping mechanism for grief. Watching Danielle discuss the power of the written word years later is proof positive that our jobs as role models impact students on a deep level. My influence is far-reaching, as is the impact of each educator in our nation. Keeping The Butterfly Effect in mind can guide educators daily in making professional decisions that will profoundly impact our students. Students imitating our behavior can also be seen in small instances. With the development of social media, students' Facebook postings mimic my daily quotes posted in class related to good character, highlight how students continue to read for pleasure, as well as reveal the jobs and important roles they are playing in their communities.

NETWORK

Network to find your school "family." Entering the school for the first time and seeing the rapid pace at which the faculty is working often leaves first year teachers feeling lost and alone. It is not that veteran teachers do not want to help—in fact, most are honored when asked. It is important to remember teachers who have been in your school for a while know the lay of the land and can help you with schedules, provide you will sample syllabi, show you where resources are housed, introduce you to other teachers, and be your proofreader for important correspondence. Reinventing the wheel will only cause angst, so asking for help will give time to make the curriculum your own with their expertise of pacing already in place.

Remember, a learning community is reciprocal. Veteran teachers can share a wealth of information, but newer teachers come with newly-acquired methods and skills that can be shared. Research in education changes constantly, so new teachers have much to offer veteran teachers who have been far removed from their methods courses. However, as a new teacher, be cautious in how you present new ideas; the veteran teachers at your school deserve respect for the years they have served. These teachers have the experience, which new teachers do not, and, because of this, they know about the practical aspects of teaching that you may not yet have acquired. When they share with you, humbly share ideas you gained from your schooling. What makes a great educator is a teacher's willingness to understand that we should be, just like our students, lifelong learners.

BE STRATEGIC

Work smart. In order to keep all things balanced, strategy is critical. Once you are aware of your students' needs, you can begin to apply the pedagogy you acquired in your teacher education program and make plans for the year. In order to avoid feeling overwhelmed, approach this first as a year-at-a-glance, then fine tune by semester. Having established a network within the school and becoming familiar with your students' strengths and weaknesses, your creative abilities can now come into play.

First, the reality of your having materials before the school year begins is highly unlikely, so prior to the first day of school, use your content knowledge to plan for essential questions you will use to teach large "Big Picture" concepts and themes in your discipline throughout the year (Burke, 2011). With these in place, you have a roadmap of where you will start and end, as well as a general idea of concepts and skills taught. Once you have your textbook, you can easily "plug in" instruction to support your concepts/themes.

Next, fine-tune the first few weeks of school. Because you have successfully conducted reconnaissance, you will have an idea of the differentiation needed, if only based on reading and writing levels. This will allow you to utilize various resources that will meet the students' needs. One of the best tips for the first week is to plan activities that can shape students' attitudes toward you and your content area. This will allow you to develop a relationship with students, as well as create community amongst students.

Reflect. Working with thousands of teachers, first as a teacher and now as a teacher mentor, has provided opportunities to reflect on what it means to be a "master" teacher, possessing the "withitness" in teaching (Kounin, 1970). It is important to think while acting and quickly respond to what is often the uncertainty of situations. Each class is different. In fact, one could go as far as to say a class of students has its own personality, and what works for one group might fail for another. One of the most difficult

Ethical Considerations

Principle II: Responsibility for Professional Competence

The professional educator demonstrates commitment to high standards of practice

skills to develop is how to be flexible and change lessons mid-stream in order to make them successful, but if this approach is seen as an exciting challenge, then becoming a master at quick responses to difficult situations can be obtained. It is important not to see this as failure but as progress. What is learned from struggles only strengthens you as a teacher.

In between classes, it is always beneficial to jot down notes regarding any needed "tweaks" in instruction. This helps for next year's instruction. Keeping a notebook for these types of reflections and adding notes about classroom behavior (both good and bad) can help equally for future planning and in your nightly review of the day.

An important note: Do not be afraid to change instruction mid-stream. The best gift a teacher can give students is to clearly articulate that a classroom is a reciprocal learning community, and teachers are learning along with students. You are not the sole source of information; the students are there to teach you, as well. With this mindset, constantly reshaping thinking (both yours and your students) is an authentic work environment, and one that will inspire not just inquiry, but the critical skills of knowing how to cope in a demanding work environment.

Rest. There is never enough time. A teacher could work nonstop, 24/7. Knowing this, it is important to keep yourself healthy and well-rested. There will always be more work to do. Make a list of what is critical for the next day, and focus your efforts on these tasks. Without rest, burnout occurs, so many teachers give up hobbies and exercise, when in fact, continuing what you love helps keep you well-balanced and healthy. Connect with people at work who share the same activities and will keep you motivated and moving each day!

COMMITMENT TO THE STUDENTS

In order for our students to reach their full potential, they must be motivated to strive for the top of Maslow's Hierarchy of Needs, towards self-actualization (Maslow, 1942). The fulfillment of the social need includes "the need to feel loved by others and be accepted" (Gobin, et al., 2012, p. 205). Because Maslow's view is holistic, it can be assumed that every element and aspect of human life works together to satisfy needs, helping people move from one level to the next in the hierarchy. With the increase in issues within family structures (Layton, 2015), what once was not paramount in the teachers' daily lives is now coming to the forefront of our thinking as educators, as students are coming to school lacking the basic needs. There are ways to assist students in moving towards this self-realization, which gives the students the power to have a strong self-efficacy that will allow them to eventually work independently. What is often forgotten is that students will have different needs and will progress at different rates (Sherwin & Stevenson, 2010). Therefore, it is necessary to get to know your students and provide space and time for them to develop.

LISTEN

Armed with the knowledge of how your classroom of students is achieving based on prior assessments, it is now time to file that information in a safe place to ensure confidentiality. Although you have gathered some student information, as we all know, people continually grow and change, and the beginning of a school year is the perfect time for students to come into your classroom with a clean slate and fresh start to learning. Listening through observations and writings, as well as direct interactions are all ways to listen to students.

Preparing an interest inventory for your students informs you on many levels. With the right questions, a teacher can find out about the interests of the students, the students' daily activities and home environment, the feelings the students have towards learning different content areas, and what you, as the teacher, can do to assist the students in their learning. Adding two questions to the interest inventory can provide more insight into the students' minds than any other: "What can I do to help you succeed in my class? What do I need to know about you that will help me be the best teacher possible?" Knowing these answers places you at a strong advantage and allows you to plan instruction that is suitable for each student. Again, think smart. There are many interest inventories for your discipline already created and online for your use.

CONNECT

Research has found that other than the students' motivation and desire to learn, the one factor most important in the success of our students is the teacher (Hattie, 1992a, 19931, 1993b, 1996, 2003), and a large part of this is due to whether or not the student feels connected to the teacher. There are many small and easily managed ways to help teachers bond with students.

First, learn student names the first day. This might mean planning team-building activities and studying school pictures on the school's database, but it is well worth the effort. The surprised looks on the faces of the students as you use names the second day of class immediately shows you the advantage to this gesture. They know you care enough to know them and can easily use their names to hold them accountable.

Another step in creating community relates to learning with your students. Whether it is reading with them while they are reading independently, writing and sharing your writing, or researching a topic together to find answers, students will have "buy-in" once they see you are an active part of their learning community. Staying behind your desk, checking email or Facebook, or any other activity that does not relate to what the students are doing must be reserved for another time. There is no stronger way to connect than to share in the joy of learning.

Another simple idea is to acknowledge students. Keep a calendar for special events (birthdays, concerts and game dates, etc.), and model writing to the students by penning a quick note in recognition. This is easier than one would think. Also, if you start every class with "Good News," allowing students to share their outside events, this becomes a routine that shows students you care. It is not feasible to be at every event for each of your students, so again, work smart. Use the methods to at least acknowledge what the students do outside of the class, and make an attempt to attend one event for each sports/club offered in which your students are active.

Another way to connect and interact with students is by using a "What I See in You" card (Figure 11.1), which allows a check of boxes and a short narrative to reinforce good behavior or hard work. Remember the reconnaissance you completed? Notating those who have not been successful in school and looking for prime situations that you can award a "What I See in You" card can be a game-changer for students. With the fast pace of our lives and our growing concern over family stressors affecting our students (Layton, 2015), these types of small gestures can pave the way for a connection between students and teacher that allows for a productive learning environment.

What I've Seen In You...

- articulate
- bright
- caring
- celebrate life
- committed
- confident
- considerate
- corageous
- devoted
- discerning
- disciplined
- emphatic
- encouraging
- enduring
- engaging
- entertaining
- enthusiastic

- expressive
- faithful
- fearless
- friendly
- funny
- genuine
- good listener
- graceful
- helpful
- humble
- inspiring
- joyful
- loving
- merciful
- nice
- obedient
- others-oriented

- perceptive
- persistent
- positive
- respectable
- responsive
- serving
- spunky
- steadfast
- strong
- teachable
- thoughtful
- understanding
- unselfish
- upbeat
- warm
- welcoming

©Boumen Japet/Shutterstock.com

FIGURE 11.1 *What I've Seen in You*

CREATE COMMUNITY

The payoff that comes from taking the time to create a classroom family far exceeds what some see as loss of instructional time. In accordance with the latest Bloom's Taxonomy (Bloom, et al., 1994), "remembering" is at the bottom rung of the pyramid, so when we give students a list of rules to remember, they are, sadly, not part of the community development process. Allowing for student involvement in "creating" (top of Bloom's) a definition of respect and defining what it means to be part of a learning community is sadly not the norm. Instead of telling kids what constitutes good communication, conversations revolving around what it means to be a good community member, a friend, and learning partner must be discussed collaboratively. Although there are many team-building activities that can be utilized to achieve a sense of community, the activities presented below not only create the community needed for a successful learning environment, but are ones that allow students to feel accepted unconditionally, a feeling that leads to a sense of equity in the classroom.

Respect activity. The first day of class, students are given the following questions:

1. What is respect?
2. Who is your hero? Why? What characteristics does this person exhibit?
3. How does it feel when someone disrespects you?
4. What can you do to ensure respect is shown to all classmates?
5. What can your teacher do to show respect to all classmates?

After collecting all student responses, a script is created. At the top of individual pages, one question would be typed. Next, every response to the question given by each student would be bulleted under the question headings. This script would be several pages long. Students were given anonymity, as no names were attached to responses. The scripts were handed out, and each student was told to read one bullet, rotating throughout the classroom, giving each student a "voice" in detailing what this particular class found to define and epitomize respect.

The first time I facilitated this was as a second grade teacher, and it was planned due to my witnessing disrespectful behavior occurring in the classroom. Then, as I moved into middle and high school education, it became a collaborative beginning-of-the-year activity that allowed for defining "respect" and, in a written agreed upon document, it grounded each of us in what we believed and stood for, as well as reminded us of what our classroom family would use as our daily guidelines. Even at the high school level, pride could be seen on the faces of each student as his or her statements were read aloud by someone else. It became apparent that for many this was the first time since elementary school that the class had collaboratively created a written document that came from the hearts of each individual student. When anyone strayed from our contract, all that would have to happen was for a classmate to nod towards the wall that held the ideas that we held sacred.

Stick figure activity. Just like instruction, building community needs scaffolding. It takes students time to trust their classmates and be willing to share with themselves, and if we want to truly create a classroom of respect that will foster collaborative learning, moving from an activity of anonymity like that of the respect exercise to something like the Stick Figure (Figure 11.2) works well, especially when modeled by the teacher. Students are taught literal and figurative language by first looking at my model, as I share my "words" (mantra and/or belief system), what I "see" (my vision of a respectful world), what I want to hear (my vision of how we communicate as humans), what I "love" (what is important to me, what are my strengths and weaknesses, and what, if I could, "stomp out" or eliminate). It was always amazing to see my students far exceed what was expected, as they took time to share of themselves, and even go as far as to show ownership by "dressing" their figure to match their likeness. These figures were proudly displayed on the wall, and students spent time talking about themselves and their lives, as they slowly began to trust and open the door to a healthy working environment.

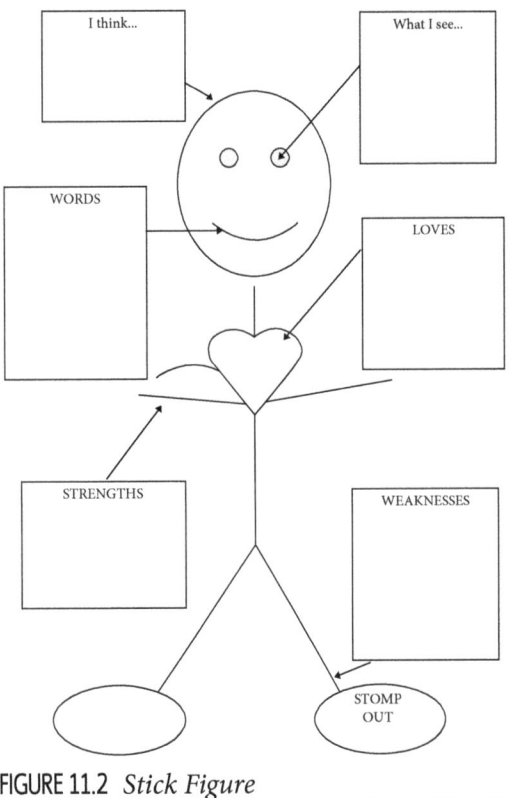

FIGURE 11.2 *Stick Figure*

Commitment to Job, Students, and Profession

When teachers hear of these activities, their concerns generally relate to loss of instructional time. With the issues that plaque our society, teachers cannot afford not to take this valuable time with students in order to become a working unit. Building a community of learners starts by getting to know one another. In order to see the multi-faceted sides of students, it is important to talk as a class about who each student is outside of school. It is not unheard of for students to arrive at the end of the school year and not even know one another's names. First sharing of self and then applying this type of character to analyze what is read in class is what makes this a solid instructional tool.

Classroom contracts. Creating classroom contracts is another great way to build community. This can be done as young as kindergarten or even in the college classroom, as students work collaboratively to make a list of what a classroom needs in order to be an effective high-functioning community. Students work in small groups to discuss and agree on three of their best ideas. They use chart paper to write these contractual agreements, while discussing how to evaluate, analyze, and synthesize ideas into a concise contract. Students sign their names to this, and it is kept on the wall along with consequences for breaking the contract. This type of collaborative work allows students to have open dialogue that gives students a voice and allows for a feeling of family.

RENEW YOUR COMMITMENT DAILY

You have committed to being the best teacher you can be for a group of students and it takes daily effort to renew this commitment. So far, you have laid the groundwork to make the year successful by becoming part of your school family and learning as much as possible about your students. The real commitment comes in continuing to keep this level of commitment going the entire school year. What you have learned about collaboration with other teachers and your students, assessing students, planning for instruction, and reflecting on your practices has to be a daily event. This will allow for the critical step of adjusting instruction to meet the changing needs of students. The best teachers are constantly assessing the needs of the students and adjusting curriculum to meet those needs.

MONITOR, DIAGNOSE, REFLECT, ADJUST, REPEAT

When interviewing teachers who have completed their first year, a common theme is revealed regarding continuing the momentum. One teacher said it well, "I am just surprised at how my mind is constantly working and trying to find solutions to problems." She went on to say that teaching is constantly monitoring students' progress, reflecting on instruction given, adjusting and fine tuning lessons, and then starting over again the next day. You make a commitment to perform triage daily, as you monitor, diagnose, reflect, adjust instruction, and repeat. Keeping this in the forefront of your mind helps to keep you focused and realistic about your school day.

COMMITMENT TO THE PROFESSION

Learn. Know that you, just like your students, are constantly learning and growing. Make sure you join the professional organization(s) that are the best for your content area. These organizations print journals and have web sites with resources for teachers. With today's technology, there are even communities of teachers set up on the web for support, as teachers can post questions and get answers from one another.

Ask the principal to allow you to attend yearly conferences in order to stay current in your field, meet educators who share your passion, and attend workshops to expand your arsenal of teaching tools. Administrators are given a pool of money for these types of professional development activities, and the old adage of "you won't receive if you don't ask" holds true.

Most of the conferences have exhibit halls and, at many of these, publishing companies provide free resources. As a language arts and reading teacher, I built an entire library of independent reading books from these conferences. Be prepared with an empty suitcase or mail them back via pony express to your school.

These trips provide a much-needed time for renewal and invigoration, as well as allow you to keep up with current trends and research-based strategies. The free resources are helpful, but what is the most rewarding will be the connections you establish with other educators. Not many professionals understand the commitment of teaching, so having someone who does recognize your hard work and efforts also fulfills your needs, as we must realize Maslow's Needs hold true for teachers, too.

Legislate. Learning also means staying aware of current legislation related to education. With all the changes in education at all levels, now is the time for teachers to legislate to share personal experiences that will hopefully assist our government in making better decisions about our students. Funding, standardized testing, and implementation of technology in our schools are all ripe for change, and unless teachers' voices are heard, people who are not trained as educators are going to make the decisions for our profession. In the spirit of Dr. Seuss, "Unless someone like you cares a whole awful lot, nothing is going to get better. It's not." We cannot sit and hope someone else will do this for us; we have to work together as a professional community who knows best about our educational arena.

Lead. Share your commitment to students with your community in leading by example and modeling professional behavior. As the facilitator in your classroom, collaborator with colleagues, and the face of education in the community, it is always important to remember to lead by example. As you start your career, remember that you are in the most honorable profession. It is challenging, but no other career is as fulfilling and stimulating, filled with as much exciting learning and many years of strong ties with students. Never forget

> ### Leading the Way
>
> *A greater level of commitment is often required of those who lead. Leadership is a great way to expand your influence, but usually requires more time and decision-making based on what is best for others.*

the impact you have on the lives of our youth. They are our future, and you are the one who develops them into our future workforce. This alone should remind us the value of our teachers. It might be the most challenging job on the planet, but, by far, it is the most rewarding.

FAVORABLE PRACTICES

To find balance in teaching that is every teacher's dream; it all comes back to keeping The Butterfly Effect in mind in all that you do. As a teacher, you serve as a role model to so many students and, eventually, you impact future generations. Failing to act professionally sets a bad example and may also cause you to lose the respect of your students. Demonstrating professionalism in all aspects of your career will allow you to not only gain respect and credibility from your students, but also from your colleagues. Following is a list of those critical practices that must be practiced daily:

- Dress up (includes dressing up your speech, appearance and interactions)
- Show up (on time, to professional development trainings, and students' events)
- Take initiative to build a network (create a school family)
- Learn about school resources
- Create a classroom learning community
- Renew your commitment daily
- Provide rich, relevant instruction for students
- Go with the flow by learning with the students, constantly reshaping thinking
- Learn, Legislate, and Lead
- Remember the Butterfly Effect

COMMON MISTAKES

What is important to remember is that we all make mistakes (even experienced teachers), but we must learn from them. If always keeping The Butterfly Effect in mind, the worst of the mistakes can be avoided. Knowing the critical role that you play in many students' lives, here is a list of the worst common mistakes you can make:

- Silo yourself in your classroom
- Have "Casual Fridays" every day
- Be your students' friend instead of an adult role model
- Create a classroom of fear and unfamiliarity
- Act like teaching is a "job" versus the noble career it is
- Teach what you like versus teaching to the needs and interests of your students
- Think one bad day means the end of your career
- Use only the textbook
- Stay with the plan, even when it is failing
- Ignore the political arena around you
- Forget how many lives you are touching and changing

CONCLUSION

Many factors contribute to a student's academic performance, including their life experiences, family background, and personality traits, but research suggests that, among school-related factors, teachers matter most to students (Hattie, 1992a, 19931, 1993b, 1996, 2003). From the moment you are hired, to your first days of pre-planning, all the way to the end of your first year of teaching, focusing on your commitment to your job, students, and the profession of teaching is critical to your success. Each of your actions creates a powerful impact on your students and school community. By staying well-balanced in all you do as a teacher and seeing your workplace as a support system you need, you will be able to provide the best instruction possible for students, while staying true to the commitment of professionalism in all you do.

HITTING YOUR MARK

Ralph Waldo Emerson once said, "We aim above the mark to hit the mark." This mantra is a good one to keep in mind, even prior to preparing for a new job. Without constant focus, professionalism can be forgotten due to the often tiring and challenging work of being a teacher. It is important that we, as professionals, keep each other in check by always striving to do better than the previous year. Teachers can take many actions in preparation of a school year. In considering the 10 favorable practices given in this chapter, focusing in on preparation before the fall bell rings can make "hitting your mark" an easier proposition.

QUESTIONS FOR DISCUSSION

1. Being a committed teacher often requires long hours and personal sacrifice. What are some ways you can balance a healthy personal life outside of school with being a committed teacher?
2. How might your commitment level change with years of experience? How do some veteran teachers maintain their energy and commitment while other seem to experience "burnout"?

ACTIVITIES FOR ENRICHMENT

Dress for Success:

Prepare correspondence to parents regarding your class, so as to give enough time for editing and review by one of your colleagues. Doing this the first week of class can cause careless errors.

If appropriate clothing is an issue, spend the summer collecting professional pieces for your wardrobe (and don't forget there are very nice second-hand clothing stores that have professional clothing with price tags still attached!).

To "dress" your classroom, leave the walls blank to prepare for displaying of student work (even at the high school level) and word walls. This will alleviate a lot of stress and is great for building community.

To procure classroom supplies, spend time at local garage sales. You would be surprised at the classroom library you can create for pennies, as well as supplies and furniture you can find.

Once you see your classroom, use technology tools, such as Classroom Architect, to arrange furniture and save for possible substitute teachers (also, go ahead and make those emergency substitute plans to include with the seating chart).

For the staple items you use in class (such as the "What I Saw In You" forms), prepare first and make copies, so that once planning begins, you can focus on curriculum.

Build Community:

To build community early, visit the school several times before fall

Make an effort to meet guidance counselors, English as a Second Language (ESL) and Exceptional Student Education (ESE) Specialists, and all administrators.

Summer is an excellent time to ask those veteran teachers to share sample syllabi, parental contact letters, and yearly plans and slowly beginning to perfect these for your students.

Ask for a tour of the school, including supply rooms.

First-Week Connections:

As soon as you possibly can obtain a roster, use index cards for pictures of your students (most schools have these pre-printed). Begin to memorize names. You can also use these cards to record yearly parental contact.

Ask for a yearbook from the previous year. This piece of advice can help you learn quite a bit about your students prior to your having them in your class. It also helps you learn the names of the faculty members.

Widen your professional world:

Over the summer, find the professional organizations you wish to be part of and get involved. There are blogs and groups that can be helpful.

Organizations and web resources, such as The Teacher Channel, has links for new teachers with excellent tips.

If a mentor is not provided, ask for one.

REFERENCES

Bloom, B. S. (1994). "Bloom's taxonomy: A forty-year retrospective". In Kenneth J. Rehage, Lorin W. Kenneth J.; Anderson, & Lauren A. Lorin W.; Sosniak, Lauren A. (Eds), eds. *Yearbook of the National Society for the Study of Education 93* (p. 2). Chicago: National Society for the Study of Education.) 93 (2).

Burke, J. (2011). *What's the big idea? Question driven units to motivate reading, writing, and thinking.* Portsmouth, NH: Heinemann.

Densmore-James, S. (2011). *The art and science of teaching literacy: Empowering the literacy leaders of tomorrow: A study of pre-service teachers' beliefs, self-efficacy, and knowledge of literacy instruction.* (Electronic Theses, Treatises and Dissertations). Paper Retrieved from 3632.http://diginole.lib.fsu.edu/etd/3632).

Fuchs, D., & Fuchs, L. (2006). Introduction to response to intervention: What, why, and how valid is it? *Reading Research Quarterly, 41(1),* 93–99.

Gardner, H. (2011). *Frames of mind: The theory of multiple intelligences.* LOCATION: Basic Bbooks.

Gobin, B., Teeroovengadum, V., Becceea, N., & Teeroovengadum, V. (2012). Investigating into the relationship between the present level of tertiary students' needs relative to Maslow's hierarchy: A case study at the University of Mauritius. *International Journal of Learning, 18* (11), 203–219.

Hattie, J. A. (1992a). Towards a model of schooling: A synthesis of meta-analyses. *Australian Journal of Education, 36,* 5–13.

Hattie, J. A. (1993a). Measuring the effects of schooling. *SET,* 2, 1–4.

Hattie, J. A. (1993b, July). *What works: A model of the teaching-learning interaction.* Paper presented at the Annual Conference of the Australian Teacher Education Association, Fremantle.

Hattie, J. A. C. (2003). What are the attributes of excellent teachers? In *Teachers make a difference: What is the research evidence?* (pp. 3–26). Wellington: New Zealand Council for Educational Research.

Hattie, J. A. Association for Research in Education. Johnson, E., Mellard, D., Fuchs, D., & McKnight, M. (2006). *Responsiveness to intervention. (RTI): How to do it.* Lawrence, KS: National Research Center on Learning Disabilities.

Kounin, J. (1970). *Discipline and group management in classrooms.* Huntington, N. Y.: R. E. Krieger.

Layton, L. (2015, May 19). Poverty, family stress are thwarting student success, top teachers say. Retrieved from http://www.washingtonpost.com/local/education/poverty-family-stress-are-thwarting-student-success-top-teachers-say/2015/05/19/17f2e35a-fe3c-11e4-833c-a2de05b6b2a4_story.html?hpid=z11

Lorenz, E. N. (1963). Deterministic nonperiodic flow. *Journal of the atmospheric sciences, 20*(2), 130–141.

Maslow, A. (1943). A theory of human motivation. *Psychological Review 50(4),* 370–396.

Sherwin, S., & Stevenson, L. (2010). Creating an optimum environment for learning. *British Journal of School Nursing, 5(9),* 455–457.

Sources of Insight: Better Insights, Better Results (Meier, J. D.) Retrieved from http://sourcesofinsight.com/dr-seuss-quotes/

Stecker, P., Fuchs, L.S. & Fuchs, D. (2005). Using curriculum-based measurement to improve student achievement: Review of research. *Psychology in the Schools, 42,* 795–819.

Stencel, J. (2001). Note-taking techniques in the science classroom: Focusing on the important concepts in science. *Journal of College Teaching, 30(6),* 403–405.

Witte, S. (2015, June 10). *The Butterfly Effect: Finding our voice through R(r)esearch.* Lecture presented at National Writing Project in University of West Florida, Pensacola.

CHAPTER **12**

SOCIAL AND COMMUNITY RESPONSIBILITY

Chris Amos

"We make a living by what we get, but we make a life by what we give."

~ Winston Churchill

INTRODUCTION

We have all heard the old adage "To whom much is given, much is required." Have you ever really stopped to ponder that statement? Teachers have many responsibilities and yet, sometimes being socially and community responsible is forgotten. In the midst of lesson plans and trying to shape young minds, we sometimes lose sight of the bigger picture and our responsibilities as a person who can invoke change and positively affect our culture. A 2012 study found a lack of social responsibility awareness among teachers and students and indicated that unless teachers are able to communicate and motivate their students to emulate social responsibility, students will not develop an understanding of the need to be socially responsible (Sihem, 2012).

Courtesy of Chris Amos. Copyright © Kendall Hunt Publishing Company.

WHAT IS SOCIAL AND COMMUNITY RESPONSIBILITY?

It would seem that a concept such as social responsibility would have a clear-cut definition. However, this is simply not the case. In 2008, Dahlsrud identified 37 different definitions for the term "social responsibility." One of the better definitions comes from researcher Karen Palmer (2008) who defined social responsibility as "an ethical framework which suggests that an entity, be it an organization or individual, has an obligation to act for the benefit of society at large" (p. 120).

With the many versions of this term, then, what really is social and community responsibility? Social and community responsibility seems to be a requirement that lies within each of us, especially those who work as public figures. As teachers (i.e., members of society/public figures), we have a moral obligation to try to help better our community, students, and constituents with whom we interact. Most of us go through ups and downs in any line of work; having a community that is present to help us when we hit those "downs" makes us more productive members in our society. As teachers, we have a duty to recognize problems within our community and larger society, determine ways we can help solve those problems, and then contribute in a useful and meaningful way. It can be as simple as helping your elderly neighbor carry her groceries inside and as complex as designing and implementing fundraisers to help build a new community center. If every member of your community was socially minded, just imagine how incredible your community would become and the amazing things that could be accomplished.

WHY SOCIAL AND COMMUNITY RESPONSIBILITY MATTERS

We live in an inherently selfish day and age. People seem to be more self-absorbed than ever before. A 2013 study shows that Americans are more focused on themselves now than they were 200 years ago (Greenfield, 2013). The study identified language that has been published in various research materials and determined that there has been a fairly steady increase in selfish terms and verbiage over the last 200 years. Sadly, this research shows that we are a society that is more focused on getting everything we want as opposed to giving to others in need. This "Me-Generation," as a result, has permeated our culture and has led to more self-absorbed, narcissistic people.

How does this self-absorbedness affect us as teachers? For some of us, we have a much greater appreciation for the blessings that we have: a college education, a vehicle, a roof over our head, but often we take these things for granted. Now, let's think about the students that you will teach. Some will have iPhones or other "Smart" devices, and have had such since they first began to talk. They have the Internet at their fingertips, and have never had to look in a dictionary for a definition, or sift through an encyclopedia to find factual information.

The Internet has an abundance of information that is required for any school or personal project at the click of a few buttons. Those students may expect to always have the latest and greatest gadgets and beg their mom or dad to spend thousands more on upgraded phones, stylish clothes, or gaming consoles.

Ethical Considerations

Principle IV: Responsibility to the School Community

The professional educator promotes effective and appropriate relationships with parents/guardians

Other students may not have the same luxuries. They may not even know where their next meal is going to come from. These students may come from broken homes and some may have experienced bouts of abuse. They might not understand the pleasures of playing video games or of owning a top-of-the-line baseball bat. As teachers, we know that depending on our school environment and location, these two types of students may be co-existing in the same classroom; they may be sitting side-by-side on a daily basis. Understandably, their viewpoints on community and social responsibility will probably be drastically different.

Regardless of the personal environment and the situation that a student comes from, most appear to have one thing in common: the feeling of entitlement. This is an unfortunate outcome from the "Me-Generation", who appear to expect favorable treatment with little effort. Because of this entitlement mindset, people may look at others and determine the value another person is based solely on what that person can do for them. Members of the "Me-Generation" are not inherently looking at ways to help others. They are not automatically looking at how they can contribute to their community or society. While this does not apply to every member of the "Me-Generation", the shared mindset appears to be true for the majority of the members within this group.

As a teacher, you might not have experienced some of the mentioned behaviors about this type of student. The "take away" here is understanding that teaching is a fundamentally selfless profession. People do not become teachers to become rich or famous. They do not do it because the hours are great and they never have to take work home. They also do not do it because the parents and students are always so grateful and kind to them. Teachers seek this profession because they feel called to this wonderful and admirable role. Some teachers view education as a way to give back or pay it forward because of an influential educator that they once had in their own lives. Others enjoy working with children and having an opportunity to positively influence lives. We all have different reasons for teaching, but it is fairly evident that we want to be a positive catalyst for students; we want to see our students succeed. This success not only impacts our students in our classrooms and schools, but it impacts society as a whole. We want to see students achieve great things in life and become contributing members within their communities. Therefore, teachers already have more of a social and community focus than a lot of other professions.

We know that learning is a holistic process. Students do not just study American Literature or Biology their entire academic careers. As teachers, we are not just providing instruction in academics, but we are also teaching our students the life lessons that will surely make them successful well into adulthood. We, as teachers, have the privilege to help shape students' views of the world, of their society, and of their community. For this reason, it is important to make sure students learn how to be socially and community minded.

How are students going to learn to be socially and community minded? Through the teacher . . . but not in the ways you may think. Actions speak louder than words. Students are looking to their teachers as examples for everything. They are carefully studying and analyzing our roles and behaviors in the classroom to ensure accuracy in our behavior and speech. As you move into your new role, you must be certain that if you are attempting to teach your students to be socially and community responsible, you must also act in that manner as well. If not, your students will see right through the façade, which could cause you to lose credibility and respect. We must lead by example.

As we become more comfortable in the classroom and with our students, we can show our support of our students in simple ways, yet ways that have a major impact. Something as simple as attending extracurricular activities can have lasting, positive effects on our interactions and relationships with our students and their families. When students see a teacher at their game, concert, or fundraisers, it demonstrates to the students that the teacher cares about them and what they are doing outside of the classroom. It makes the students feel that they are more than just a grade to the teacher.

Lastly, if you examine communities and their structure in the United States, you will find that many communities revolve around the local schools. The schools are essentially a centerpiece of the community. Therefore, what happens in the schools can have a significant impact on the local community. If teachers and students are more socially and community minded, then the effects can be enormous.

TYPES OF SOCIAL AND COMMUNITY RESPONSIBILITY

We have established the need for teachers to be socially and community responsible. The next step is to determine in what ways you as a teacher can be socially and community responsible. Often it comes down your individual community. Different communities have different needs. It is important for you determine what the greatest needs are within your community and then assess how your own personal skills and passions can help meet that community need.

DONATIONS

One of the most common ways that people try to have a positive influence is through charitable donations. Charitable donations generally come in two forms: cash donations and in-kind donations. The nature of giving often depends upon the type, size, and mission of the charitable organization. Donations are made to charities whose programs' influence on the community is felt daily. An example would be a homeless shelter that works year-round to house, clothe, feed, and provide job training to homeless populations. Other times, donations are made because of a particular fundraising effort. An example of this would be a community center trying to raise funds to build a new gymnasium. Another possibility could essentially be a combination of the previous two examples. Donations are often made because of a certain event or tragedy. For example, the Red Cross often generates fundraising initiatives after natural disasters. People are able to donate to the Red Cross, but earmark their money to go exclusively towards specific relief efforts surrounding the natural disaster.

In-kind donations are gifts given to a person or organization instead of cash. These types of donations are quite common in the business world and typically involve a donation of a product or service as opposed to physical currency. The advantage to businesses is that the donated value of a product is not the same as the actual cost of the product. A company may donate a television that retails for $1,000 but it only costs the manufacture $500 to produce. This type of exchange works out well for both parties as the donor saves money and the recipient gets a product that they would have had to pay for otherwise. If the charity chooses to sell the product, they can often get more than the retail value of the product in an auction setting.

All of this may sound interesting, but you are probably wondering how this would apply to a teacher. While teachers are typically not going to donate goods or products, they can donate services. These services involve a teacher's time and effort. Giving your time is considered an in-kind type of donation. Many charities just need manpower help. Whether it be Habitat for Humanity needing volunteers to help build homes, or a local Boys and Girls Club trying to build a new public playground, or a homeless shelter needing educators to help teach residents, there are many ways people can donate their time and energy to meet the needs of a charity.

VOLUNTEERING AND SOCIAL CAUSES

When it comes to giving your time and effort, teachers need to find the causes that have the greatest need in their local community and discover a role that helps capitalize on talents and interests. If you are not passionate about solving literacy issues among adult populations in your area, then volunteering with an organization that works to solve literacy issues is probably not the best idea for you. You will not be giving maximum effort and will not reap the intrinsic rewards that come from contributing to the betterment of your community. In addition, if you are a high school music teacher who does not have formal training on how to teach people to read, then this particular charity may not be a good a place for you to provide services.

On the other hand, if you have a passion for the environment, then getting involved with a charity that is trying to make your local community more eco-conscious would be a great idea. Your passion for the subject matter will fuel your drive and enable you to be much more effective. As a teacher, you can then start discussing environmental issues with your students and make them aware of the importance of protecting the environment. You can design lessons that teach students the importance of recycling and reducing carbon emissions. You can teach history lessons on how poor environmental laws and loosely regulated industrial manufacturing led to acid rain issues in the 1980s. You can incorporate science lessons on how carbon emissions are produced and what can be done to reduce them. Students will begin to see your passion for a particular cause, begin to develop an understanding of the subject matter, and may become passionate themselves. They will see the volunteer work that you are doing and want to contribute as well. Students may begin recycling initiatives at their school and then eventually spread these initiatives into their homes and the community. This is what makes social and community responsibility so important for teachers. The impact that you, as one teacher, could have on a community is exponentially multiplied when your students follow your example and begin making an impact themselves.

Besides just volunteering with one singular charity, teachers may find themselves with the ability to almost create their own charitable program that may not only have an impact on the community, but can also provide a platform for students to gain first-hand knowledge in community service. For example, at one school in Virginia, a teacher whose son has autism, organized and hosted a 5K race benefitting Autism Speaks, which is an autism advocacy organization that sponsors autism research and conducts awareness and outreach activities aimed at families, governments, and the public (AutismSpeaks, n.d.). As the teacher began organizing the race, he decided to include his students in the planning process. Students were able to be a part of the organizational process and then help see the race through to fruition. As the event began to grow, the teacher began to involve his students in much more detailed capacities. Students were assigned roles and titles involve marketing, promotions, advertising, social media, registration, and finance. The students were able to experience these roles and apply them, not just learn about them in theory. The students had real responsibilities and were a vital part of the entire event. The students came away not only learning an immense amount about events and all the components of an event, but they also developed a passion for charitable causes and saw how their hard work and efforts have a real impact on the community. The race has turned into an annual event, with students from the founding teacher's class contributing every year.

When it comes to charity work, it does not have to be as complex as a large-scale charity race. Sometimes it just involves identifying needs and seeing where you can contribute. At one elementary school in North Carolina, a student's home burned down. Teachers, students, and parents all pitched in to help provide clothes, toys, and money for the family as they dealt with the recovery process. In California, a similar situation occurred when a middle school student and his family lost their home in a fire. The school put together a play and charged admission; all of the money raised contributed to helping the displaced student and his family relocate. There are lots of examples where teachers and administrators identify a need and put together ad hoc initiatives to help address societal interests. Some events are simply on-going fundraisers. Students often sell wrapping paper or cookies to help benefit a school or a particular cause. These programs also teach students the value of social and community responsibility.

EXTRACURRICULARS

Teachers can also donate their time and effort through extracurriculars. While being involved in extracurricular activities may not seem glamorous, teacher involvement is very important. Most sports teams are coached by teachers at the school and there never appears to be a shortage of needed help because extracurriculars include not only sports, but clubs, too; faculty sponsors are in high demand. These are all great opportunities for a teacher to demonstrate a social and community responsible attitude. For many students, extracurricular activities are where their passions lie and where they find meaning. Beyond helping keep students on track academically, extracurricular activities also provide a context for many students to develop their talents and passions.

Education is not just confined to the classroom. Learning can occur at any place and any time. Some of the strongest life lessons can be learned through extracurricular activities. Important traits like perseverance, dedication, teamwork, hard work, how to deal with failure, and how to deal with success can easily be learned through extracurricular activities. Teachers who choose to coach a team, direct the school band, or sponsor a science club are able to connect with students on a level that does not typically occur in the classroom. As teachers, we probably all remember former teachers, coaches, band directors, and other extracurricular leaders with whom we had a personal connection. As you develop in your professional role, your involvement in extracurriculars may provide the opportunity to better connect with your students. It allows you the opportunity to invest in their lives and help shape character, making them better members of society.

HOW TO SUCCESSFULLY DEVELOP A SOCIAL AND COMMUNITY RESPONSIBLE PROGRAM OR INITIATIVE

Understanding and identifying a need for a Social and Community Responsible Program is great for teachers. After you have identified an area where you can be involved in some capacity, you must, then, be able to successfully develop a program or initiative. Let us examine some key aspects to developing an effective program.

BEGIN IN THE CLASSROOM

Teachers can begin teaching social responsibility by allowing students to take ownership of the decision-making process. If a teacher allows his or her classroom to take on a more participative and democratic climate, students can begin to learn how the decisions they make influence outcomes that affect not just them, but the entire class.

Along this same line of thinking, whenever people are allowed to make decisions in a participative climate, conflict is likely to arise. Conflict is inevitable in life, and students will more than likely encounter some trials. Many children, who are still in the early developmental stages of reasoning and communicating, may have a tendency to respond in a manner that does not help resolve the conflict. Whether it be lashing out at others or shrinking into the background, students will find their own methods to cope. Creating a safe classroom environment where students feel a sense of social and community responsibility opens the door to allow students learn proper conflict resolution. This does not mean that students are going to leave your class as conflict resolution experts, as most of us as adults still struggle when it comes to conflict resolution. What it does mean, though, is that they will improve their conflict resolution skills and, therefore, improve their school community. Students will, hopefully, be less likely to get into fights, or let teenage drama create a significant negative impact on their school community. Students will be more confident standing up for what is right, such as not allowing bullying to occur. Helping students develop the skills necessary to create a socially-responsible environment could possibly help prevent school violence, deter teenage suicides, or decrease the effects of cyberbullying. The sense of accountability that is developed through conflict resolution skills could have untold positive consequences.

Within a safe classroom environment, students may also feel more at ease discussing controversial topics. Having open and honest dialogue with students enables them to better understand societal issues and allows discovery in addressing these issues.

INVOLVE PARENTS, ADMINISTRATORS, AND COMMUNITY LEADERS

In order to develop an effective social and community responsible program, it is imperative to have school and community support. Think back to the example we used earlier in the chapter about creating an environmental initiative at your school. If the school administration does not support it, then how successful do you think the program is going to be? Involving administration in your plans helps insure a supported, effectual program. After all, who is going to purchase the recycling bins necessary for each classroom? Who is going to give you the platform necessary to spread your message? Who is going to encourage other teachers and students to get on board? Having the administration buy-in and support your vision will immediately provide credibility to your program. If your program is supported by administration, people are a lot less likely to question the validity of the program.

Besides administration, it is a really good idea to get parents or guardians on board, as well. Programs and initiatives can only go so far without parental support. While kids care about their teachers and their teachers' interests, it does not mean quite as much if their parents display zero interest in the initiatives. In many scenarios, children appear more influenced by their parents than their teachers; therefore, their parent's opinion matters more. While this does change as the child ages, it still seems to apply, no matter what type of demeanor a teenager may exude. For this reason, teachers should strive to get parents involved. Once parents get involved in a program, it has the potential to grow by leaps and bounds. Children will be encouraged to be involved in and advance the program both at school and at home. Parents may even be willing to volunteer their time or funds to help further the initiative. This type of experience improves the parent-teacher relationship and improves the community as a whole.

Some parents show little interest in their child's schooling or academic achievement. In these scenarios, developing a program that benefits the community directly can encourage these parents to begin taking an interest in their child's schooling in a manner they may not have otherwise. This strategy could be one of the ways you are able to effectively reach out to uninvolved parents and bridge the gap.

In addition, parents may need to sign waivers or permission slips to allow their children to participate in some aspect of the program. If a parent or guardian does not approve of the program or initiative, they may not allow their child to participate. It may have nothing to do with the viability or safety of the program, but rather a parent who has not bought in or has a belief system that goes against whatever the program is supporting. These can be tricky scenarios to deal with and you should consult with your school administration before taking any drastic steps.

The final group you should focus on is the community itself. The community is obviously the group we are trying to positively influence, but if you cannot get them to buy into your program, then the likelihood of it succeeding is minimal. If you start a program that provides job training to unemployed, homeless people in your area and no unemployed, homeless people show up, then your program is not going to be successful. If you and your class make immense strides to clean up a local park and then everyone continues to litter there, your efforts will have been in vain. This does not mean that everyone in the community has to buy in, but if enough people get on-board, then your initiative is much more likely to succeed. If people who use that park begin using the new trash receptacles you installed, more and more people will take notice.

Sometimes, all it takes to garner community support is to raise awareness. If the community is not aware that a student's house burned down and that you are hosting a fundraiser to support that student and their family, then the event will not be successful. In this digital age, it is easier than ever to get your message heard but it is also harder than ever to get noticed. Invoke the help of local civic leaders to generate community support for your cause. If you can garner support from your administration, parents, and community, then the sky is the limit for your program.

FOLLOW THE FILES GUIDE

In 2007, Greg Johnson, founder of the Sport Philanthropy Project, presented a methodology for creating effective social and community programs. Johnson used the acronym *FILES* as a handy way to help guide those developing these programs (Stoldt, 2012):

> **Focused.** A program should be focused on a particular issue. As established earlier, teachers must determine areas of need when developing a social or community responsibility program. If the whole goal of a program is to simply help the community or school, then there is no clear purpose or direction to the program. Each individual might form his or her own opinion of what areas in the community or school need the most help and what they should be doing. However, if the focus of a program is to provide social interaction and activities for isolated seniors within the community, then everyone has a clear focus on what groups are being impacted and, through the development of the plan, they will also know how to accomplish the goals.
>
> **Impactful.** Teachers must choose a cause that needs to be addressed and that will be impactful. If a teacher chooses a social need and develops a program, then the program should have an impact. Social and community issues that have little to no impact on the community

should probably be avoided, as there are likely more relevant and pressing issues that can have a much greater positive impact on the community once they are resolved. If the goal is to increase literacy rates among local homeless populations and after six months the literacy rate has not changed or, even worse, declined, then the program is clearly not working and should be revaluated and reworked or simply discontinued. If there are specific objectives and outcomes that you would like to achieve and that are established before the program begins, then it gives everyone involved even more sense of direction and determines how success will be evaluated.

Leveraged. The whole point of social and community responsibility is to get people involved in bettering their community. Why should a program be limited to only students in your own class? Consider creating partnerships that will take your program to the next level. It may be difficult to get students to show up for a voluntary safe-driving seminar, but if you partner with a local gaming store to give away two gaming consoles to two random attendees, then students are much more likely to come. You would not be able to afford to purchase the gaming consoles on your own, but by bringing in a local business who is receiving commercial exposure and positive publicity for being involved in a great social cause, you are enhancing the viability and potential success rate of your program. Consider working with local police and EMS departments, other teachers' classes at the school, and the local news to help leverage your program. Reaching out to others and creating partnerships does not cause you to lose ownership of your program, but adds to the community mindedness of it.

Evaluated. After any program is developed and implemented, it should be evaluated for efficacy. As we established in the Impact section, you should develop goals and objectives for your program before implementing it. Once the program is completed or goes through a particular cycle, stop and evaluate whether or not you achieved your goals and objectives. If you did not, examine why. Analyze the situation and try to develop ways to improve the program. Program evaluation should take place on a regular timetable.

Leading the Way

Community and charity based organizations and activities can be great opportunities for educators to develop and practice leadership skills.

Sustained. To create a meaningful, impactful, and lasting program, you need to sustain it. Creating and hosting a 5K charity race is great, but imagine how much success the race would have if it were a yearly event. Participations rates would theoretically increase as the race grows in recognition and popularity. Research shows that long-term programs are likely to be more effective than short-term programs. Create a program that will continue to positively impact your community for years to come.

FAVORABLE PRACTICES

When it comes to developing Social and Community Responsibility, there are several favorable practices that have been mentioned in this chapter. **Remember that success begins in the classroom. Let your students be a part of the process of choosing a social or community cause and allow them to help develop a response and an action plan.** You will obviously be guiding the process but should still allow them to come to realizations on their own, taking ownership of the plan.

Be sure to involve parents, administrators, and community leaders. Getting your administration on board with your plan and having their support can often be the difference between unsuccessful or mildly successful initiatives compared to extremely successful programs. Parents can also provide support and choose to volunteer with the initiatives. With parents' support, it may be easier to get overall community support as well, especially from community leaders. Getting the community to buy in to positive initiatives and help further a cause is a tremendous way to ensure the success of a program.

COMMON MISTAKES

One of the most common mistakes made with social and community responsibility programs is starting off too big. Programs take a lot of support and often a lot of time to flourish. Creating a program with an objective of improving reading literacy rates in your community by 80% in one year is probably a little too ambitious. While a program to improve reading literacy over a one year time span is not unrealistic or over the top, the objective associated with it can be. In this scenario, the plan may not need to be adjusted, just the outcome. Shifting the goal from 80% down to 15% would be a much more realistic and achievable objective.

Just as it is a good idea to get the right people on board with your initiative, it is a bad idea to get the wrong people on board. You want counsel that is realistic and wise, but do not be swayed because one person does not support your plan. Sometimes, all it takes is one loud, negative person to sway people from a good cause. Be realistic, but be realistic in both positive and negative ways. It can be good to have a dissenting voice in the room but do not let that dissenting voice be the most influential.

Last, put together an initiative that blends your passions and the needs of the community. Sometimes people get wrapped up in their own agendas and start pushing for initiatives that are either not needed or are self-serving. The whole purpose of social and community responsibility is to benefit those around us in the community, not ourselves.

CONCLUSION

There are immense benefits to being socially and community minded. Students, parents, colleagues, administrators, and your community as a whole will benefit from this mindset. Not only will you get intrinsic value from volunteering or developing programs but you will also be improving the reputations of your school and students. Citizens within a community, especially citizens with influence like teachers, can have a significant impact on the local population and help to create a "super community." Whether it be a program to solve local problems or simply bringing in members of the community to serve as guest speakers, the influence is a positive one. This type of civic mindedness helps create the type of environment of which we would all like to live.

HITTING YOUR MARK

Social responsibility has become a buzz topic lately and for good reason. As the world becomes more connected through advancements in technology, we can sometimes lose sight of those who might need help the most. Enabling students to learn the value of social responsibility and the influence that they can have is the first step towards empowering the next generation to be more socially-conscience. As educators, we must implore our young people to understand the obligation needed to improve the world around them, moving past any sense of entitlement or selfishness. Teaching social responsibility and involving students in service projects will provide our youth with the framework and understanding that is necessary for a positive impact on our world.

QUESTIONS FOR DISCUSSION

1. Why should educators teach about social responsibility? In what ways can teaching about social responsibility and civic mindedness benefit your students? How can teaching social responsibility in schools improve the quality of life in your area?
2. What are some ways you can integrate social responsibility into your teaching? Start with devising rudimentary methods such as placing a recycling bin in your classroom and then develop your ideas further into more advanced and impactful projects.
3. What are your passions and how can you implement these passions into a community service project?
4. Can you think of ways that students can get involved in their own schools? What are some types of social responsibility initiatives that can be performed internally within a school to help benefit the school itself?
5. How can you assess the validity and effectiveness of a community service project once it has been completed? How will you establish objectives to determine success before a project is implemented? What are some assessment tools or techniques that you can use to determine how much students learned from their experiences involved in a project?

ACTIVITIES FOR ENRICHMENT

Select a charitable organization or cause and find ways that you can get involved with that organization. When selecting an organization, really take time and reflect on causes that you feel most passionately about. As most organizations have a need for volunteers in a variety of different roles, find out what ways you can assist that organization based on the skills and strengths that you have.

Research your current or potential school district. Determine what areas of need are the greatest in your particular district. Then brainstorm activities or programs that your class could conduct to provide support for these areas of need. For example, if you teach younger grades, the students can participate in a fundraiser that benefits a local food bank. Older student populations could be involved in revitalizing a park or local sports fields.

REFERENCES

AutismSpeaks.org. (2015). *Mission.* Retrieved from https://www.autismspeaks.org/about-us/mission

Dahlsrud, A. (2008). How corporate social responsibility is defined: An analysis of 37 definitions. *Corporate Social Responsibility and Environmental Management, 15,* 1–13.

Greenfield, P. (2013, August 7). The changing psychology of culture from 1800 through 2000. *A Journal of the Association for Psychological Science, 24(9),* 1722–1731.

Palmer, K. (1995, September 1). Tightening environmental standards: The benefit-cost or the no-cost paradigm? *The Journal of Economic Perspectives, 9(4),* 119–132.

Sihem, B. (2012, November 23). The social responsibility of teaching. *Social Science Research Network.*

Stoldt, G. C., Dittmore, S.W., & Branvold, S.E. (2012). *Sport Public Relations: Managing Stakeholder Communication* (2nd ed.). Champaign, IL: Human Kinetics.

CHAPTER **13**

CLASSROOM MANAGEMENT

Pamela P. Randall

"The single greatest effect on student achievement is the effectiveness of the teacher."

~ Henry Wong

INTRODUCTION

Most of us have at least one memory of a year in which we were students in the "perfect" classroom. For many, this classroom was in an elementary grade, but not for all. Some of us had that amazing teacher as a high school student. Wherever and whenever it was experienced, it probably heavily influenced our decision to become a teacher.

In all likelihood, this classroom was filled with engaging and challenging work. It contained an adult who expected great things—things that pushed our minds, our bodies and our emotions. This adult also provided us with the necessary structure, safety, and encouragement to take a chance. We spent time in this class doing work for which we were proud; work that we knew was valid, authentic, and worthwhile. We also knew that our teacher held us accountable for producing high quality work by providing a classroom atmosphere that was structured and encouraging. What was their secret? How did these teachers create a sense of

---

Courtesy of Pamela P. Randall. Copyright © Kendall Hunt Publishing Company.

community—one that challenged us, supported us, and made us want to learn? Were they born with that talent, or can it be learned? Can *you* re-create this same sense of security, challenge, and engagement? YES!

PROACTIVE CLASSROOM MANAGEMENT

Let's clarify one issue up front—discipline and classroom management are not synonymous. Discipline is a reaction to an undesirable behavior problem; classroom management is the procedures and policies that guide the classroom. A well-crafted and implemented classroom management plan should, therefore, reduce the incidences of disciplinary issues in the classroom! If not, a readjustment of the management plan is needed. This does not imply harsher disciplinary procedures and policies. Children rise to the expectations set in the classroom, both academically and behaviorally. If the expectation is that students will succeed, and structures provide for them to do so, they will be successful.

Wong (2014) reminds us that, "Good classroom management is based on the behavior of teachers—what the teachers do—not the behavior of students" (p. 5). These critical behaviors for teachers must include well-designed, engaging lessons and structures and procedures that allow student self-regulation. They are not created by the luck of the draw or the throw of the dice. They take serious consideration and pre-planning on the part of the teacher. The habits developed and behaviors modeled can promote a positive learning environment in any situation. Keep in mind, though, that the following list is not exhaustive, but highlights some habits that I believe are critical for a teacher. Teachers should:

- Know and own their personal management style
- Establish and clearly articulate classroom policies and procedures
- Consider the physical arrangement of the classroom
- Develop and promote engaging, challenging and appropriate content

Let's take some time to look at each of these and see how they can help us create that classroom where the children look forward to attending and the teacher looks forward to leading.

PERSONAL MANAGEMENT STYLE

Each teacher has a preferred management style. However, yours may change over time. As you practice your craft, you will modify and grow into a style that best works for you and your students. In 1966, Diana Baumrind determined that parenting styles could be broken into three broad categories: Authoritarian, Laissez-faire/Permissive, or Authoritative. These have since been broadened and applied to classroom teachers. While there have been others who have added subcategories to this list, such as democratic, nearly all styles can be connected back to one of these three original categories.

Authoritarian teachers are characterized as those who "establish and maintain order through the use of controlling strategies" (Cooper, 2014, p. 243). Classrooms that contain teachers with this style are often seen as "punishers." These teachers are often viewed by students as being mean and somewhat emotionally cold and withdrawn, no-nonsense. At the extreme, the Authoritarian teacher gives no indication that he\she cares for the students. Teachers view themselves as being strict and, therefore, in control. They see themselves as enforcers of the rules. These teachers are quick to blame anyone but themselves for academic or behavioral issues in the classroom. Humiliation, detention and other punitive consequences are often a highly utilized tactic. Student autonomy is not valued, nor practiced. Students have little control or voice in this classroom. Generally speaking, educators who utilize this strategy believe, "my way or the high-way." Academic achievement, as is measured by standardized testing, may actually be quite high in some of these classes.

Laissez-faire or Permissive teachers, in comparison, place few demands on students, either behaviorally or academically. They often feel that class preparation is not worth the effort. This teacher simply will not take the necessary preparation time. Often, they will use the same materials, year after year. Classrooms such as these are simply going through the motions. This teacher may lack the skills, confidence, or courage to discipline students. Permissive teachers are popular, but have a low control threshold; their primary objective is self- centered rather than other-centered. They are apathetic toward student progress. This particular style is suitable, ironically, for a learning situation in which advanced students, the kind that need little or no supervision, complete independent studies or advanced projects on their own. Teachers who employ this strategy rely on students to self-regulate. Students will often take advantage of these teachers and academic achievement is often very low.

Our final management style is Authoritative, (not to be confused with Authoritarian). The Authoritative teacher has both high academic and behavioral expectations of their students. The Authoritative teacher places limits and controls on the students but simultaneously encourages independence. This teacher often explains the reasons behind the rules and decisions. This type of teacher is also open to considerable verbal interaction. The students know that they can interrupt the teacher if they have a relevant

Ethical Considerations

Principle V: Responsible and Ethical Use of Technology

The professional educator maintains confidentiality in the use of technology

The professional educator promotes the appropriate use of technology in educational settings

question or comment. This environment offers the students the opportunity to learn and practice communication skills and is often seen as a democratic classroom. Additionally, Authoritative teachers provide the structure and consequences to allow students to practice self-management and academic growth. Self-reliant and socially competent behavior is encouraged, which fosters higher achievement and motivation. Teachers who consider themselves to be Authoritative believe that a warm and caring environment is critical to creating a positive climate and community for everyone in the classroom, including themselves. They are open to revising their policies and strategies if the desired results are not attained; they are flexible, responsive, and encouraging; and they have high expectations for every member of the classroom community.

Consider the following infraction: A student is using a cell phone in class. How would a teacher, exhibiting the previous classroom management styles react?

Authoritarian

(In front of everyone), "YOU KNOW BETTER THAN TO HAVE A PHONE WITH YOU IN CLASS. HOW COULD YOU BE SO STUPID TO BRING IT TO MY CLASS??? GIVE IT TO ME NOW AND HEAD DOWN TO THE PRINCIPAL'S OFFICE. "

Laissez-faire/Permissive

(To self, definitely not out loud), Ignore it, you do not want to deal with the drama and they are not going to pass your class anyway, so why bother?

Authoritative

(Away from other students), I will need you to turn in your phone. I will give it back to you at the end of the day, just like the handbook says.

Keep in mind, regardless of where you fall in the assessment, ultimately you will determine how you will relate to and interact with your students. Always strive to find that balance of challenge, support, respect, and warmth.

Teachers who have high demands of all students and respond to learning differences in an appropriate manner, but who are also responsive, respectful and caring are the best combination of leadership styles. Is this not the ideal classroom you remember? The teacher, who engaged, challenged and motivated you to do your best? Keep in mind, regardless of where you fall in the continuum, ultimately, *you* will determine how you will relate to and interact with your students. Always attempt balance.

POLICIES AND PROCEDURES

Let's go back for just a moment to the dream classroom . . . were there many student disruptions in class? Was the teacher clear regarding behavioral expectations? What happened if someone crossed the line? Most importantly, how do we re-create that level of student accountability and resilience in our own classrooms?

We can all agree on the following: We want our students to love learning, be good decision makers, be responsible, self-sufficient, resilient, kind, considerate, and comfortable with accountability (Nelson, Lott, & Glenn, 2013). This is not a small task! How do we turn these concepts into logical, enforceable classroom rules, procedures, and policies? For that matter, should we refer to them as something else entirely, such as expectations or agreements? Again, this will be a reflection of your own management style, as well as the disposition of your classroom. No two classrooms will be alike, but will rather be a reflection of the community that inhabits them. Ultimately, you must decide how your classroom community will function.

Rules and expectations

Mackenzie and Stanzione (2010), refer to three different types of rules: (1) General Rules (i.e., respect the rights and property of others); (2) Specific Rules (i.e., raise your hand before speaking); and Rules in Theory (i.e., general or specific but are not enforced). Keep in mind that general rules are often those placed in student handbooks and even on school walls.

Consider the school rule, "respect one another." All of us agree that the phrase "respect one another" sounds good, and in theory, is a rule we would like everyone to follow. Consider, however, that this statement is open to multiple interpretations depending on the socio-economic, ethnicity or even age of the student. Rules such as this will require lengthy discussions as to exactly what the expectation is and is not. What does that mean, what does it "look like?" How do you teach it? Does it only mean students have to respect you or does it mean that the entire classroom community will be respectful to each other? How will you teach, practice, and correct this rule? How will you know it when you see it, and what will be the repercussions of not following the rule. These are all critical questions that you will need to answer, before deciding what your classroom expectations will be.

Generally speaking, rules should be short, enforceable, written positively, include student opinion and input, and not be subject to interpretation. Keep in mind, when you allow students to participate in the creation of classroom rules you are valuing their voice in the creation of a classroom community. Your rules should be easy to explain, demonstrate, and enforce. Likewise, consequences for not abiding by the rules should be appropriate, tiered, applied consistently and without undue emotion. While the child's action, or lack thereof, may trigger an emotional response in you, your reaction to the child should not be fueled by anger or frustration.

Policies and procedures, as we discussed earlier, are the backbone of any successful behavioral management plan. You must create the plan for the day, week, and year. You are not just creating the academic plan, but the daily living and functioning plan for your classroom, as well. Wong (2014) reminds us of this by using an effective acronym—PROCEDURES.

> P – Plan for success
> R – Rehearse and reinforce
> O – Organize before students arrive
> C – Costs nothing to do
> E – Extra time gained for teaching and learning
> D – Don't wait until next year: do it now
> U – Make a difference in students' lives
> R – Rehearse some more
> E – Experience a class that hums with learning
> S – Success is yours because procedures work (p. 50).

Many of the daily procedures that occur in a classroom will need to be reflected upon carefully and in advance. These will then need to be discussed, practiced and consistently enforced by the teacher. A few examples of common procedures that a teacher might consider when designing classroom rules include:

- How will students enter the room?
- What constitutes being late?
- What procedure will the teacher use to get students' attention?
- How will missed worked be handled?
- How will students exit the classroom?
- How will students ask for help from the teacher?
- What noise level is acceptable?
- How will students transition into cooperative learning groups?
- How will students get supplies?
- How will students turn in work?
- How will students pick up or distribute work?

This is just the beginning! Keep in mind, however, that it is imperative to establish, teach, and practice your procedures to help ensure that everyone knows and understands the expectations and consequences. This will, in turn, save you and your students countless hours of frustration! It will also provide students the structure to practice self-reliance and accountability.

> **Leading the Way**
>
> *Many new and experienced teachers struggle with some aspects of classroom management. Lead in this area by searching best practices and sharing successful strategies with others.*

In addition to the procedures and policies already discussed, we should also remember that the daily routine in school includes policies for emergencies, guest speakers, substitute teachers and other extracurricular activities. Teachers should have clear policies for any foreseeable circumstances, and most importantly provide students with the opportunity to practice those procedures.

PHYSICAL ARRANGEMENT OF THE CLASSROOM

In a perfect world, teachers would have the opportunity and funding to create a room that meets the needs of their particular students. For elementary students, this might include lots of areas for stations, kidney shaped tables for group work, or cubbies for supplies. This luxury may or may not be available in the school at which you work. Regardless, here are some well established guidelines in setting up your room that I have found helpful. In general, teachers should ensure that:

- Teachers can see all students at all times, and likewise, students can see the instructional area that the teacher is using at all times.
- Travel between obstacles can be navigated quickly and safely without disruption.
- Student seating encourages engagement and cooperative learning.
- High-use materials and equipment, such as a smartboard area, are easily accessible.

Keep in mind that, depending on the age of your students, you might need instructional areas for whole-group instruction, small-group instruction, reading/writing centers, computer/iPad centers, or smartboard area. Knowing the needs of your students and your teaching style will help you determine the arrangement that best suits your classroom community.

If you are curious about how various arrangements might look in your classroom, consider creating a virtual classroom. Sites such as "Classroom Architect" will allow you to create and arrange common classroom furniture pieces. You can then assess whether or not your "ideas" will actually be feasible, functional, and safe.

APPROPRIATE CONTENT

While this is not a chapter on curriculum development or lesson plan writing, the importance of educational planning must not be neglected. Unfortunately, many of the disruptions and disciplinary issues teachers face in class are a direct consequence of inadequate or inappropriately planned lessons. While you have not been hired to entertain students, you have been hired to meet the needs of *every* student. You cannot be successful in this endeavor without taking the time to get to know your students. This time spent in building positive relationships will invariably lead you to create lessons that are engaging and challenging for each of the unique young people in your classroom. Students attend school to master content and learn social skills that will prepare them to be successful in society. You, as the teacher, are given the responsibility to meet each student where he or she is, not where you think he or she should be, and take them as far as he or she can go. This means providing instruction that is appropriate for their level, content that is appealing, and expectations that are high. This is not easy, but you did not sign up for an easy job; you signed up for one of the most important jobs in our society. You are building the future, so bring your very best to class every day and expect the same of your students.

BEHAVIOR INTERVENTION

Notice, I did not say, "behavior management." In the best of situations, many of us have our hands full just managing ourselves, let alone "managing" a room of youngsters. The ability to control oneself, socially interact appropriately, and actively engage with peers are all skills that students must learn. You, as the teacher, are expected to teach these skills, as well as your academic curriculum. Social skills require time, space, and encouragement to practice. They also require teachers to remain calm, be highly organized, and offer educational settings that are structured with purpose and engagement. Children are just that—children. We should not expect them to act like small adults . . . they do not have the skills to do so, nor should they. They must be given the time to move, collaborate, and practice appropriate social interactions with each other and adults. When correction or redirection is needed, it should be just that, and not a judgment statement or punishment. Students will rise to the occasion when given clear expectations and the opportunity to practice the external and internal gratification of succeeding.

There are many resources to help teachers create classroom management plans. Ultimately, teachers must pick the style that works with their particular personality and management style. They should also strive to create a positive, cooperative community within the classroom, which allows respect for themselves and the students for setting clear expectations and consequences for everyone's behavior, the teachers included.

FAVORABLE PRACTICES

As we have discussed in this chapter, behavior management is crucial to the overall success of a teacher. If the classroom atmosphere is hostile or too relaxed, students will not have the support systems, encouragement, or expectations to be successful. While this list is by no means comprehensive, it should help you begin to create a true community in your classroom. In turn, you will be on a path, with the help of your students, in creating a classroom atmosphere that will help ensure that you and your students will have a productive and rewarding school year. Here are some things to remember as you move into your new position:

- Take time to know your students and families, their dreams, talents and fears. The most successful classrooms are communities, not dictatorships.
- Be consistent and fair to everyone.
- Remain emotionally calm; do not bait or bully your students.
- Admit when you are wrong. Students will appreciate that you are indeed a member of the community and are above mistakes.
- Allow students to make mistakes. Give them time to fail and grow, change will not happen overnight, so do not give up on them.
- Set high expectations, in behavior and academics, then hold everyone, including yourself, accountable.
- Create rules and expectations that can easily be modeled, learned, and enforced. Be mindful of diversity.
- Be clear about consequences. Allow students a voice in creating the rules and the consequences.
- Allow students, and yourself, time to calm down before determining consequences.
- Design instruction that is respectful, engaging, and challenging for everyone! This means you must have first mastered point one!

COMMON MISTAKES

Your classroom setting will be a place of trial and error. Some of your very best intentions will not work. It is ok! Teaching, like some many vocations, is a journey. It will take time for you to solidify your own personal management style. That style preference will drive your classroom management choices. You will become more confident in your ability to create a cooperative and caring classroom community.

Having said that, there are some "tried and true" mantras to keep in mind as you create that classroom management plan, including:

Do not forget that you are the adult and they are the student—act appropriately. This can be especially difficult if you allow your emotions to gain control. Take a moment to calm down and think objectively before interacting with the student. Many times students are "pushing your buttons" to see if you are going to actually follow through with the expectations you have set for your community classroom. Will you be fair? Do students have a voice? Will you follow through? Do you believe in second and third chances?

Do not come to work with baggage—check it at the door and allow students to do the same; each day should be a fresh start. Everyone, including you, deserves a fresh start. Do not hold grudges and do not base your opinion of students on what other adults tell you. They will give you a clean slate; extend the same courtesy to them. If you make a mistake, apologize, model the behavior you want you students to exhibit.

Consider, very carefully, the use of behavior charts in the classroom, particularly for younger students. While these charts are a very popular addition to many classrooms, consider the following:

- Charts track behavior; they do not correct it. Only you and the child can do that.
- They can be quite stressful to students, particularly those who are tender-hearted and concerned about their classmates.
- They can be quite demoralizing.
- They announce the expectation that we expect everyone to misbehave at some point.

Refrain from writing referrals. Do not relinquish control by sending students out for someone else to deal with. This is your community, and all communities have issues and problems to address. Ask for the help you need, but stay invested and involved in the resolution. Remember, we are kidding ourselves if we think we are sending them out for the benefit of the class. What message is this sending to the other members of the classroom community? Tough kids are just that, tough, they still deserve your best, not someone else's. Writing a referral rarely helps a child; it is simple a temporary fix. If students are struggling, they need more teacher intervention, not less. Always remember, you were hired to teach; you cannot teach them if they are not in your class! Finally, and most importantly, when you send a child out of the classroom, you are telling them you give up; you are announcing to that child, and the rest of the class, that they are not worthy to be a part of the classroom community and you will not be bothered with them.

Do not give up. This is not an easy profession, but one that has endless blessings!

CONCLUSION

As an educator, you are in a very noble profession. One that is rewarding, exciting, challenging, and, at times, exhausting. You will spend many hours fretting over creating the perfect lesson plans, designing engaging and rewarding projects, assessing student outcomes and attending school events. All of these tasks are key components of a teacher's life. However, I would argue that the success you have, in and out of the classroom, will most depend upon whether or not you can first create a classroom that welcomes, encourages, challenges, and celebrates the individual achievements of its members. A classroom where clear educational and behavioral expectations are defined for every member of the community and all are held accountable. All have a voice, and all feel needed. This requires you to take a reflective look at what you believe about students and how they learn and should be treated. As you design and modify your classroom expectations for behavior, always be mindful because "they do not care what you know, until they know you care."

HITTING YOUR MARK

While classroom management is often seen as a means of "controlling" the students, it is, in reality, more about organization and relationships. Classrooms that contain teachers who set high expectations, engage children in meaningful and rewarding work, and celebrate community are effective and successful. This skill takes time and patience to develop and requires upfront planning on your part. Consider completing the following project (see Activities for Enrichment) to help you solidify your personal classroom management style, strengths, and weaknesses.

QUESTIONS FOR DISCUSSION

1. What components of your classroom structure and procedures should you plan before the first day of school? Why is this important?
2. Why is it important to develop positive relationships with your students, both as individually and as a class? How will you work toward building these relationships?
3. Discuss the importance of student engagement in teaching and learning and its positive impact on reducing behavioral issues. What is most likely to occur if we fail to engage students and why?

4. When we argue, bargain, or negotiate with students about our rules and their behavior choices what are we saying about our rules? How will you enforce and adapt your behavioral expectations for students?
5. Do you believe that developing social skills and social responsibility are a part of your job? Why or why not? How will your beliefs manifest themselves in your classroom?

ACTIVITIES FOR ENRICHMENT

Design a classroom management plan for your future classroom. Keep in mind the requirements listed below:

- A visual layout of all furnishing for the room (i.e., desks, tables, smartboard, centers etc.)
- Posters and visuals
- List of procedures and how they will be completed such as:
  - Dismissal
  - Collecting notes and papers
  - Absences
  - Unfinished classroom assignments
  - Getting the attention of your students
  - Transitions
  - Bathroom breaks
  - Finishing work early
  - Working in groups
- Rules, what will they be and how will you create them? Collaboratively?
- Communication with home and community
- Substitute plans

Consider using resources such as Pinterest, teacher to teacher, and others to inspire you!

REFERENCES

Baumrind, D. (1966). Effects of Authoritative parental control on child behavior. *Child Development*, 887–907.

Classroom Architect. (2016). Retrieved from http://classroom.4teachers.org/

Classroom management styles. ACES. (2016). Retrieved from http://aces.www.esu13.org/modules/locker/files/get_group_file.phtml?gid=3789920&fid=25852827

Cooper, J. M. (2014). *Classroom teaching skills.* Belmont, CA: Wadsworth Cengage Learning.

Mackenzie, R. S. (2010). *Setting limits in the classroom.* New York: Three Rivers Press.

Nelson, J., Lott, L., & Glenn, H. S. (2013). *Positive discipline in the classroom.* New York: Three Rivers Press.

Wong, H. K. (2014). *The classroom management book.* Mountain View, CA: Harry K Wong Pulications, Inc.

CHAPTER **14**

TIME MANAGEMENT

Michael D. Kelly

"Time is the most valuable coin in your life. You and you alone will determine how that coin will be spent. Be careful that you do not let other people spend it for you."

~ Carl Sandburg

INTRODUCTION

Everyone has said it: "There's just not enough time in the day." The challenge of everyday life is to use your time effectively; this is never truer than in the life of a school teacher. Each day teachers are challenged with a number of different issues that will pull from the limited time they have available. In order to be effective for the school, and more importantly the students, teachers must learn techniques that will make their days operate as fluidly as possible. This means dedicating time to the areas of greatest need and effect. Time is the one resource that truly does come in limited supply so it is essential that you make decisions based on what is going to be best for the students and make the most effective use of this very limited resource.

Courtesy of Michael D. Kelly. Copyright © Kendall Hunt Publishing Company.

WHAT IS TIME MANAGEMENT?

According to the Oxford Dictionary, (2015) "Time management is the ability to use one's time effectively or productively, especially at work." This applies to all career fields, including education, but it is exceptionally important to school teachers. Teachers are faced with numerous demands on their time each day, and their ability to balance and discern what issues garner the use of their time will determine not only their individual success, but the success of a school as a whole.

WHY IS TIME MANAGEMENT IMPORTANT?

You will often hear that it is critical to manage your time wisely in your personal and professional life. It seems logical, but why is time management important? There are several reasons why school teachers must effectively manage their time. There are so many tasks that teachers will be required to complete, and numerous individuals that they will need to meet, that without effective time management they will not be as nearly successful as they could be with an effective plan. Effective time management provides teachers with both professional and personal gains that could not be achieved without it. According to Carnegie (2011), there are several reasons why time management is important:

It helps you prioritize. If you do not review all of the important tasks you have in advance, you will not truly know what is the most important work to be done and, therefore, could easily miss a vital deadline or commitment. Effective time management helps you to prioritize what is most important all the way down to what is least, which will aid you in decision-making throughout the day and the year.

It makes sure you stay on task. One of the most common mistakes people make when it comes to time management is that they get off task. This happens through distracting conversations, or completing less important tasks instead of completing what really needs completion. A strong time management plan will help mitigate this type of behavior.

It helps you complete undesirable tasks. Most people have duties that they do not necessarily like to do in their career. That being said, these are often the most necessary duties to complete in order to be effective. Time management helps to ensure that these responsibilities are completed so that you become much more efficient in your work.

It will provide you a sense of accomplishment. Getting things completed and off of your desk feels great. Getting the right things finished on time feels even better. In this way a good time management plan will help you to feel even more accomplished in your career.

It provides a route to self-discipline. Finally, the best benefit of a strong time management plan is its ability to develop self-discipline. By doing the work to create a strong time management plan, you are much more likely to follow through on the schedule of events. This will help develop your own self-discipline, which ultimately will lead to greater success as a teacher.

WHAT WE DO TAKES TIME

Everything a school teacher does throughout the day takes time. In order to better understand how to make the best use of this precious resource, we need to understand the common activities that school teachers participate on a regular basis. It would be impossible to list all of the tasks a teacher participates in daily, but in an effort to organize and plan a schedule, one must start somewhere. With all of the tasks that need to be completed, it is vital that teachers understand what types of activities take up their time on a regular basis. There are countless tasks a teacher will need to complete in the job, and organizing these tasks helps the teacher finish the most important ones first. The following table helps to categorize these activities to better organize the use of a teacher's time.

TABLE 14.1: *Teacher Activities*

STUDENT ACTIVITIES	INSTRUCTION	MANAGEMENT
Art class	Unit planning	Materials preparation
Physical Education	Lesson planning	Parent meetings
Music class	Interdisciplinary planning	Student issues
Other electives	Special education	School duties (halls, buses)
Field trips	Standardized testing	Faculty meetings
PTA events/meetings	Grading assignments	Professional associations
Sporting events	Other instructional initiatives	Other teachers
Computer lab	Professional development	Administration requirements

You are welcome to use the table above, or create your own that will better identify the impeding demands you may face as a teacher. What is important is that you create some type of a list to facilitate organization. From this list, you will now begin to prioritize what is most important to you as a school teacher. This can be done in a number of ways either through a numeric list, a color-coding, or other system you develop on your own. What is important is that you prioritize. Many teachers choose to use color-coding, as it is easily transferable into electronic calendar. For the purposes of this chapter, we will refer to color-coding as the option of choice. As an example, the following colors will be used in determining priorities on our calendar:

- Red – essential tasks
- Orange – important tasks
- Yellow – moderate importance
- Green – things to do that can wait if needed

PLANNING FOR TIME

If you want to make the best use of your time on a daily basis, you must take time to plan for its use. This almost sounds counter-productive, but when teachers take the time to plan effectively, both long-term, as well as daily, much more will be achieved throughout the year. The most effective time management occurs when you take the time to set long-term goals, develop a schedule, prioritize events and stick to the schedule.

Schools are busy places almost every day of the year, and the summer time is no exception. As school teachers, there is a lot more to do in the summer months than the public understands. This being true, it is still good practice to be reflective on the past year, and plan for the future. Effective time management for school teachers begins in the summer months. Following these easy steps below will help teacher candidates develop effective long-term time management plans for the school year.

BEGIN WITH THE BIG PICTURE

To start your time management planning, begin by laying out the entire year at a glance. Here, the use of technology in planning out your calendar will make things significantly easier, but if you like the old-style paper and pencil, that technique works just fine as well. Once your schedule is in front of you, start by placing the most critical items on your calendar first. Each of the categories listed in the chart above contain some critical items that need to be placed on your schedule; you will need to determine which areas are most important to you, but the following will provide you some basic guidelines;

Main office requirement. Usually in or before August, the main office will provide teachers and staff with a list of required meetings that will run throughout the year. This is a great place to start when planning your long-term schedule. In most instances teachers are required to attend these meetings, so it makes sense to put these dates and times on your schedule first and highlight them as critical. Any meetings that you must attend without exception should be coded red on your calendar.

Long-term lesson planning. This is also often referred to as unit planning. If we claim that instruction is most important, then the activities and processes involved need to be of critical importance to us as teachers, and as such should be identified is critical on our schedules. Begin by reviewing your curriculum guides,

> **Ethical Considerations**
>
> Principle IV: Responsibility to the School Community
>
> *The professional educator promotes effective and appropriate relationships with employers*

along with the pacing guides. Identify how long each unit is allotted for instruction. Place each unit on your calendar with a beginning date and an end date. We know that instruction is fluid, and some units may take longer than planned, and others less, but by placing the units on your calendar you are providing yourself with a beginning framework.

Team meetings. Each school has a variety of planning and instructional teams that meet on a scheduled basis. This would include faculty meetings, grade level meetings, department meetings, school safety meetings, school planning council meetings, and a variety of other team meetings. Place these meetings on your calendar next and color-code them appropriately. These meetings may be either red or yellow, depending on the circumstance.

Faculty meetings. This includes any professional development days or times that have been pre-planned by the administration. Important information is usually shared at these meetings and attendance is almost always required.

Reoccurring events. These events are things that occur on a daily basis that you plan to accomplish. Examples such as bus duty, lunch duty, hall duty, and other types of student supervision occur daily. Even though you may conduct these activities on a daily basis, it is important to place them on your calendar as a reminder that you are blocking off the time for the activity. You would color-code these events based on your own personal priorities, and that of your administrative team!

SHORT-TERM EVENTS

Now that we have the big picture items out the way, we can begin focusing on smaller items that are still important but may or may not be as critical. These items often cannot be planned in advance during the summer time, but may need to be added to the schedule each quarter, by teaching unit, monthly or even weekly.

Lesson planning. If instruction is a priority, you need to set aside time in your schedule to effectively plan your lessons. With the unit planning now on your calendar, it is important to add time to your schedule for weekly and daily planning. Generally it is common to plan a week's worth of daily lessons in advance. As such, it is critical to set aside time in your calendar to plan the lessons for the coming week. Completing plans for the next week as you are finishing up the current week, can help make curriculum adjustments more appropriate. Some schools may even require teachers to complete and submit these plans on a specific day. Here you should identify what you will teach each day, the materials needed, assessments used, and any other resources necessary for the week (i.e., library time, computer labs, laptops, etc.). At the beginning of the year it is also helpful to plan several weeks out, knowing that the pacing of lessons may need adjusting depending on the students' needs.

Materials preparation. Once your lessons are in place, it is time to prepare your materials for the coming week. This may include printing copies of worksheets, preparing materials for a lab, and ensuring computer labs (or any other resources needed for daily instruction) are available.

Grading assignments. You should also set aside time each day to grade any student assignments you have received. If you have a large assignment that will take more time to grade, such as term papers or projects, plan to "eat the elephant one bite at a time" by splitting the work over a number of days and timeframes. Timely feedback for students on their work is a vital piece in achieving mastery of a subject. A good technique is to have a different colored folder for each class you teach. Use each folder to store the work to be graded. This will also help you stay organized between classes.

Special education and guidance office meetings. These meetings include annual and triennial Individualized Education Plan (IEP) meetings, manifestation meetings, and child study team meetings, to name a few. Some of these you will be able to plan months in advance, while others are on much shorter notice.

Events. Regardless of the school level in which you work, there will always be events that you will need to attend. These include sporting events, musical concerts, theatrical plays, open houses, and Parent-Teacher Association (PTA) events, to name a few. These events should go on your calendar next. You will need to decide how to color-code the events in terms of your own personal priority. Some teachers feel they have to attend all of these events, while others will delegate some of the events to assistant teachers. The key is that all of these events should go on your calendar to remind you to attend.

Parent and/or student meetings. These meetings are often only planned a day or two in advance, but it is clearly important to make sure they are included on your calendar and that you prepare in advance to attend. You should have all grades and assignments for the student ready to present to the parents in advance. Nothing will cast doubt on your ability as a new teacher more than showing up unprepared for a parent/teacher conference. Those parents will leave unimpressed, and they will tell others.

Now that you spent the time needed to successfully plan for the coming year, the students will soon be back into their routines, and daily issues will start to take precedence over the visionary ideas you had in the summer. It is important to make sure that you review your schedule on a regular basis in order to prepare for the events to come. A good practice to achieve this is to take a few moments each Friday at the end of the week to look at your schedule for the coming days. This will help remind you of important events as you move forward. Then, Monday morning, be sure to not only look at what is coming up for the day, but also review the week in its entirety. Items will be added and subtracted from your calendar as you progress through the year, but a well-developed schedule will help reduce the challenge of not having enough time to get the work completed. Using technology also can be a huge benefit here; the use of a smartphone calendar option, outlook calendar, or other option can be a significant help because alarms can be set in advance for reminders.

> **Leading the Way**
>
> *Those who lead should put a high value on others' time. Try to avoid holding unnecessary meetings or assigning tasks that take up inordinate amounts of time or cause disruptions to the workflow.*

DAILY PLANNING

Great long term planning can be dismantled by poor execution on a daily basis. This is why it is critical to have a solid plan each day, and for each lesson. Be certain to have established routines each day for yourself as well as the students. Daily routines provide structure for not only you, but they help the students as well. Assigning roles for students will also provide them a sense of belonging in the classroom, which is critical to their success. Scholastic (2015) has identified six ways for teachers to better make use of their time during the day.

Find out which aspects of school time you can control. In some schools, teachers discover they can change the scheduling of class periods, pull-out programs, extracurricular activities planning time, and outside interruptions. Ask your principal to help you control time-wasters such as unexpected visitors and frequent intercom announcements.

Schedule solid blocks of teaching time for each day. You might hang a "Do Not Disturb" sign outside your door during those times. Also, secure your principal's help in scheduling pull-out programs around those blocks and ask parents not to schedule medical or dental appointments during academic class time.

Plan for smooth transitions between lessons and always try to have materials ready for each lesson or activity. A good technique here is to gather all of your needed materials before leaving school for the day and having them ready for the next day.

Assign homework to extend practice time. Homework should allow students to practice skills they have already learned, but should never be used for new instruction.

Consider how and when you schedule restroom breaks for maximum efficiency. Students will invariably need to use the restroom throughout the day, but planning this time as part of the lesson (i.e. during transition time) can make far better use of the time, and allows for a natural transition.

Improve student attendance. Attendance has a big effect on teaching and learning. Impress upon parents the importance of good attendance and teach an actual lesson on how it hurts to miss school. "At the end of each day, I try to tell kids what we will be doing the next day," notes first-grade teacher Susie Davis. "I emphasize the kinds of activities they look forward to, such as hands-on activities. This seems to encourage attendance."

FAVORABLE PRACTICES

Thus far in this chapter, we have discussed a number of ways to effectively lay out a strong time management plan. Inside of this plan are a lot of little nuances that will make your time management plan even more effective, if implemented appropriately. Below is a general list of favorable practices that will help guide you in the process:

Prioritize. Prioritizing is a benefit of a strong time management plan, but how does one go about doing so? Dale Carnegie (2011) identified the following steps to effectively prioritize your work:

- Record All Activities: Write down all your multiple demands, competing priorities, tasks, and activities for the day or week.
- Determine Primary Goals: List your primary goals for the day or the week.
- Consider 80/20 Rule: Determine which 20% of activities will yield 80% the results, bringing you nearer to your goals.
- Evaluate Important vs. Urgent: Decide which activities are the most important versus the most urgent. At this stage, take into account how certain items affect others and the consequences for not accomplishing certain tasks (for example, someone might need something from you in order to do their job).
- Rank: Use a ranking system to begin planning. For example:
  - "A" tasks have high priority and must be completed immediately.
  - "B" tasks are moderately important but can be done after the "A" tasks.
  - "C" tasks are of low-level importance and can be tackled in spare time.

- Create a Schedule: Indicate deadlines for each task and estimate the time involved to complete the task. Create a schedule, keeping in mind any tasks that may be linked together to increase productivity. For example, can you couple something of lesser priority with something of greater importance?
- Revisit Goals and Adjust: Review your goal(s) and the rewards of doing the task on time, and make any necessary adjustments.
- Purge: Get rid of items on your list that remain at the bottom and will realistically not be completed.

Connect electronically. While keeping a daily calendar is clearly important when it comes to time management, you can significantly increase its effectiveness through the use of an electronic calendar or similar technology. Electronic calendars provide a means to remind you in a timely fashion of events that are going to occur. Placing these calendars on devices such as tablets or smart phones makes the process more beneficial.

Stick to the schedule. Do not waste the good work you have done creating a schedule by not following the calendar. It is easy to put aside tasks that are not viewed as positive and move on to other tasks, but at its core time management is about following through on what you have scheduled. Teachers will sometimes put off grading papers, as an example, and complete other tasks instead. This has a negative effect in two ways: the teacher gets behind on the tasks that need completion, and more importantly, the students do not receive timely feedback on their work.

Plan a little time for the unexpected. Each and every day in a school setting a crisis will arise; some will be small, some will be larger. In any event, all of these circumstances will maximize the schoolteacher's time. In order to address these important issues, it is vital that teachers include time in the schedule to allow for the unexpected. This may mean that some of the lower priority issues on your schedule have to be shifted, but make sure you do not change the critical areas on your schedule unless it is essential to the safety and well-being of your students and school.

COMMON MISTAKES

There are many mistakes teachers make when dealing with time management. Most of these mistakes can be overcome by using a few effective techniques that will make better use of your time. All of the mistakes that can be made could not be listed in this chapter, but here are a few of the most common ones that new teachers make.

We do not stick to the schedule. This is the easiest mistake to make, and is the most common one that is made. If you follow the guidelines above in terms of planning over the summer, then not sticking to your schedule is not only wasting the time you have spent developing the schedule, but also the time you used planning in the summer. Whatever method you used to identify the most important parts of your daily schedule, color-coding or highlighting, these critical areas must be maintained in order to effectively do the work of a school teacher.

We do not disconnect. Just as was mentioned in the previous section that it is important to connect with technology to make your job easier, it is equally important to disconnect at appropriate times and leave the technology behind. As a school teacher, one of the greatest mistakes we make is to constantly read our emails throughout the day, taking away our attention from what is really important. As a general rule, you can successfully do your job as a teacher by checking your email only three to four times a day maximum. Once in the morning when you arrive, once during midday just to make sure there is nothing important coming from the main office or a parent, and once after the students have left the building. If you're so compelled you can also check work email before you go to bed at night but I do not recommend it!

We put off what we do not like. For some teachers, it is grading papers; for others it is entering grades into the computer; and yet others do not like preparing materials. Whatever the task, there is always one (or two) we do not favor in our jobs. This dislike lends itself to not completing the task in a timely fashion. When we avoid these tasks, we are not fulfilling our responsibilities and we are also creating a backlog of work to be completed.

We do not have an agenda. A significant mistake is made when teachers go into meetings and do not have a clear agenda prepared identifying what is to be accomplished. A well-planned, thoughtful agenda will help save enormous time and keep the group on task. The optimum agenda also includes the amount of time that will be spent discussing each item. It is also important to assign someone in the group the duty of refocusing the conversation back to the agenda topics when the discussion goes off in an irrelevant direction.

CONCLUSION

If you want to be successful as a school teacher, you have to effectively manage your time. A well-developed calendar will make your daily tasks easier to finish, and your professional life much more fulfilling. The ability to prioritize what is important each day, coupled with the confidence to delegate tasks to others in your building will help make the duties of a school teacher attainable. A well-planned day, week, month, and year will make the experience of teaching that much more rewarding for you, and your students will benefit immensely as well.

HITTING YOUR MARK

It is Sunday night, and you have a full week ahead of you filled with students, lessons, meetings, and numerous other duties. Do you feel excited and prepared for the tasks ahead, or are your head and heart filled with anxiety over the overwhelming responsibilities you have this week? If you are excited, chances are it is because you have spent the time on the front end preparing your schedule, prioritizing tasks, and effectively managing your time. Remember that effective time management makes everything else you have to do in a day much more attainable, and less intimidating. Spend your Thursdays and Fridays effectively preparing for the week ahead, and your Sunday evenings can then be a time of rest and regeneration!

QUESTIONS FOR DISCUSSION

1. Consider a time when you felt stressed because you did not have enough time to complete all of the tasks at hand. What proactive steps could you have taken to minimize the stress?
2. What are strategies or habits you could develop to better manage you time on a daily basis?

ACTIVITIES FOR ENRICHMENT

The Mason Jar:

- Divide your group into teams of 3-4 members.
- Give each group an empty mason jar and a variety of different sized items (you can use stones, pebbles, and sand as an example).
- Tell the group they have 10 minutes to get as much of the material in the jar as they can (do not provide much more in terms of instruction).
- Teams may empty and refill the jar as often as they can in the time allowed until they feel they have the most in.
- Have each group share out the different trials they had in filling the jar, and what they ended up with.
- Students should then be allowed a few minutes to reflect on the items in the jar, and have them write independently about how the items could be related to time management (larger items [most important] should go in first, etc.)
- Share out their thoughts. (Baily, 2016)

Four Puzzles, Four Types of People:

Preparation – you will need four identical children's puzzles, a timer, and blindfolds. Open the boxes and place the puzzle pieces into four different zip lock baggies.

Divide your group into four teams.

Group A gets a bag of puzzle pieces, as well as the box cover from the puzzle.

Group B gets a bag of puzzle pieces, but nothing else.

Group C gets a bag of puzzle pieces and the timer.

Group D gets a bag of puzzle pieces and the blindfolds.

Each group will need to solve the puzzle as quickly as possible once you say go. There are three restrictions; Group B will not have the cover to look at; Group C will need to set the timer to 3 minutes, and may not begin the puzzle until the timer goes off. Group D will need to wear the blindfolds when solving the puzzle.

Have the groups try to solve the puzzle.

Change group roles once or twice to allow groups to experience each group.

Reflection:

- Ask the groups in terms of time management, what kind of person is the blindfolded group? (no plans, no schedule, etc.)
- What about the timer group? (procrastinators, people who put things off)
- What about Group B? (those somewhat prepared, but without a good road map, etc.)
- Group A? (well-planned out, effective time management.)

$86,400:

You have $86,400 to spend, but there are restrictions:

- Once you use a portion of the money you can't get it back
- You cannot bank any of the money

Write down how you will spend your money.

1. What did you choose to spend it on, and why?
2. How did you decide what to buy first? Last?

(Links to time management: 86,400 is how many seconds are in each day

Knowing this, relate how you spent the money to how you spend your time

Could you do better with either your money or your time? How? (Argenio, J. 2016).

Ribbon of Life:

Take a colored ribbon length approximately 1 meter/100 cms and scissors.

Start with the following questions:

Explain that each cm is one year of life. Ask how long most people live. If the response is only 75 years, then cut 25 cms from the 100 cm ribbon and throw it away.

Ask the average age of the participants. If it is 25 to 30, cut another 25 cms of the ribbon and say that is gone. You cannot do anything with it.

Ask how much is left. If people will say, "50," explain what that isn't correct. Every year we have 52 weeks, and 52 Sundays. If we multiply that by 50 years, it comes to 7.14 years. Reduce the ribbon by another 7.14 cms.

We also usually have Saturdays off, so reduce another 7 cms.

Public/National holidays are 10 each years. That comes to another 1.5 years. Reduce ribbon by another 1.5 cms.

Your casual leave, sick leave and annual holidays are approxiimately 40 days a year, multiplied by 50. Cut off another 5 cms.

Now you are left with about 29.5 years. But, the calculation is not over yet.

You sleep average 8 hour daily; multiple 365 days again by 50 years (122 days x 50 = almost 17 years). Cut off another 17 cms.

You spend time eating lunch, breakfast, snacks, and dinner total for a total of 2 hours daily (i.e. 30 days a year X 50 years= 4 years or so). Cut off another 4 cms.

Last, let's figure we spend about 1 hour a day traveling from place to place for activities and such. (That is about 2 more years).

We're down to SIX years of life to make it or break it! Make use of your six years! (Anthony, J. 2016).

REFERENCES

Carnegie, Dale. (2011). Time management tips guide. Retrieved from http://www.dalecarnegie.com/ebook/time-management-tips/

Oxford Dictionary. (2015). Time management. Retrieved from http://www.oxforddictionaries.com/us/definition/american_english/time-management?q=time+management

Scholastic. (2015). *Time management strategies*. Retrieved from http://www.scholastic.com/teachers/article/time-management

CHAPTER 15

REFLECTIVE PRACTICE AND PROFESSIONAL DEVELOPMENT

George Parker

"Without continual growth and progress, such words as improvement, achievement, and success have no meaning."

~ Benjamin Franklin

INTRODUCTION

The field of education is saturated with an abundance of research that supports a direct correlation between the preparedness of the classroom teacher and student achievement. In fact, researchers such as John Hattie, who conducted a meta-analysis study that synthesized research findings from over 800 educational studies, determined that the quality of teacher professional development had a greater impact on student learning than factors such as the home environment or socio-economic status of a student (Hattie, 2009). Consequently, it is understandable that in many school divisions today there is an emphasis on teacher professional development.

Unfortunately, professional development alone will not cure all of the problems that schools face today in improving student achievement or teacher performance. If this were the case, we could reasonably argue that any teacher in the teaching profession who was employed by a school division that provided some degree of consistent professional development would eventually obtain the equivalent rating of an exemplary or master-level teacher as measured

Courtesy of George Parker. Copyright © Kendall Hunt Publishing Company.

through division performance ratings and student results. This is not the case. In reality, classrooms around the country are filled with teachers of varying years of experience who have either declined, remained stagnant, or made moderate growth in their ability to positively impact student learning since entering the teaching profession.

Why is it that some teachers become highly effective teachers in only a few years, while others do not see significant gains in their abilities to impact student learning? If you are a novice teacher, it is critical that you adopt these key principles of professional development that will lead to your continued growth as an instructional leader in the classroom. This chapter will provide insight into two important fundamental principles of teacher development: **Reflective Practices and Establishing a Mindset of Continuous Learning.**

REFLECTIVE PRACTICES

Why is reflection important? It is important that we, as educators, consistently reflect on the impact that our decisions may have on the educational experiences of our students. For example, when two teachers independently plan a lesson that addresses the same curriculum standards, the resulting lessons may be very different. Decisions such as how the topic is introduced, strategies to employ, or assessment practices may result in a uniquely different learning experience for students in each of the two classrooms. Therefore, it is important that teachers reflect on their instructional decisions regularly to ensure that they are effective in meeting the educational needs of their students.

REFLECTING ON DAILY LESSON PLANNING

The following questions will provide you with substantial input for improving the quality of your daily lessons. If used consistently, your daily lessons will become more engaging, rigorous, and impactful for students:

1. What worked in today's lesson?
2. What did not work in today's lesson?
3. What was the level of engagement during the _____ activity? (assess each activity)
4. Did I meet the objective(s) of the lesson at the appropriate level of rigor?
5. What level of mastery did my students exhibit in relation to the objective(s)?
6. Based on my review of today's assessment, what information should I reteach, clarify, or reinforce through additional examples for my students?
7. How could this lesson be improved?

REFLECTING ON CLASSROOM INSTRUCTION

While planning is an important component of effective instruction, often little effort is made to reflect on other important areas of teacher effectiveness such as classroom management and pedagogy. For most teachers, reflecting on all three areas would ensure that they are not only developing effective lessons, but that they are equally capable of implementing their plans.

Three practices that teachers may utilize to increase opportunities for reflection in the areas of classroom management and pedagogy are classroom observation, videotaping, and student surveys.

1. Classroom Observations

Whether a teacher is being observed in the act of teaching or observing another teacher, the opportunity to reflect on real-time classroom evidence can be impactful to future classroom management or teaching practices. When being observed, it is important that teachers reflect on any feedback that is provided by the observer. Often, feedback will be provided in writing in the form of an observation report. Upon receiving the report, you should ask yourself whether the suggestions will lead to either better management or delivery of instruction in your classroom.

When you are observing another teacher, it is important to observe both teacher actions and student actions. A simple approach to doing this is to draw a line down a single sheet of paper and record what the teacher is doing (teacher actions) on one side of the sheet, and what the students are doing (student actions) on the other side. This will enable you to reflect on how the actions of the teacher impacted the student behavior in the classroom.

For example, in Figure 15.1, Mrs. Martin is modeling the process of checking for the correct solution for a two-step equation in an algebra classroom. It is important that you, as the observer, notice not only how the teacher effectively models the skill for the class, but also how the students respond to the teacher's actions. Are the students engaged or off-task? Is the teacher actively involving the class through questioning and discussion throughout this process? Are there any checks for understanding?

Ethical Considerations

Principle I: Responsibility to the Profession

The professional educator promotes and advances the profession within and beyond the school community

Mrs. Martin	
Algebra I	
Teacher Observation Notes:	
Today's Learning Objective—Students will be able to solve and check two-step linear equations	
Teaching/administrative experience	
Teacher Actions	**Student Actions**
Mrs. Martin selected three problems from the class assignment sheet to model for her students. Students were asked to record the examples in their notebooks and follow along with her as she solved the problems on the whiteboard. While solving each problem, she called on students to provide the next step in the process. Additionally, she discussed each step of the process and identified potential mistakes that students might make. After each problem, Mrs. Martin solicited the students for any questions before moving to the next example.	Students took notes and responded to Mrs. Martin when called upon. It appears that an expectation has been established that classroom examples should be recorded into the notes for the day. No off-task behavior noted. Two students asked questions during the activity.

FIGURE 15.1.

2. Recording Your Classroom

Recording your classroom is an excellent way to reflect on classroom management and pedagogy. When filming, it is important that sound quality and camera coverage are arranged in advance in order to minimize any distractions during the instructional period. Self-recording is an effective process for assessing your body language, vocal responses, and interaction with students while engaged in teaching. It is important to document actionable next steps as you critique your video.

3. Student Surveys

In business, it is common practice to survey customers to solicit input on improvements in customer service or product quality. If the customer is always right, why are we not consistently listening to our number one customer, our students? Student surveys are an effective way for teachers to gain a better understanding of their impact on student learning. In developing or adopting a student survey, it is important to take into consideration the age of the students being surveyed. For instance, younger students may require age-appropriate text and response selections, such as a smiley face, which correlates to agreement. For older students, survey questions may be used to assess areas involving:

- Classroom climate
- Content mastery
- The teacher's delivery of instruction
- The teacher's responsiveness to the individual needs of students
- Classroom engagement
- Consistency of rule enforcement
- Consistency of communicating expectations

It is important that student surveys be administered in a way to ensure that the identity of individual survey respondents remains anonymous. While teachers may share general information from a completed survey with students, addressing individual comments or marks on a survey with individual students is strongly discouraged.

DEVELOPING A MINDSET OF CONTINUOUS IMPROVEMENT

As mentioned in the introduction to this chapter, years of service and simply participating in professional development will not guarantee that a teacher will reach the highest standards of performance. In order to accomplish this, there must exist a commitment to continuous improvement. As educators, we want our students to aspire to become life-long learners who have a thirst for the acquisition and application of knowledge. Therefore, it seems rather hypocritical that professional educators would not model similar qualities.

In her ground-breaking book, *Mindset-The New Psychology of Success*, author Dr. Carol Dweck examines the differences and implications of a *growth* and *fixed* mindset (Dweck, 2006). Since having a growth mindset involves building a level of resilience and understanding in relation to failure and change, educators who exhibit the qualities of a risk-taking and continuous learning have also adopted a growth mindset. When educators become fixed in their thinking, they become resistant to the change (Dweck, 2006). Consequently, innovation is stifled and creativity takes a back seat to organizational norms of teaching.

Establishing a mindset of continuous improvement ensures that you will never see an end to professional growth as an educator. Rather than simply attending required professional development sessions, you will seek out opportunities for professional growth while challenging yourself to take risks by trying new strategies or approaches to teaching. Educators who acquire a growth mindset are more likely to become high performing teachers than those who simply do the bare minimum.

PROFESSIONAL LEARNING COMMUNITIES

Collaboration among classroom teachers is rapidly becoming a common expectation in many schools around the country. School administrators often structure teacher schedules to include common planning time. This enables teachers who are assigned either the same content area, grade, or students to meet and engage in collaborative activities that focus on improving student learning. Professional Learning Communities (PLCs) are structured instructional meetings designed to improve learning outcomes for all students (DuFour, 2004). During PLC meetings, teachers examine curriculum standards, develop assessments, and utilize data-driven decisions to improve learning outcomes in the classroom. In addition to scheduled meetings, teachers may participate in a variety of job-embedded learning opportunities such as lesson study, learning walks, and peer observations.

In addition to receiving an assigned school mentor, PLCs provide teachers with an appropriate venue to address classroom issues that may impact the learning of their students. Many times, for instance, novice teachers may need some assistance in developing lessons that match the level of rigor of the curriculum standard. Activities such a lesson study, where teachers collaboratively develop a lesson, teach the lesson, and then reconvene to reflect on their experiences can be a powerful experience for many teachers.

SCHOOL-BASED PROFESSIONAL DEVELOPMENT

In addition to professional learning communities, many schools develop site-based professional development opportunities for their teachers throughout the school year. These sessions may be led by teachers, school administrators, division instructional specialists, or external consultants. School-based professional development will usually focus on a specific area of interest or need for the school. Sessions are usually provided either before the start of school, after school, or on days when classes are not in session.

DIVISION-SPONSORED PROFESSIONAL DEVELOPMENT

While schools may provide professional development opportunities that are unique to the needs of the school, many school divisions offer additional professional development opportunities that are targeted on areas of focus for the entire school division. Division-sponsored professional development may be mandatory for a specified group of employees when a focused effort is made to build capacity in a specific area. School divisions may also develop mandatory or voluntary professional development sessions based on the interests of teacher or other staff. Mandatory sessions are managed through a sign-in procedure to ensure that participation is monitored for all required personnel.

EXTERNAL GROWTH OPPORTUNITIES

For many educators, developing a mindset of continuous improvement involves looking beyond their school or division for great ideas and innovation. Many organizations offer opportunities for professional development, additional qualifications, or networking. National organizations, such as the Association for Supervision and Curriculum Development (ASCD), support educators both at the state and national level by providing professional workshops, conferences, instructional videos, and materials. Professional organizations such as National Council of Teachers of Mathematics (NCTM) or the National Science Teachers Association (NSTA) offer teachers an opportunity to learn, network and share best practices with colleagues from around the country and abroad.

In addition to association memberships, other growth opportunities such as the National Board Certification, which is sponsored by the National Board for Professional Teaching Standards (NBPTS), provide teachers the opportunity to join thousands of teachers nationally who have completed a voluntary and rigorous teaching certification program. National Board Standards are comprised of four components of the certification process: a content knowledge assessment; reflections on student work samples; classroom video and analysis; and documentation of the teacher's impact as a teaching professional. Because this process is both labor intensive and costly, it is recommended that you consider any support offered for National Board Certification when comparing potential employment opportunities.

FAVORABLE PRACTICES

In this chapter, we have reviewed several items that can make you a better educator. Here are some important "take-a-ways" that you may reflect upon as you strive to improve your personal growth:

Consistently reflect on your educational decisions and practices. Reflect on the effectiveness of your lesson planning daily by asking thoughtful and reflective questions. Consider using videotaping, observations, and student surveys to gain a better understanding of your classroom management and pedagogical abilities.

Develop a mindset of continuous improvement. Great teachers understand the importance of continuous Improvement. Adopting a growth mindset involves seeking additional professional development opportunities and taking risks by trying new strategies and practices.

Establish your professional network. Whether through professional learning communities, assigned mentors, or professional organizations, communication and collaboration with experienced colleagues will provide you the opportunity to adopt proven strategies while continuing to grow as an educator.

COMMON MISTAKES

Within this chapter, we have also reviewed several items that can hinder growth. Below are some key items to thoughtfully consider:

Do not be afraid of receiving feedback. Simply put, feedback is your friend. You should avoid the appearance of being defensive or confrontational. Whether the feedback comes from a colleague, instructional coach, mentor, or administrator, listen attentively and ask questions to gain a clear understanding of what is being communicated.

> ### Leading the Way
>
> *When planning professional development activities, seek the input of others to identify needs. PD will be much more effective when those involved see the value in the activity.*

Do not isolate yourself. Effective educators understand the importance of collaborating with their colleagues and learning from one another. Be available and prepared to share your ideas and strategies with your fellow teachers. Establish norms on your team that enable the group to establish trust and collegiality.

When it comes to professional development, do more than the minimum. While schools and school divisions offer professional development, there are many additional opportunities beyond the school division such as professional organizations, conferences and National Board Certification, that provide educators opportunities to grow, learn, and share innovative practices.

CONCLUSION

Whether you are an experienced teacher or new to the profession, how you view professional development may have a significant impact on your future development on student learning. It is important to that you reflect on instructional decisions daily to determine whether changes are needed. Reflecting on lesson plans, video, surveys, or observation reports can be powerful practices for novice and experienced teachers.

In addition to reflective practices, adopting a mindset of continuous improvement will ensure that you continue to grow as a teacher. In addition to school and division sponsored professional development, you are encouraged to join professional organizations and attend workshops and conferences.

HITTING YOUR MARK

Years of teaching or participating in required school or division professional development do not guarantee that you will become an exemplary teacher. Establishing healthy habits such as reflective practices and a growth mindset will ensure that you are consistently seeking opportunities for professional growth and improvement. The following activities provide an opportunity to expand on the learning from this chapter, allowing you to hit your mark:

QUESTIONS FOR DISCUSSION

1. The author believes that years of experience or participation in mandatory professional development is not a guarantee that a teacher will improve their performance. Do you agree or disagree? Explain your response.
2. The author emphasized the importance of professional learning communities (PLCs) in support of an environment of growth and professional development. Discuss your experience with PLCs.
3. Mr. Ellis is a new science teacher at Linkton Middle School. Over the past two weeks, he has shared with you his frustrations in keeping his classroom on task for the full 95-minute class period. Additionally, his recent first-quarter benchmark assessment scores indicate that 45% of his students failed to meet the cut-score on the benchmark assessment. As a result, Mr. Ellis expressed a feeling of being defeated. Discuss what advice you would provide to Mr. Ellis.

ACTIVITIES FOR ENRICHMENT

Reflecting on the results of a student survey can be a powerful practice for a teacher. Create five sample questions that you would ask your students on a survey. Discuss how you would respond to the feedback on each question.

Conduct some online research on PLCs using search engines or accessible printed materials. Write a one-page paper on PLCs explaining in your own words what constitutes a PLC and provide an example of what a PLC is not.

Visit http://www.nbpts.org/ to learn more about the process for becoming a National Board Certified teacher. Interview a National Board Certified teacher to discuss the process leading to certification and their experience in completing this process. Discuss your findings with the class and/or write a one-page report on your findings.

REFERENCES

DuFour, R. (2004, May). What is a professional learning community? *Educational Leadership*, *61*(8), 6–11.

Dweck, C. S. (2006). *Mindset: The new psychology of success.* New York: Ballantine.

Hattie, J. (2009). *Visible learning: A synthesis of over 800 meta-analyses relating to achievement.* New York: Routledge.

CHAPTER **16**

THE HATS TEACHERS WEAR

Bunnie Claxton

"Each item has merit, and all have their ardent supporters, but the truth is that we have added these responsibilities without adding a single minute to the school calendar in six decades."

~ Jamie Vollmer

INTRODUCTION

The phrase "wearing many hats" usually refers to a person that has many or varying responsibilities in their job or position. Teaching is a profession often associated with this phrase due to the variety and multitude of roles a teacher performs. I once heard of an assignment in a teacher education course where a classroom full of preservice teachers were asked to make a hat out of craft supplies. The preservice students were then asked to name their hats based on the many roles and responsibilities of a teacher. The purpose of this exercise was to emphasize to these teacher candidates that the roles of a teacher go beyond preparing and teaching a lesson; it involves so much more. In another situation, several teachers were asked to name the roles of a teacher. Interestingly, the first role named was janitor, followed by nurse, parent, disciplinarian, security officer, referee, communicator, police, politician,

---

Courtesy of Bunnie Claxton. Copyright © Kendall Hunt Publishing Company.

administrator, manger, and researcher. Interestingly, not one role was mentioned in regards to the communication or transmission of knowledge. Max Depree (2004) states that the first role of a leader is to define reality. For teachers, the reality is that they will wear a plethora of hats on any given day which must be defined. These hats are defined by administrators, students, parents, and circumstances in the classroom. Teachers are often the executors of other people's decisions (Ballet and Kelchtermans, 2008) and are expected to achieve more, in less time, and with fewer faculties.

In his book *Schools Cannot Do It Alone*, businessman Jamie Vollmer (2010) discusses the challenges that teachers face fulfilling the many additional roles and responsibilities added to teaching across our nation in recent decades. Furthermore, he emphasizes that the length of the typical school day, and the number of days per year that students attend school has remained constant. So what are the implications of this phenomenon for teachers? For one, it means that teachers can no longer close the door to their classroom and "just teach." The job requires so much more in our modern-day classrooms. Additionally, it means the school day can sometimes be more hectic, teachers may have to remain at school longer, and sometimes work might have to be completed at home. Most current teachers have never known it any other way.

The purpose of this chapter is to raise awareness of the potential variety of roles and responsibilities that you may face and help prepare you mentally for those roles and responsibilities. It is not the intention to make judgments about how hard teachers work, which responsibilities are appropriate and necessary, or recommend what schools might need to do differently. Regardless of whether you teach elementary, middle, or high school, or whether you teach in a specialized classroom, the reality is, that you will wear many hats. In order to do so effectively, you must prepare to hit your mark! The categories in this chapter are broad, and by no means are meant to be an exhaustive list of the roles of a teacher. However, it can be helpful for you as a teacher to teach with realistic expectations of the many tasks that may be competing for your time. If you teach with an attitude of flexibility, a willingness to be a team player, and an awareness that you will be called on to do many things beyond teaching your curriculum content, you will most likely be more content, and thus more effective, in your role as a teacher.

Many factors affect the roles and responsibilities of a teacher in a particular educational setting. The size of the school, the community, the academic structure of the school, and the philosophy of the school's leadership can all have an impact on those roles. For the sake of this chapter, we will look at most of the common hats teachers wear based on the age of the students. The items listed may not be exclusive to one age group, and there is some overlap, but the roles and responsibilities of an elementary teacher typically look very different from those of a secondary teacher.

ELEMENTARY LEVEL

In the early elementary grades, students were once given very little autonomy. Much of the teacher's time was spent doing things for their students, while the students were learning to do things for themselves. However, in today's elementary classroom, the students are expected to arrive at school with more independent learning skills than in the past. This may create challenges for the kindergarten teacher who receives students with a wide variety of skills dependent on home dynamics. Though students begin kindergarten on the same day, a tremendous gap may already exist between the skill levels of the students. Close supervision, clear instructions, support and assistance, and caring relationships are critical. In many ways, what is taught in the classroom should be an extension of what should be taught in the home. Below are some of the common hats worn by an elementary teacher.

NURSE

As a teacher of young children, you can expect instances of sickness, injury, or various other major or minor physical infirmities. Although it is common for most elementary schools to have a school nurse, teachers should also have some basic first aid skills. In recent years, school nurse reductions, coupled with minimal teacher training in healthcare procedures, has led to confusion as teachers attempt to decipher their role as teacher and healthcare provider (Pufpaff, Mcintosh, Thomas, Elam, & Irwin, 2015). Most of the medical services required of a classroom teacher are for minor instances of nausea, headaches, scratches or bruises. A teacher's response might require a few basic questions, the evaluation of an injury, and a decision of whether the situation warrants a visit to the nurse's office. In many cases a smile and a hug is all that is needed.

There may occasionally be situations that require a more serious medical response. An allergic reaction, a serious injury, or unconscious student may require quick and decisive action. It is important to know the school's processes and procedures for dealing with a medical emergency and having critical information on hand. Whether it is a requirement of a particular school or not, it is a good idea for a teacher to have formal first aid/cardiopulmonary resuscitation (CPR) training. Although it is something you never want to have to use,

Ethical Considerations

Principle III: Responsibility to Students

The professional educator maintains student trust and confidentiality when interacting with students in a developmentally appropriate manner and within appropriate limits

an emergency that requires a timely response is always a possibility. Organizations such as the Red Cross offer this training at little or no cost, and some states and school systems offer or even require this type of training.

DECORATOR

An elementary classroom should promote a friendly, welcoming environment that is conducive to learning and free from unnecessary distractions. For a teacher, learning to decorate a classroom in such a way that it promotes curiosity and excitement, but does not distract or detract from learning, is a meaningful skill. Taking an empty classroom with blank walls and turning it into a place of discovery requires creativity. The posters, letters, shapes, colors, content-related materials, and student work, can all be used to teach and reinforce instruction. However, a recent study revealed that students spent significantly more instructional time off-task and made significantly less educational gains in a high-decorated room as compared to a sparsely decorated room (Fisher, Godwin, & Seltman, 2014). The study (2014) also noted that the younger the student, the more distracted they were due to "still-developing and fragile ability to actively maintain task goals and ignore distractions" (p. 1363). Ironically, the younger the student, the more the typical teacher tends to bombard the student with classroom decorations. The way teachers decorate their classrooms makes a statement about their personality, their academic emphasis, and the overall classroom environment they are promoting. It is essential that teachers keep learning objectives at the forefront of their decorating goals in order to maximize learning.

Just as decorating a home is more than the color you choose to paint the walls, decorating the classroom is more than just putting a few posters up on the walls. How the desks are organized can affect supervision and student interaction. Providing optimal lighting and reducing unnecessary noise should be considered when arranging a classroom, and the concept of neatness, or at least "organized clutter" should not be dismissed when decorating. Teachers should ask themselves, what does the appearance of my classroom say about me, the expectations and my classroom, and what I will be teaching?

PARTY PLANNER

A significant part of encouraging young children is learning to celebrate accomplishments, both large and small. Having a party does not always mean food and decorations, although sometimes that is the case. Some schools allow significant celebrations for birthdays, end-of-the-year, or for certain holidays, while others may not. Even if a "party" just means taking a few minutes to pause, go outside, sing a song, or socialize, these activities can be a source of encouragement and fun. Celebrating achievement is necessary to encourage the learning process.

HEALTH CONSULTANT

During the early years of their education, children are still learning to take care of themselves physically. Even when parents are actively involved in this process, students often need reminders and support at school. Most schools today have a school nutrition program and teach health education (sometimes integrated into Physical Education). However, relationships and "teachable moments" often afford teachers additional opportunities to discuss health issues. Developing good eating and exercise habits can be discussed in a group setting. Requiring students to wash their hands before lunch and after restroom breaks is essential to minimize illness. Other issues, such as personal hygiene, might need to be discussed more discreetly. In some situations where these issues are not discussed in the home, the teacher may be the only one telling a student to go outside and play, brush their teeth, or eat their vegetables.

ACTIVITY COORDINATOR

A typical school day usually involves a number of transitions from one activity to another. These activities can occur inside or outside of the classroom. Keeping the day on schedule and helping students transition smoothly can improve the instructional process. Activities in the classroom can be simple and routine, but school-wide or off campus activities usually require more thorough planning. For example, helping plan a field trip may require communicating with outside organizations, obtaining transportation, collecting money and permission slips, coordinating plans with school or district officials, enlisting parental chaperones, and closely supervising students during the trip.

CUSTODIAN

It is amazing how quickly a group of children can make an orderly classroom look like it has not been cleaned in weeks. Even as teachers try to emphasize the importance of students cleaning up after themselves, the potential for messes can be never ending in a classroom. To keep a neat and clean environment conducive to learning, a teacher cannot always wait for a custodian to clean up a mess. Even when students have the best intentions, accidents can happen, things get broken, spilled, and dropped. Even outside of the classroom a teacher can show pride in their school and set a good example for students by picking up trash or tidying up little messes around campus when possible. An orderly classroom promotes learning just as s disorderly classroom detracts from the learning process.

DISCIPLINARIAN

Discipline and behavior management are often perceived as a negative part of being a teacher. However, discipline is used for correction and teaching and true discipline can be a great opportunity to teach valuable lessons and develop positive relationships with students. The behaviors exhibited by teachers significantly impacts their effectiveness in the classroom and, ultimately, the influence they have on students (Stronge, 2007). Some students may receive strict discipline at home, while others seem to have very little. The challenge is discovering what type of discipline has the greatest impact on each individual child. Discipline can be both proactive and reactive, and can be applied to individuals, or an entire group. While most schools have disciplinary processes in place, it is important to seek out additional strategies that fit your teaching style. Improving your behavior management techniques will be a career long process, and an area that can always be improved. In order for learning to take place, a teacher absolutely must be able to manage the behavior of the students in the classroom. The importance of this hat cannot be stressed enough if a teacher is to hit the mark in teaching!

ADVOCATE

Children do not always know what is best for them, or what they need to be successful in school. Sometimes they need an adult who knows them and wants what is best for them to serve as their advocate (Jones, 2010). Sometimes a teacher has to be a student advocate before school administrators to voice school or classroom needs or concerns. At other times a teacher needs to be an advocate for the child in the home or in the community, understanding that a student's performance in school is impacted by what happens outside of school.

SURROGATE PARENT

It is easy to look at some of the teacher roles above and think that these should be the responsibility of the parent, and for the most part they are. As the teacher of a young child, you are coming alongside the parents to help meet the basic needs of the child and teach basic life skills, while adding subject matter to the other lessons they are learning. Most teachers are aware that the amount of collaboration in this process varies significantly from one parent to the next. Your role as a teacher may be to reinforce lessons that are already being taught at home, or it may be to fill in the gaps when these needs are not being met at home.

In addition to the learning needs of your students, you may have students with other basic needs that are not being met at home. Students may come into your classroom hungry, without sufficient clothing, or lacking necessary school supplies. Although you will not find this requirement listed in the faculty handbook, many teachers feel compelled to try to help the students in whatever ways possible. Even though most teachers would like to see these needs met by parents or guardians, educators understand the concept of Maslow's Hierarchy and the challenges a student will face finding academic success until these basic needs are met.

It is easy to be critical when we perceive that the parent expects us to raise their kids. Although the frustration that many teachers feel is understandable, it is important to avoid blaming the parents and focus on addressing the needs. We should work to get parents more involved, but be prepared to address needs when parental support is lacking. Even if the student does come from a home where the above needs are being met on a regular basis, there will most likely be a time during the course of the day, or a school year, when a child has a need for a surrogate parent.

SECONDARY LEVEL

Although there are some roles and responsibilities that are similar for both elementary and secondary teachers, the hats a teacher wears are usually significantly different at the secondary level. As students progress through middle and high school, they become more autonomous, and although they still require some supervision, teachers' interaction with students changes significantly. Hats commonly worn by secondary teachers may include the following.

ACADEMIC ADVISOR

Students usually begin to get more involved in the course selection process around middle school. This involvement often starts with the selection of elective courses or difficulty levels of their core subjects. At the high school level, students not only become increasingly involved in the course selection process, but they must also begin to consider how their selection of courses can affect their future plans and academic goals. Some students know from an early age exactly what they want to do when they grow up, and they do not waiver from that plan. However, the more common scenario is the student who is still trying to identify strengths, weaknesses, interests, and career goals. The students can benefit not only from the advice of professional school counselors, but from their formal and informal conversations with teachers. A casual conversation with a student about his or her strengths and helping to identify possible careers where those traits would be beneficial, or even a conversation about your own career choices, can provide helpful guidance. Teachers can encourage or discourage a student from a particular career path, even if the comments are inadvertent. It is important

Leading the Way

Leaders, like teachers, also wear many hats. When starting a new position, seek to understand the formal and informal requirements and expectations of the position.

The Hats Teachers Wear 215

for teachers to consider the potential impact of their comments, and attempt to assist students in making these decisions, while avoiding making the decisions for them.

COUNSELOR

As students develop academically, socially, and physically, their concerns become more significant, or at least that is their perception. As is the case with academic advising, there are usually professionals in the building who specialize in this area, but much of the counseling that occurs in a secondary school occurs outside of the counselor's office. The life of a typical teenager is often filled with drama. When students are dealing with relationship issues, employment challenges, academic struggles, and numerous other topics, it can be helpful just to have an adult (who is not their parent) to talk to. This does not mean that a teacher is responsible for solving the problems of their students, but it can be an appealing quality for a teacher to be an effective listener.

It is important to note that some counseling functions are better handled by, even legally required to be reported to, a school counselor or official. Issues of child abuse, illegal substance use, or potential mental or physical harm to a student should not be handled through informal or casual counseling. Make sure you know what topics are appropriate to discuss with the student, and do not be afraid to ask if you are unsure.

COACH

Athletic activities are prevalent in most high schools, and many middle schools. It is not unusual for a school to have 15 to 20 athletic teams competing during the course of a school year, and every team needs a coach. Some schools incorporate coaches from the community who are not employees of the school, but for the most part coaches come from the ranks of the faculty. Teachers with an athletic background are prime candidates to fill a school's coaching positions. However, finding those teacher/coach candidates to fill every position can be difficult. Teachers who are willing to coach, even with a limited athletic background, can be a valuable asset to the school. "Additional tasks that go beyond their regular teaching duties include managing sports teams, writing athletic budgets, training athletes, and teaching the fundamentals of sports. At certain times of the year in particular, athletic coaches devote large blocks of time to organizing practices and travelling to games" (Egalite, Bowen, & Trivitt, 2015, p. 3).

In addition to training students in the skills of a particular sport, coaches teach many valuable character traits such as teamwork, commitment, dedication, and respect for authority. Athletic competition can complement, instead of compete with, what is being taught in the classroom. In addition to the service that coaches provide to student athletes, teachers who coach can also develop personal and professional skills in leadership, time and resource management, budgeting, and community relations.

CLUB SPONSOR

Similar to coaches, club sponsors fulfill a vital need in a secondary school. Clubs allow students to develop skills and interests beyond the classroom and there are an unlimited number of club titles. Clubs vary in content and each will require work, but some require more work than others (Kelly, n.d.). A club may enhance an academic subject, such as an art or math club, or it can just promote common interests such as photography or video games. A club may bring students together for a mental activity, such as a book club, or physical activity such as running or hiking. Although the topics of clubs may vary, the common purpose is that they bring students together to learn about and enjoy common interests. A club sponsor may be required to schedule and plan activities, serve as a liaison between the club and school administration, manage club accounts, and provide overall supervision. But beyond those common functions, a club sponsor has the opportunity to share their own interests and experiences with the students.

FUNDRAISER

In today's educational climate of budget cuts and limited resources, most schools, clubs, athletic teams, and PTAs participate in some type of fundraising along the way. Athletic teams and fine arts programs may receive funding from the school budget, but there is often a desire to raise money for additional resources such as uniforms, equipment, or travel. Clubs may receive little or no school funding, and may conduct fundraisers just to have a budget. A school may even decide to have a schoolwide fundraiser to fund projects that potentially benefit the student body as a whole. A teacher's participation in a fundraiser may include motivating the students, organizing activities, or recording and collecting the money raised.

BOOKKEEPER

Anytime a teacher is involved in an organization or an activity that requires funding, there is a possibility that the teacher will have to handle money. Most schools employ an official bookkeeper to process school receipts, pay bills, and manage various school accounts, but it may not always be reasonable for the school bookkeeper to collect money directly from the students. When students are required to pay for field trips, lockers, optional activities, lunches, or books, teachers may be required to collect fees and keep records. Fortunately, most teachers are usually given clear directions from the administration regarding the collection and handling of money, and it is usually involves only small amounts.

TECHNICAL SUPPORT SPECIALIST

It can be difficult for most schools to keep up with the constant changes in educational technology. Teachers use technology in most aspects of their job, and most students use the school's and/or their own technology for learning. As technology has increasingly become prevalent in the K–12 classroom, the ability of school or district level tech support to address classroom needs quickly has become more challenging. Increased technology use also increases the probability that teachers will experience "technical difficulties" during the school day. A teacher who can troubleshoot, identify, and rectify these difficulties, will increase the beneficial use of the technology.

CROWD CONTROL

Whenever a group of students comes together in a school setting, a proportional number of adults should be in close proximity. Even the most mature and responsible students can display foolish behavior when they are in unsupervised groups. The larger the group, the greater the propensity for brief lapses in judgment. In a secondary school setting, there are numerous times and locations when the presence of adults is important, just to be visible. During the few minutes between class periods, there may be hundreds, or even thousands of students in the halls of the school with no particular teacher responsible for them. Many school cafeterias hold hundreds of students at a time, several periods a day. At the end of the school day, a school may have hundreds of students flowing through the halls, into the parking lot, and onto the school buses. Student supervision does not always end with the last bell of the day. Afternoon and evening activities often attract large numbers of students mixed in with parents and community members. All of the scenarios above require formal and informal supervision by teachers.

Teachers sometimes perceive supervision duty as an inconvenience or even a waste of time. They may pass the time by grading papers or talking to other teachers. However, supervising a large group of students can be an excellent opportunity to build relationships and get to know kids on a more personal level. Great teachers are masters at developing solid relationships with students which are vital in fostering academic success (Meador, 2014). A teacher may never know the influence he or she can have just by starting a conversation with a student who is sitting alone at lunch. Even when inappropriate behaviors must be addressed, these interactions can provide opportunities to encourage maturity, responsible behavior, and appropriate interaction with others.

FAVORABLE PRACTICES

As mentioned earlier in this chapter, the hats a teacher wears can vary significantly from one teaching assignment to another. Below are a few favorable practices and common mistakes to consider in regard to teacher roles and responsibilities:

Have a good attitude. Most people appreciate those who work with a positive attitude, especially in less than positive situations. Those who not only avoid complaining, but actually learn to "make the best" of situations, often gain favor among their peers and leaders. Your attitude during activities outside of class will either improve or detract from how you are perceived as a teacher.

Address concerns with those who make the decisions. If you have a question or concern about something you are being asked to do, go to the person who made the decision. It is possible that the person was not aware of all the possible implications or your specific situation. Understand that these decisions are usually not personal and leaders are often just trying to get things accomplished. Additionally, if you share a concern, you should also be prepared to suggest a solution.

Take advantage of situations where you can interact with students outside of the classroom. Instructional time is usually focused on course material and in most cases casual conversation is limited. During many of the additional duties that teachers are assigned there is less structure and teachers may have time to just talk to students. These conversations can be helpful, interesting, or just indicate to students that you care. Students enjoy seeing their teacher at their sporting events, theatrical productions, and sponsored competitions. If you are unable to attend their events, it is still thoughtful to ask the student about the activities they participate in outside of school.

Choose to serve according to your strengths. Some additional duties are assigned to teachers based on need, such as general supervision. However, when teachers are needed to fill coaching, club sponsor, or activity coordinator positions, volunteer for those that fit your interests, strengths, and personality.

Ask questions. When asked to complete a new task or take on an additional assignment that you are unfamiliar with, do not be afraid to ask others for help. Most of the time the expectations and guidelines are already established, whether in writing or by some informal means.

Take the task seriously. Most additional duties are assigned, not suggested, because they need to be done. If you are given an assignment, you are expected to complete the assignment, or communicate with someone if there is an issue. For example, if you are assigned to supervise a group of students and you do not show up for the duty, you may be held liable if something happens to one of the students.

COMMON MISTAKES

Complaining to other teachers. When you complain to other teachers it only intensifies negative feelings. It is likely that those around you feel busy as well. In most cases your peers can not help the situation but complaining to each other can increase a sense of injustice or feelings of anger.

Complaining to students. Complaining to students sets a bad example of how to approach unpleasant tasks. Consider how your students might feel if you complain about all you have to do for them. Furthermore, it is unlikely that they will be able to respond with helpful comments.

Complaining to parents. Most parents like to feel that their children are being taught by caring and positive adults. Complaints could cause parents to question your commitment or could cause them to have negative views toward those making the decisions. Try instead to gain their support.

Complete the task in less that professional manner. Showing up late to a duty post, inattentiveness while supervising, or poorly organizing and activity might seem like effective ways to oppose an assignment, but these responses may cause damage to your reputation and/or reduce your chances of continued employment.

CONCLUSION

Hopefully, you were aware of many of the expectations placed on teachers before reading this chapter. If not, the concept of additional responsibilities is not something to be concerned about; it is just part of being a teacher. Learning to consider additional duties and responsibilities as part of the profession, and not as tasks that interfere, can make completing these tasks seem less of a burden. Wearing many hats can add variety to the job of being a teacher.

HITTING YOUR MARK

Whether you are an elementary or secondary teacher, it is important for you to be aware that teachers wear multiple hats. The ones listed in this chapter are hats commonly worn by teachers, but are by no means exhaustive. The following activities will help you to personalize the concepts of this chapter.

QUESTIONS FOR DISCUSSION

1. Some teachers wear the disciplinarian hat way more often that they would prefer. What skills can you develop to ensure that you do not wear that hat too often?
2. Taking a proactive approach to teaching will help you to be intentional about which hats you wear the most. In order to hit your mark as a teacher, the hat that you should wear most often is the teacher hat. What steps can you take to maximize the time you wear your teacher hat?

ACTIVITIES FOR ENRICHMENT

Make a list of every possible hat that you think you will wear when you are in your own classroom, and briefly describe each one. This may prove to be an eye-opening exercise.

After making a list of the possible hats you believe you will wear in your classroom, interview a teacher who currently teaches in the area in which you intend to teach. Discuss the hats you anticipate wearing in the classroom as compared to the ones actually worn by the teacher you interview. You may discover a whole new set of hats with which to accessorize.

Once you have identified most of the hats you will wear, identify three that you believe are the most challenging and are potentially the most significant hindrance to teaching and learning. Identify proactive steps to minimize these potential challenges.

REFERENCES

Ballet, K. & Kelchtermans, G. (2008). Workload and willingness to change: Disentangling the experience of intensification. 40(1) 47–67. doi:1.01080/00220270701516463

DuPree, M. (2004). *Leadership Is an Art* (4th ed.). New York, NY: Doubleday

Egalite, A. J., Bowen, D. H., & Trivitt, J. R. (2015). Do teacher-coaches make the cut? The effectiveness of athletic coaches as math and reading teachers. *Education Policy Analysis Archives, 23*(54) 1–24.

Fisher, A. V., Godwin, K. E., and Seltman, H. (2014). Visual environment, attention allocation, and learning in young children when too much of a good thing may be bad. *Psychological Science 25*(7), 1362–1370. doi: 10.1177/0956797614533801

Jones, B., (2010). *The Many Hats of a Teacher*. New Horizons. Retrived from: http://education.jhu.edu/PD/newhorizons/Journals/spring2010/themanyhatsofateacher/

Kelly, M. (n.d.). *Being a club sponsor: What teachers need to know about being a club sponsor.* Retrieved from: http://712educators.about.com/od/teacherresources/a/Being-A-Club-Sponsor.htm.

Meador, D. (2014). *Tips for developing positive teacher student relationships.* About Education. Retrieved from: http://teaching.about.com/od/Information-For-Teachers/a/Tips-For-Developing-Positive-Teacher-Student-Relationships.htm

Pufpaff, L. A., Mcintosh, C. E., Thomas, C., Elam, M.m & Irwin, M. (2015). Meeting the health care needs of students with severe disabilities in the school setting: Collaboration between school nurses and special education teachers. *Psychology in the Schools*, 52(7) 683–701.

Stronge, J. H., (2007). *Qualities of effective teachers* (2nd ed.). Association for Supervision and Curriculum Development, Alexandria, VA. Retrieved from: http://www.ascd.org/publications/books/105156/chapters/Section-II@-Teacher-Responsibilities-and-Teacher-Behaviors.aspx

Vollmer, J. R. (2010). *Schools Cannot Do It Alone: Building Report for America's Schools.* Enlightenment Press, Fairfield, IA.

CHAPTER 17

ENVISIONING AND ENACTING A SERVANT LEADERSHIP JOURNEY

Tamie Pratt

"The first and most important choice a leader makes is the choice to serve, without which one's capacity to lead is severely limited."

~ Robert Greenleaf

INTRODUCTION

The decision to become a teacher is often made based on a fundamental desire to help others reach their goals. Some choose teaching because they love children and want to be role models for them. Some choose teaching because they truly enjoyed school as a child, had wonderful educational experiences, and dreamed of having their own classroom one day. Still, for others, teaching is the best way to share their knowledge in a particular content area such as math, art, biology, or physical fitness.

Why did you choose teaching? What fundamental beliefs do you hold related to education and where did they come from? What unique gifts and talents do you have to share with others? Do you view yourself as a potential school leader? Spending time reflecting on these questions will unearth personal perspectives that will help you navigate the myriad of choices you will confront along your career journey. We'll begin with unpacking a few roles, responsibilities, and attributes of educators.

Courtesy of Tamie Pratt. Copyright © Kendall Hunt Publishing Company.

AMBITION AND STAMINA REQUIRED!

Teaching is a profession that requires foundational content knowledge, instructional skill, and a commitment to continuous learning to meet the ever-changing needs of students, parents, colleagues, and the community. It is a demanding profession when you do it well! Physically, it requires constant moving about the classroom, distributing materials, orchestrating group work, and keeping an organized and engaging classroom environment. Mentally, teachers must be proactive and reactive in all that they do including assessing, planning, instructing, and evaluating. In addition to these more cognitive attributes is the definite need for personal motivation: purposeful and self-driven; constantly seeking out innovative ways to convey content. Teachers must also be motivators for learning by seeking and creating opportunities which instill a love of learning in students. This means that students not only see the value in the content, but realize that the gift of education is just that: a gift we are provided by others. Don't misunderstand, much of the learning is the responsibility of the learner! As we learn, we must be actively and cognitively engaged in the process by predicting, questioning, making connections, and applying what we know to new situations. However, teachers are more often than not "the others" in the classroom. We take on the responsibility for modeling and leading learning experiences. In essence, we are learning leaders! Now, let's put this in more practical terms situated within a classroom context.

Lesson scenario. Imagine you are a high school biology teacher creating an experiment on how bacteria grow in different environments. First, you may give your students a pre-assessment to see how much they already know about bacteria. Of course, you have to score it and analyze the results to make an appropriate plan for learning and groups (yes, write that lesson plan!). Then, you need to decide what types of materials you are going to need to create a really engaging lab. Perhaps you already know how to create a great experiment or maybe you spend some time chatting with colleagues or surfing the web to see what creative ideas are available. Once you reach a decision, you will have to gather up the lab materials needed. Hopefully, your school has the necessities on hand. If not, you may need to purchase them with school or personal funds, or even seek out donations from businesses or parents. Might you need to do some or all of this on your own time? At home? After school hours? Chances are, yes! With all your planning and preparation, you are now ready to teach the bacteria lesson. This may entail distributing materials, explaining directions, modeling processes, monitoring groups, asking and answering individual questions, and redirecting students, just to name a few. So, are you leading students' learning in this scenario or doing more than that? According to Greenleaf (1977), you are doing something else remarkable: you are serving others. As a teacher, you are a servant leader. Let's explore this concept further.

UNDERSTANDING SERVANT LEADERSHIP

Servant leadership is a term that holds a bit of a paradox when first encountered. The individual words seem contradictory in meaning; however, unpacking each separately and then collectively will help us in understanding how and why they apply to teaching. Let's start by getting the elephant out of the room. You may be thinking that the word servant is a derogatory term that should not even be associated with education. This is certainly a natural reaction as historically, a servant was considered less than others and often beneath those being served in terms of the value that society placed on his/her wealth, class, race, etc. For our purposes, this type of interpretation is not the way to look at the term servant. The term servant as explained by Greenleaf (1977) means simply that you have an inherent desire to serve others before yourself. In other words, you have a passion to engage in work that puts others' needs before your own. Serving in this sense is your natural inclination. Does this sound like the mindset of a teacher? Does this reflect your thinking?

> **Ethical Considerations**
>
> Principle IV: Responsibility to the School Community
>
> *The professional educator promotes effective and appropriate relationships with the community and other stakeholders*

Moving forward then, the term leader is secondary to servant. Leading others is not your first personal or professional disposition. Put another way, you did not necessarily choose the education profession to be a leader in the school although this may be a future goal. If so, you have set that goal based on a desire to put others before yourself. You are servant first so that others' needs are met and a leader second so that your work and commitment can move an agenda, a vision, a set of policies, or institutional norms forward for the common good (Keith, 2008).

Following Greenleaf's lead, Sipe and Frick (1993) further expanded the concept of servant leadership by describing seven pillars or personal characteristics one must possess or strive for as a servant leader. Just as pillars offer support for a heavy building, Sipe and Frick's (1993) pillars serve as not only the foundation of servant leadership, but also useful benchmarks for our own personal behavior. As such, Table 17.1 briefly describes each pillar and provides representative examples of character traits and behaviors (Sipe & Frick, 1993, p. 5). Blank spaces are provided for you to reflect on your own practice in education to determine if any particular pillar warrants more personal or professional attention to grow in your own servant leadership. Use the spaces to document your own example, make a short-term goal, or rate yourself using a Likert rating scale of 1 (not me) to 5 (highly me).

Table 17.1: *Pillars of Servant Leadership*

PILLAR	DESCRIPTION	EXAMPLES	REFLECTION
Person of Character	Makes insightful, ethical, and principle-centered decisions	Integrity Humility Higher Purpose	
Puts People First	Helps others meet their priority needs	Servant's heart Mentor-minded Care and concern	
Skilled Communicator	Earnestly listens and effectively speaks	Empathy Seeks feedback Persuasive	
Has Foresight	Imagines possibilities and anticipates the future with a purpose	Visionary Creativity Decisive	
Systems Thinker	Thinks and acts strategically; leads change effectively and with balance	Comfortable with complexity Adaptable Focused on the common good	
Leads with Moral Authority	Worthy of respect; inspires trust and confidence; establishes performance standards	Accepts and delegates responsibility Shares power and control Creates a culture of accountability	

As Table 17.1 demonstrates, there are numerous personal characteristics associated with servant leadership. As you reflect on your own standing within each of these pillars, you may feel somewhat intimidated by all that is required of a servant leader; however, it is important to keep in mind that becoming a servant leader is just that. It is a process rather than a distinct I am or I am not. It is also a skill-based journey. So for each example, you may consider your options for increasing your competence in that area, such as a book study, online course, or working with a respected mentor. Additionally, servant leadership is a contextualized art-form requiring the servant to practice the art in different to types of situations to assist his/her development and confidence as a servant leader.

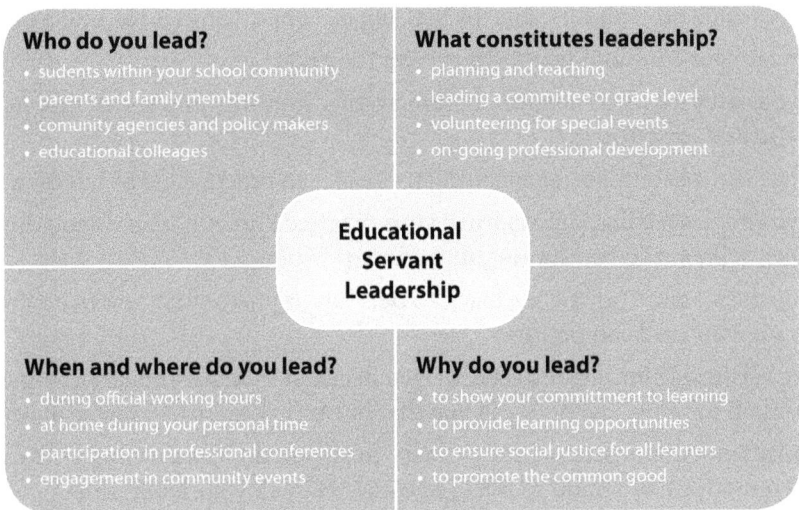

FIGURE 17.1 *Demonstrating servant leadership*

As illustrated in the biology scenario above, remember that you do not have to have an official or defined leadership role or responsibility to exhibit the pillars of servant leadership. Rather, for educators, it is imperative to understand how to situate servant leadership in the context of our daily work. Figure 17.1 illustrates several ways you may be positioned to demonstrate servant leadership within your professional life.

Opportunities for demonstrating servant leadership exist in all educational contexts. Keep this in mind so that you are routinely self-monitoring your attitudes and behaviors to ensure that your visibility as an educator is reflective of service at all times. Greenleaf (1998) states that "the ultimate model of servant is one whose service is rendered in one's own personal time for which one is not paid," (p. 155). Educators know this all too well! So much of what we do is unseen, and therefore, often unacknowledged by others. Do not let this be a deterrent to your service, but rather know that your efforts are ultimately nurturing others beyond ways you can imagine. Find joy in not being recognized! Finally, consider additional contexts in which you can embed and embrace servant leadership opportunities within your own work.

FAVORABLE PRACTICES

One of the most crucial aspects of servant leadership is its application in practical terms (Greenleaf, 1977). As an educator, you are positioned to demonstrate intentional integration of the pillars in your work. **Below is a list of behaviors and attitudes, which will support your growth as a servant leader.**

- Work beyond your comfort zone by seeking out opportunities for leadership roles
- Volunteer your time and talents to exhibit the pillars
- Ask for assistance when needed, demonstrating humility and respect for others' expertise and experience
- Embrace the role of follower, enabling the leader to practice his or her own servitude
- Receive and use feedback to improve your practice knowing that as you do so, your students, school, and community ultimately prosper
- Provide useful and realistic feedback to peers to improve their practice refraining from judgment and competition
- Practice critical thinking and data-driven decision making, remembering justice and compassion for all; a just policy is one that harms no one and benefits at least one
- Be transparent and maintain authenticity in all you do by assuming a servant's heart; trust from others will build as they see consistency in your leadership
- Stay visible when needed, but do not seek the spotlight or take it away from others; instead, lift others up so they can shine and grow in confidence
- Be open to change by remaining flexible to other leaders' requests; focus on strengthening relationships
- Engage in productive conversations at all times, and practice listening; silence can be golden and sends the message that you value others' perspectives

These practices certainly do not represent an exhaustive list, but they provide a starting point for your servant leadership journey. As you may already know, education is a stressful profession; therefore, a heightened need for empathy applies in all situations. Empathy is the opposite of rejection. According to Greenleaf (1998), the servant leader always accepts the person, but may refuse to accept their effort or behavior. In the classroom, the "educator may be rejected by students and must not object to this. But one may never, under any circumstances, regardless of what they do, reject a single student" (p. 34). We are called to respect and build up one another, and although sometimes difficult, refraining from judging any person does just that.

COMMON MISTAKES

As educators, one of the best parts of our jobs is starting each school year with the fresh promise of new and sometimes unique professional roles; however, the process of assuming these roles can be a double-edged sword. On the one hand, we are forced to learn and think in different ways; on the other hand, we are bound to make mistakes. Thankfully in both situations we are bound to grow! **In order to fully realize your potential as a servant leader, make intentional attempts to avoid the following roadblocks along your journey:**

- Saying yes all the time: pace yourself by not taking on more than you can successfully handle
- People-pleasing: servant leadership is not about letting others control you, so make professional decisions with moral authority keeping the common good in mind
- Asking others to do tasks you would not do yourself: practice the Golden Rule
- Engaging in non-productive conversations about students and colleagues: remove yourself from situations where this occurs; be forthright in your preference not to participate in this behavior
- Being defined by your work: you are more than what you do, so remember how multi-faceted you are; engage in health-promoting physical and mental activities outside of work
- Negativity: assume good in people; seek out and demonstrate joy as you lead and serve
- Staying in a position too long: be timely in your discernment of work knowing that there is often a time to move on to new learning opportunities (grade-level, school, position)
- Accepting unsupportive leaders: be confident in asking for what you need in order to do your best professional work
- Accepting the status quo: if you see a problem, search and communicate a solution to colleagues to colleagues who may be unaware

Serving and leading others will definitely present challenges, but it is your reaction to those challenges that will come to define you as a servant leader. As adult learners, and particularly as educators, one of the most crucial aspects to our ability to move forward from challenging situations is reflective thinking. Merriam and Bierema (2014) distinguish between two types: reflection-on-action, which occurs after the experience and impacts future decisions, and reflection-in-action, which takes place during the experience to immediately reshape the course of events. Both are valuable, however, mastering the latter positions you as a more effective servant leader because you are able to read people, think on your feet, and make responsive decisions. This flexibility illuminates your skill in professionally managing tough situations.

> **Leading the Way**
>
> *A good leader must first be a good follower. Make it your goal to make those who lead you "look good." Whether you receive credit or not, this attitude will most likely result in long-term success.*

CONCLUSION

The Hebrew word *abodah* has multiple meanings including work, service, and worship. Hopefully, you can now realize how that one word is so representative of servant leadership. As you embark on your personal journey of servant leadership, remember to embrace a growth mindset (Dweck, 2006) about yourself and others, understanding that every individual has the capacity to change, learn, and reflect light in this world when light is illuminated on them. So, be the light by choosing a mindset where you are not solely working for yourself, your family, financial gain, power, or prestige, but primarily to serve others in whatever ways you can. Remember, work is a privilege; education is a privilege. Not everyone gets either or both. Your chosen work and the ways in which you enact that work is a testimony to who you are and what you believe. Set your moral compass and stay the course on your servant leadership journey!

HITTING YOUR MARK

As teachers and educational leaders, our primary goal is to have a positive effect on student learning. We do this by utilizing multiple measures at intervals spaced throughout units of study and individual lessons. We assess *before* units to determine depth of content, student groups, and timeframes for instruction. We assess several times *during* lessons to ensure that students grasp concepts before moving on or to check our pace of instruction. Finally, we assess *after* units or lessons to ensure that we "hit the mark" with all students, and if not, to create action plans for re-teaching content in novel ways to individuals or groups.

Consistent assessments and resulting actions are the hallmarks of a professional teacher, so have you ever considered *assessing yourself*, particularly in terms of your servitude? There's no better way to determine and develop your enactment of servant leadership than developing a process and timeline for measurement. In doing so, you may choose to go it alone at first, and then as you become more comfortable in the process, solicit feedback from colleagues and critical friends. Make it an interesting and fun part of your professional development, and remember that the best leaders are the best learners. Keep learning about yourself, and your students and schools will reap the benefits, allowing you to hit your mark every time!

QUESTIONS FOR DISCUSSION

1. What opportunities do you currently have throughout each day to demonstrate one or more of the servant leadership pillars? In what environments may you seek more and different opportunities?
2. Are you finding joy in all aspects of serving as a teacher? If not, what can you do within your circle influence to live joyfully?
3. Are you authentic in your servant leadership at school, home, and in your community? What measures are in place to let you know?
4. What learning tools exist which will help you develop as a servant leader? What is your timeline for enacting your newly acquired skills?
5. As a colleague who contributes to a positive school culture, how are you serving other teachers so that they may do their best work?
6. What do you envision for your future as a teacher 3, 5, or 10 years down the road? How does servant leadership play into this goal? What do you need to do today to realize this goal?

ACTIVITIES FOR ENRICHMENT

Keep a reflective servant leadership journal for a specific length of time that works with your schedule, for example, 30 days or for a particular six-weeks or semester. Purchase a "special journal" that speaks to you (leather bound, flowery, inspirational cover, etc.), and commit to writing in the journal daily, every other day, or at a minimum, at the end of every week. Find quiet time to do so and just start writing about the day's/week's activities. Be specific about what you did, said, and how you reacted. Above all, be honest. Just write! Then, at the end of your journaling project, start analyzing your servant leadership. Utilizing the pillars, reread what you wrote looking for instances of each pillar. You may want to create a tally sheet or a spreadsheet to keep track of the pillars you enacted and how. Afterward, look for overuse and underuse of each pillar. Are you really adept at one pillar, but rarely utilize another? Is there a pillar that wasn't used at all? After this period of analysis, make a plan for increasing your servant leadership. Include a vision, goals, objectives, timelines, and resources. Finally, hold yourself accountable by enlisting the support of an accountability partner who can check in with you to remind you or nudge you as you move along this journey.

Create a critical friends servant leadership group comprised of teachers or leaders who may want to learn more about servant leadership and how to practice it within your workspace. Consider getting together informally either in-person or virtually with online video conferencing. You may choose to study a servant leadership text or participate in a school event that allows you to focus on one or more of the pillars. Share your successes and challenges as a servant leader, and encourage one another along the journey.

REFERENCES

Dweck, C. (2006). *Mindset: The new psychology of success.* New York: Random House.

Keith, K. (2008). *The case for servant leadership* (2nd ed.). Atlanta: Greenleaf Center.

Greenleaf, R. K. (n.d.). *Center for servant leadership.* Retrieved from http://www.greenleaf.org

Greenleaf, R. K. (1977). *Servant leadership: A journey into the nature of legitimate power & greatness.* New York: Paulist Press.

Greenleaf, R. K. (1998). Servant: Retrospect and prospect. In L. C. Spears (Ed.), *The power of servant leadership.* San Francisco: Berrett-Koehler.

Merrimam, S. B., & Bierema, L. L. (2014). *Adult learning: Linking theory and practice.* San Francisco: Jossey-Bass.

Sipe, J. W., & Frick, D. M. (1993). *Seven pillars of servant leadership: Practicing the wisdom of leading by serving.* New York: Paulist Press.

APPENDIX

PRINCIPLE I: RESPONSIBILITY TO THE PROFESSION

The professional educator is aware that trust in the profession depends upon a level of professional conduct and responsibility that may be higher than required by law. This entails holding one and other educators to the same ethical standards.

A. *The professional educator demonstrates responsibility to oneself as an ethical professional by:*
1. Acknowledging that lack of awareness, knowledge, or understanding of the Code is not, in itself, a defense to a charge of unethical conduct;
2. Knowing and upholding the procedures, policies, laws and regulations relevant to professional practice regardless of personal views;
3. Holding oneself responsible for ethical conduct;
4. Monitoring and maintaining sound mental, physical, and emotional health necessary to perform duties and services of any professional assignment; and taking appropriate measures when personal or health-related issues may interfere with work-related duties;
5. Refraining from professional or personal activity that may lead to reducing one's effectiveness within the school community;

© 2016 National Association of State Directors of Teacher Education and Certification (NASDTEC). Reprinted by permission.

6. Avoiding the use of one's position for personal gain and avoiding the appearance of impropriety;
7. Taking responsibility and credit only for work actually performed or produced, and acknowledging the work and contributions made by others.

B. *The professional educator fulfills the obligation to address and attempt to resolve ethical issues by:*
1. Confronting and taking reasonable steps to resolve conflicts between the Code and the implicit or explicit demands of a person or organization;
2. Maintaining fidelity to the Code by taking proactive steps when having reason to believe that another educator may be approaching or involved in an ethically compromising situation;
3. Neither discriminating nor retaliating against a person on the basis of having made an ethical complaint;
4. Neither filing nor encouraging frivolous ethical complaints solely to harm or retaliate.
5. Cooperating fully during ethics investigations and proceedings

C. *The professional educator promotes and advances the profession within and beyond the school community by:*
1. Influencing and supporting decisions and actions that positively impact teaching and learning, educational leadership and student services;
2. Engaging in respectful discourse regarding issues that impact the profession;
3. Enhancing one's professional effectiveness by staying current with ethical principles and decisions from relevant sources including professional organizations;
4. Actively participating in educational and professional organizations and associations; and
5. Advocating for adequate resources and facilities to ensure equitable opportunities for all students.

PRINCIPLE II: RESPONSIBILITY FOR PROFESSIONAL COMPETENCE

The professional educator is committed to the highest levels of professional and ethical practice, including demonstration of the knowledge, skills, and dispositions required for professional competence.

A. *The professional educator demonstrates commitment to high standards of practice through:*
   1. Incorporating into one's practice state and national standards, including those specific to one's discipline;
   2. Using the *Model Code of Educator Ethics* and other ethics codes unique to one's discipline to guide and frame educational decision-making;
   3. Advocating for equitable educational opportunities for all students;
   4. Accepting the responsibilities, performing duties and providing services corresponding to the area of certification, licensure, and training of one's position;
   5. Reflecting upon and assessing one's professional skills, content knowledge, and competency on an ongoing basis; and
   6. Committing to ongoing professional learning.

B. *The professional educator demonstrates responsible use of data, materials, research, and assessment by:*
   1. Appropriately recognizing others' work by citing data or materials from published, unpublished, or electronic sources when disseminating information;
   2. Using developmentally appropriate assessments for the purposes for which they are intended and for which they have been validated to guide educational decisions;
   3. Conducting research in an ethical and responsible manner with appropriate permission and supervision;
   4. Seeking and using evidence, instructional data, research, and professional knowledge to inform practice;
   5. Creating, maintaining, disseminating, storing, retaining and disposing of records and data relating to one's research and practice, in accordance with district policy, state and federal laws; and
   6. Using data, data sources, or findings accurately and reliably.

C. *The professional educator acts in the best interest of all students by:*
   1. Increasing students' access to the curriculum, activities, and resources in order to provide a quality and equitable educational experience.
   2. Working to engage the school community to close achievement, opportunity, and attainment gaps; and
   3. Protecting students from any practice that harms or has the potential to harm students.

PRINCIPLE III: RESPONSIBILITY TO STUDENTS

The professional educator has a primary obligation to treat students with dignity and respect. The professional educator promotes the health, safety, and well being of students by establishing and maintaining appropriate verbal, physical, emotional and social boundaries.

A. *The professional educator respects the rights and dignity of students by:*
 1. Respecting students by taking into account their age, gender, culture, setting and socioeconomic context;
 2. Interacting with students with transparency and in appropriate settings;
 3. Communicating with students in a clear, respectful, and culturally sensitive manner;
 4. Taking into account how appearance and dress can affect one's interactions and relationships with students;
 5. Considering the implication of accepting gifts from or giving gifts to students;
 6. Engaging in physical contact with students only when there is a clearly defined purpose that benefits the student and continually keeps the safety and well-being of the student in mind;
 7. Avoiding multiple relationships with students which might impair objectivity and increase the risk of harm to student learning or well-being or decrease educator effectiveness;
 8. Acknowledging that there are no circumstances that allow for educators to engage in romantic or sexual relationships with students; and
 9. Considering the ramifications of entering into an adult relationship of any kind with a former student, including but not limited to, any potential harm to the former student, public perception, and the possible impact on the educator's career. The professional educator ensures that the adult relationship was not started while the former student was in school.

B. *The professional educator demonstrates an ethic of care through:*
 1. Seeking to understand students' educational, academic, personal and social needs as well as students' values, beliefs, and cultural background;
 2. Respecting the dignity, worth, and uniqueness of each individual student including, but not limited to, actual and perceived gender, gender expression, gender identity, civil status, family status, sexual orientation, religion, age, disability, race, ethnicity, socio-economic status, and culture; and
 3. Establishing and maintaining an environment that promotes the emotional, intellectual, physical, and sexual safety of all students.

C. *The professional educator maintains student trust and confidentiality when interacting with students in a developmentally appropriate manner and within appropriate limits by:*
   1. Respecting the privacy of students and the need to hold in confidence certain forms of student communication, documents, or information obtained in the course of professional practice;
   2. Upholding parents'/guardians' legal rights, as well as any legal requirements to reveal information related to legitimate concerns for the well-being of a student; and
   3. Protecting the confidentiality of student records and releasing personal data in accordance with prescribed state and federal laws and local policies.

PRINCIPLE IV: RESPONSIBILITY TO THE SCHOOL COMMUNITY

The professional educator promotes positive relationships and effective interactions, with members of the school community, while maintaining professional boundaries.

A. *The professional educator promotes effective and appropriate relationships with parents/guardians by:*
   1. Communicating with parents/guardians in a timely and respectful manner that represents the students' best interests;
   2. Demonstrating a commitment to equality, equity, and inclusion as well as respecting and accommodating diversity among members of the school community;
   3. Considering the implication of accepting gifts from or giving gifts to parents/guardians; and
   4. Maintaining appropriate confidentiality with respect to student information disclosed by or to parents/guardians unless required by law.

B. *The professional educator promotes effective and appropriate relationships with colleagues by:*
   1. Respecting colleagues as fellow professionals and maintaining civility when differences arise;
   2. Resolving conflicts, whenever possible, privately and respectfully and in accordance with district policy;
   3. Keeping student safety, education, and health paramount by maintaining and sharing educational records appropriately and objectively in accordance with local policies and state and federal laws;

4. Collaborating with colleagues in a manner that supports academic achievement and related goals that promote the best interests of students;
5. Enhancing the professional growth and development of new educators by supporting effective field experiences, mentoring or induction activities across the career continuum;
6. Ensuring that educators who are assigned to participate as mentors for new educators, cooperating teachers, or other teacher leadership positions are prepared and supervised to assume these roles;
7. Ensuring that educators are assigned to positions in accordance with their educational credentials, preparation, and experience in order to maximize students' opportunities and achievement; and
8. Working to ensure a workplace environment that is free from harassment.

C. *The professional educator promotes effective and appropriate relationships with the community and other stakeholders by:*
1. Advocating for policies and laws that the educator supports as promoting the education and well-being of students and families;
2. Collaborating with community agencies, organizations, and individuals in order to advance students' best interests without regard to personal reward or remuneration; and
3. Maintaining the highest professional standards of accuracy, honesty, and appropriate disclosure of information when representing the school or district within the community and in public communications.

D. *The professional educator promotes effective and appropriate relationships with employers by:*
1. Using property, facilities, materials, and resources in accordance with local policies and state and federal laws;
2. Respecting intellectual property ownership rights (e.g. original lesson plans, district level curricula, syllabi, gradebooks, etc.) when sharing materials;
3. Exhibiting personal and professional conduct that is in the best interest of the organization, learning community, school community, and profession; and
4. Considering the implications of offering or accepting gifts and/or preferential treatment by vendors or an individual in a position of professional influence or power.

E. *The professional educator understands the problematic nature of multiple relationships by:*
   1. Considering the risks that multiple relationships might impair objectivity and increase the likelihood of harm to students' learning and well-being or diminish educator effectiveness;
   2. Considering the risks and benefits of a professional relationship with someone with whom the educator has had a past personal relationship and vice versa;
   3. Considering the implications and possible ramifications of engaging in a personal or professional relationship with parents and guardians, student teachers, colleagues, and supervisors; and
   4. Ensuring that professional responsibilities to paraprofessionals, student teachers or interns do not interfere with responsibilities to students, their learning, and well-being.

PRINCIPLE V: RESPONSIBLE AND ETHICAL USE OF TECHNOLOGY

The professional educator considers the impact of consuming, creating, distributing, and communicating information through all technologies. The ethical educator is vigilant to ensure appropriate boundaries of time, place, and role are maintained when using electronic communication.

A. *The professional educator uses technology in a responsible manner by:*
   1. Using social media responsibly, transparently, and primarily for purposes of teaching and learning per school and district policy. The professional educator considers the ramifications of using social media and direct communication via technology on one's interactions with students, colleagues, and the general public;
   2. Staying abreast of current trends and uses of school technology;
   3. Promoting the benefits of and clarifying the limitations of various appropriate technological applications with colleagues, appropriate school personnel, parents, and community members;
   4. Knowing how to access, document and use proprietary materials and understanding how to recognize and prevent plagiarism by students and educators;
   5. Understanding and abiding by the district's policy on the use of technology and communication;

6. Recognizing that some electronic communications are records under the Freedom of Information Act (FOIA) and state public access laws and should consider the implications of sharing sensitive information electronically either via professional or personal devices/accounts; and

7. Exercising prudence in maintaining separate and professional virtual profiles, keeping personal and professional lives distinct.

B. *The professional educator ensures students' safety and well-being when using technology by:*

1. Being vigilant in identifying, addressing and reporting (when appropriate and in accordance with local district, state, and federal policy) inappropriate and illegal materials/images in electronic or other forms;

2. Respecting the privacy of students' presence on social media unless given consent to view such information or if there is a possibility of evidence of a risk of harm to the student or others; and

3. Monitoring to the extent practical and appropriately reporting information concerning possible cyber bullying incidents and their potential impact on the student learning environment.

C. *The professional educator maintains confidentiality in the use of technology by:*

1. Taking appropriate and reasonable measures to maintain confidentiality of student information and educational records stored or transmitted through the use of electronic or computer technology;

2. Understanding the intent of Federal Educational Rights to Privacy Act (FERPA) and how it applies to sharing electronic student records; and

3. Ensuring that the rights of third parties, including the right of privacy, are not violated via the use of technologies.

D. *The professional educator promotes the appropriate use of technology in educational settings by:*

1. Advocating for equal access to technology for all students, especially those historically underserved;

2. Promoting the benefits of and clarifying the limitations of various appropriate technological applications with colleagues, appropriate school personnel, parents, and community members; and

3. Promoting technological applications (a) that are appropriate for students' individual needs, (b) that students understand how to use and (c) that assist and enhance the teaching and learning process.

GLOSSARY

Boundaries:
The verbal, physical, emotional, and social distances that an educator must maintain in order to ensure structure, security, and predictability in an educational environment. Most often, the boundaries that are transgressed relate to role, time, and place. By respecting contracted roles, appropriate working hours, and the location of the learning environment, secure boundaries are in place for all members of the schooling community.

District/school district:
This is often referred to as a "local education agency." A "district" in this document is defined as a public board of education or other public authority legally constituted within a State for either administrative control or direction of, or to perform a service function for, public elementary schools or secondary schools in a city, county, township, school district, or other political subdivision of a State, or for a combination of school districts or counties that is recognized in a State as an administrative agency for its public elementary schools or secondary schools. This can include charter schools, magnet schools, virtual magnet schools, regional educational school districts, or other entities falling under the definition above.

Culture:
The customary beliefs, social forms, and material traits of a racial, religious, or social group, including the characteristic features of everyday existence shared by people in a place or time.[1]

Educator:
Educators are the target audience for the MCEE and are defined as licensed educators. These include paraprofessionals, teachers, teacher leaders, student support personnel, and administrators. However, others who interact with students who are not under the auspices of an education-related licensing organization such as coaches, school secretaries, custodians, or other school staff are encouraged to adopt or adapt this *Model Code of Educator Ethics*. See a separate definition for "professional educator."

---

[1] http://www.merriam-webster.com/dictionary/culture

Ethic of care:

Responding with compassion to the needs of students.

Ethical Decision-Making Model:

A framework utilized by educators to guide decision-making, which includes professional dispositions; applicable laws, statutes, and policies; the *Model Code of Educator Ethics*; and other guidelines that have been adopted and endorsed by educational organizations.

Fiduciary relationship:

A fiduciary relationship is one in which a person justifiably places confidence in another whose aid, advice, or protection is assumed. Inherent in such fiduciary relationships is an imbalance of power. Educators have a unique responsibility, as the relationship between student and teacher differs from other professional/client relationships (e.g., attorneys, physicians, clergy). Educators are entrusted with the safety and welfare of students during and after school hours and serve "in loco parentis."

Implicit or Explicit Demands of an Organization:

Implicit demands are often subjective or implied and reflect the culture of the schooling environment. Explicit demands are clearly articulated through mandates, policies, or statutes.

Harm:

The impairment of learning or any potential action which may lead to physical, emotional, psychological, sexual, or intellectual damage to a student or a member of the school community.

Learning Community:

A group of educators who work with one another to achieve the shared goals of their school and engage in collaborative professional learning to strengthen practice and increase student results.[2]

Multiple Relationships:

Multiple relationships occur when the educator is in a professional role with one or more members of the school community and also has a personal relationship with that person or a member of that person's family. Multiple relationships have the potential to impair objectivity, competence, or effectiveness in performing functions as an educator.

---

[2] http://learningforward.org/standards/learning-communities#.VTVerkv7Q3Y

New Educators:

New educators include individuals in an educator preparation program or newly employed in the education profession, including paraprofessionals, teachers, administrators, and student support personnel.

Professional educator:

A licensed educator who demonstrates the highest standards of ethical and professionally competent practice and is committed to advancing the interests, achievement, and well-being of students. The professional educator is also committed to supporting the school community and the education profession.

Proprietary materials:

Materials that are protected from unauthorized use by copyright or other forms of intellectual property rights.

Safe environments/Safety and well-being:

A school setting that promotes the well-being of all members of the school community and is characterized by the absence of physical, psychological, sexual, or emotional harm.

School Community:

This term usually refers to those stakeholders invested in the welfare of a school and its community. A school community includes school administrators, teachers, school staff members, students, their parents and families, school board members, and other community members.[3]

Sensitive Information:

This includes but is not limited to student information and educational records, including medical or counseling records.

Student:

A learner attending a P-12 school.

Technology:

Tools, systems, applications, and processes that can include, but are not limited to, electronic communications networks such as the Internet and electronic devices such as computers, laptops, phones and other hardware/software that deliver text, audio, images, animation, and streaming video.

Transparency:

Openness and accountability with respect to one's behaviors, actions, and communications as an educator.

---

[3] http://edglossary.org/school-community/

www.ingramcontent.com/pod-product-compliance
Ingram Content Group UK Ltd.
Pitfield, Milton Keynes, MK11 3LW, UK
UKHW050409240426
12048UKWH00020B/1420